Myth and Reality in International Politics

Recent generations have experienced dramatic improvements in the quality of human life across the globe. Wars between states are fought less frequently and are less lethal. Food is more plentiful and more easily accessed. In most parts of the world, birthrates are down and life expectancy up. Significantly fewer people live in extreme poverty, relative to the overall population. Statistics would argue that the human race has never before flourished as it has in this moment.

And yet, even with this progress, we face a number of seemingly intractable challenges to the welfare of both states and individuals, including:

- Governmental instability undermining the lives of citizens, both within and beyond their borders;
- Persistent and recurring intrastate conflict due to ineffective conflict management strategies;
- Marginally successful development efforts and growing income inequality, both within and between nations, as a result of uncoordinated and ineffective global development strategies;
- Internecine conflict in multiethnic societies, manifested by exclusion, discrimination, and ultimately violence, the inevitable consequence of an insufficient focus on managing the inherent tensions in diverse societies;
- Global climate change with the possibility of catastrophic long-term consequences, following an inability to effectively come to terms with and respond to the impact of human activity on our environment.

These challenges require a newly collaborative, intentional, and systematic approach. This book offers a blueprint for how to get there, calling for increased leadership responsibility, clarity of mission, and empowerment of states and individuals. It is designed to transform lofty but often vague agendas into concrete, measurable progress. It believes in the capacity of humanity to rise to the occasion, to come together to address these increasingly critical global problems, and offers one way forward.

Jonathan Wilkenfeld is Professor of Government and Politics, and Director of the ICONS Simulation Project at the University of Maryland. His research and writing has addressed conflict and crisis, negotiation and mediation, with regional foci in the Middle East and China.

International Studies Intensives

Series Editors Mark A. Boyer and Shareen Hertel

International Studies Intensives (ISI) is a book series that springs from the desire to keep students engaged in the world around them. ISI books pack a lot of information into a small space—they are meant to offer an intensive introduction to subjects often left out of the curriculum. ISI books are relatively short, visually attractive, and affordably priced.

Titles in the Series

The Rules of the Game: A Primer on International Relations
Mark R. Amstutz

Development Redefined: How the Market Met Its Match
Robin Broad and John Cavanagh

Protecting the Global Environment
Gary C. Bryner

A Tale of Two Quagmires: Iraq, Vietnam, and the Hard Lessons of War
Kenneth J. Campbell

Celebrity Diplomacy
Andrew F. Cooper

Global Health in the 21st Century: The Globalization of Disease and Wellness
Debra I. DeLaet and David E. DeLaet

Terminate Terrorism: Framing, Gaming, and Negotiating Conflicts
Karen A. Feste

Watching Human Rights: The 101 Best Films
Mark Gibney

The Global Classroom: An Essential Guide to Study Abroad
Jeffrey S. Lantis and Jessica DuPlaga

Democratic Uprisings in the New Middle East: Youth, Technology, Human Rights, and US Foreign Policy
Mahmood Monshipouri

Sixteen Million One: Understading Civil War
Patrick M. Regan

Forthcoming in the Series

Myth and Reality in International Politics

Meeting Global Challenges through Collective Action

Jonathan Wilkenfeld

Routledge
Taylor & Francis Group

NEW YORK AND LONDON

First published 2016
by Routledge
711 Third Avenue, New York, NY 10017

and by Routledge
2 Park Square, Milton Park, Abingdon, Oxon, OX14 4RN

Routledge is an imprint of the Taylor & Francis Group, an informa business

Library of Congress Cataloging in Publication Data
A catalog record for this book has been requested

ISBN: 978-1-61205-567-1 (hbk)
ISBN: 978-1-61205-568-8 (pbk)
ISBN: 978-1-315-67401-8 (ebk)

Typeset in Sabon
by Sunrise Setting Ltd, Paignton, UK

Printed and bound in the United States of America by Publishers Graphics,
LLC on sustainably sourced paper.

Contents

Figures

About the Author

Jonathan Wilkenfeld is Professor of Government and Politics, and Director of the ICONS Simulation Project at the University of Maryland. He was a founder with Michael Brecher of the International Crisis Behavior Project. His research and writing has addressed conflict and crisis, negotiation and mediation, with regional foci in the Middle East and China. His recent research has been supported by the National Science Foundation, the US Department of Homeland Security, and by the Folke Bernadotte Academy (Sweden). His recent books include *Peace and conflict 2014* (with David Backer and Paul Huth), *International negotiation in a complex world* (4th edition, with Brigid Starkey and Mark Boyer), and *Mediating international crises* (with Kathleen Young, David Quinn, and Victor Asal).

Acknowledgments

This book pulls together challenges to human security that I have written on or at least thought about carefully at various stages of my academic career—conflict, ethnicity, democratization, development, and climate change. With this book, I hope to reach academic and policy readers, as well as the public at large. Only through a concerted collective effort by scientists, policy makers, and an informed public throughout the world will we make sustained progress on the many global challenges facing us now and for future generations.

Readers will note that for each of the topics covered in this book, the academic, scientific, and policy literature has been combed for insights into all aspects of these areas. I want to acknowledge the outstanding support provided by my two graduate research assistants at the time: David Quinn and Roudabeh Kishi. Their careful work has allowed me to make what I hope are credible contributions to our understanding of the complex topics covered in the book.

In recent years, my research has been supported by grants and contracts from: the National Science Foundation; the US Department of Homeland Security, through its support of the Center of Excellence for the Study of Terrorism and Responses to Terrorism at the University of Maryland; the US Army Research Laboratory and the US Army Research Office; and the Folke Bernadotte Academy (Sweden). I am very grateful for their support. None of these agencies is responsible for the views and recommendations expressed in this book.

My wife Suzanne Stutman has read every word of the manuscript at least once and has been a wonderful source of insight. If the book makes sense to a broad audience of nonspecialists, then much of the credit goes to her.

Introduction
Dramatic Progress and Daunting Challenges

The current human condition presents us with an unparalleled opportunity to address pressing issues on a global scale. The frequency and lethality of interstate conflict is on the decline. There are dramatic improvements in agricultural production and means of distribution. There has been a significant decline in global birthrates and increases in life expectancy. The proportion of people living in extreme poverty across the globe has shown an enormous decline. Our ability to communicate freely through a wide range of easily accessible social media has increased opportunities to identify and track key challenges to the human condition by creating global communities that cross national boundaries, cultures, and languages.

Yet key long-term challenges to human security remain stubbornly in place. Unstable governments, often coupled with underperforming economies and unresolved domestic tensions, negatively impact the lives of citizens and often constitute a threat to neighboring states. In extreme cases, these conditions can become a threat to regional and even global security through the cross-border spread of violence and terrorism. Even as we have seen a dramatic decline in conflict between states in recent decades, ineffective conflict management at the local sub-national level in seemingly intractable *intrastate* conflicts has meant that conflict recurrence is on the rise with the accompanying localized human suffering. Uncoordinated global development strategies, insufficient or mismanaged funding, and corruption have resulted in uneven development and a widespread public perception that development aid is a waste of precious resources. Insufficient focus on the tensions that diversity can spawn in multiethnic societies can often lead to political, social, and economic exclusion and a rise in tensions and conflict. Our inability to deal with the impact of human activity on climate in a timely manner has meant that we leave unaddressed very clear deterioration of environmental conditions both in real time and for future generations. And the list of challenges goes on: outdated global financial institutions that are ill-equipped to deal with crises; inattentiveness to obvious threats to health and well-being;

mass migration and the attendant human rights issues that both spawn them and then accompany them to their next destination; and terrorism, which has sown fear and suspicion, and diverted resources from more productive endeavors.

Key long-term challenges to human security remain stubbornly in place: unstable governments, ineffective conflict management, uncoordinated global development strategies, and unaddressed human impact on climate.

This book sets out to assess a number of these challenges in terms of a series of beliefs about how the international system operates—call them myths—and the reality of how things actually work. Democracy is desirable, but the transition to democracy is incredibly destabilizing (e.g., Egypt after the Arab Spring); diversity enriches the culture and enhances the creativity of societies, but ethnic diversity can lead to repression and violence (e.g., Bosnia in the aftermath of the breakup of Yugoslavia); conflicts can be managed through agreements, but these agreements are often superficial and rarely lead to full conflict resolution (the jury is still out on Northern Ireland). This book will assess the performance of the international system in meeting these challenges.

Above all, this is a book about leadership responsibility, mission, and empowerment. It is about the transformation of lofty agendas into concrete, measurable progress. It is about a way forward in an age of seemingly insurmountable global challenges and associated gridlock. And it is optimistic about the ability of humankind to rise above divisions and address critical global problems through collective action.

Despite warnings about the demise of the nation state that date as far back as the end of World War II, all signs point to its continued dominance of the international system. This particular institutional form has endured while the issues facing the international system have become increasingly multi- and transnational in character. The international community and national leaders are particularly ill equipped to take on challenges where progress is difficult to define and measure, and where solutions require a long view. But unless we address the need for strong leadership with the ability to take such a long view, and unless we develop appropriate metrics for measuring progress in addressing global challenges, the most vulnerable of our populations will remain underserved by global medical advances, malnourished, poorly sheltered, undereducated, and under threat of repression by governments or by powerful majorities. How might such a long view of human security and development become the norm?

Myth and Reality

This book will address the challenges to political stability and individual prosperity noted above. It will identify the key fault lines along which long-held approaches to these challenges meet reality in the global system. It will present policy options for addressing global challenges, and metrics to help identify critical problems and assess progress (or lack thereof) in dealing with them. The following is a listing of the myths and realities that undergird the discussions in this book:

Myth 1 The international community has played an increasingly important role in the settlement of armed conflicts.

Reality Of the 39 armed conflicts that became active in the last 10 years, 31 were conflict recurrences—instances of resurgent, armed violence in societies where conflict had been largely dormant for at least a year.

With the end of the Second World War and the creation of the UN, the international community has developed a vast array of institutions to deal with armed conflict. Since the end of the Cold War, there has been a proliferation of international and regional institutions, as well as NGOs specifically charged with addressing aspects of conflict. In fact, in the post-Cold War era, almost 60 percent of all international crises have been the subjects of mediation efforts on the part of third parties, and that increases to nearly 90 percent in the case of violent intra state ethnic crises, particularly in Africa. Indeed, data show something of a decline in the number of armed conflicts since the end of the Cold War.

But in the last 10 years, the greatest threat of armed conflict has come from countries that recently resolved a serious armed conflict. The current rate of conflict recurrence is at its highest level since the Second World War. Simply put, despite the proliferation of institutions, we are not getting it right in terms of conflict resolution.

Myth 2 Diverse societies are culturally dynamic, facilitating individual and collective identity, and fostering creativity, imagination, and invention.

Reality One in every seven people on the globe is a member of an ethnic minority suffering some form of discrimination (political, economic, social, or cultural).

That in and of itself is disturbing enough. Even more disturbing, seven of the ten most lethal terrorist acts in the past decade have been perpetrated by organizations with strong ethnic links and grievances.

What are the contributing factors in moving an ethnicity-based organization from the adoption of legitimate means of political and social action to violence? These include:

- Non-democratic ideology
- Advocating self-determination
- Foreign support
- Rhetoric justifying violence
- Government repression

Recent research has shown that if all five factors are present, there is a high probability that the organization will engage in violence, often in the form of terrorism.

Ethnic diversity can be a force for innovation and creativity in society. But when ethnicity is politically mobilized in a divisive manner—as it has been in Rwanda and the former Yugoslavia, or as it is today in Iraq, Afghanistan, Pakistan, the Democratic Republic of Congo, the Central African Republic, and many other societies across the globe—it can become a very powerful means of organizing individuals for violence.

Myth 3 The significant increase in the number of democracies among the states of the international system, coupled with a decrease in the number of autocracies, bodes well for a more tranquil international system—the democratic peace.

Reality The transition from autocracy to democracy is the period most fraught with potential instability and conflict.

It wasn't until the late 1980s and the beginning of the 1990s that the number of democracies finally exceeded the number of autocracies, and that trend continues. But the problem lies in the rise of a third category: states that have hybrid political systems, with both authoritarian and democratic institutions. While strong democracies and strong autocracies are best able, obviously through differing means, to control tendencies within their societies to devolve into conflict and violence, anocracies—with a mix of democratic and authoritarian institutions and traditions—are least able to do this. Examples of these states are Niger, Cambodia, and Chad.

So the dilemma for the international community is how to promote democratic values in societies emerging from long histories of authoritarian rule, while at the same time keeping these states from slipping into instability and conflict, in this vulnerable transition period. The recent history of Egypt provides an unfortunate example of this tendency. One of the paradoxes of democracy is its complex relationship with violence.

Myth 4 The international community has been successful both in increasing the pot of international development-aid funds and in directing those funds to the places where they are needed the most.

Reality Development aid is outpaced by the economic cost of state instability, fragility, and failure by a factor of almost four to one.

By some estimates, the various institutions of the international community currently spend approximately $80 billion annually on development aid, whereas the cost of state fragility and failure has been estimated at $270 billion annually (Hoeffler 2010). One of the little-understood realities of state failure is that it is not just a local tragedy. It has widespread negative ramifications in terms of the spread of violence and terrorism beyond its borders—Afghanistan, Yemen, and Somalia are but the most recent and prominent examples. It also has serious economic consequences for their immediate neighbors.

And instability is on the rise. Over the past 2 years, the risk of instability has increased in the regions of the world where those dangers were already high. The top 25 states with the highest risk of failure are at greater risk than they were just 2 years ago. And more worrisome, 22 of these 25 are in Africa—exceptions are Afghanistan, Iraq, and Nepal.

Myth 5 While little doubt remains that human behavior has contributed to environmental degradation, a short-term technological fix is likely before this degradation becomes irreversible.

Reality The international community is incapable of coming together with sufficient urgency to undertake the collective action necessary to address human-induced climate change.

The "Tragedy of the Commons" has been proposed as an explanation for why collective action to address environmental degradation has not been possible, despite dire warnings and solid science. Also, we have seen how the impact of burgeoning threats to the environment have impacted human security. The link between climate change, famine, population movements, and conflict are just beginning to be explored. However, early evidence points to the most vulnerable of our populations suffering disproportionally from our inability to take meaningful action. This is a clear example of the weakness of the nation-state system in the face of global challenges.

Of course, there are important linkages among all of these challenging areas. Underdevelopment and conflict have an unfortunate symbiotic relationship. Climate change and stages of development are inexorably intertwined. Ethnic diversity and democratization are at the forefront of patterns of conflict recurrence in the international system today. As Thomas Friedman stated in a recent *New York Times* (*NYT*) op-ed: "You can't understand the Arab Awakenings—or their solutions—without considering climate, environment, and population trends," pointing to the roughly one million Syrian farmers and herders and their families forced off their land in recent years into already overcrowded urban centers (*NYT* January 21, 2014).

Each of these issue areas will be treated in the following chapters; and each chapter will conclude with a set of metrics and prescriptions, meant to begin to address the serious lapses in the performance of our system in meeting these challenges. For example, in the area of conflict management with the goal of transforming enduring conflict resolution, these prescriptions should include the development of sophisticated, localized early warning and monitoring systems, intervention keyed to the particular circumstances of a conflict, and postconflict reconciliation and reconstruction. Further, the postconflict phase should include sustained conflict-management processes, including tribunals, truth and reconciliation commissions, and track II processes; a focus on the role of women in the postconflict setting; and paced development of governmental institutions—including, but not restricted to, democratization. These actions, in turn, will help societies transition from tenuous conflict management to sustainable conflict resolution. See Chapter 1 for a more complete discussion of these mechanisms.

Human Security: Metrics and Policy

And finally, this is a book about human security. As Mohamed ElBaradei, former Secretary General of the International Atomic Energy Agency and 2005 Nobel Peace Laureate, recently stated:

> The modern age demands that we think in terms of *human* security— a concept of security that is people-centered and without borders. A concept that acknowledges the inherent linkage between economic and social development, respect for human rights, and peace. This is the basis on which we must "re-engineer" security. While national security is just as relevant as before, the strategies to achieve it must be much more global than in the past, and our remedies must be centered on the welfare of the individual and not simply focused on the security of the state. Until we understand and act accordingly, we will not have either national or international security.
>
> (ElBaradei 2010)

The modern age demands that we think in terms of *human* security—a concept of security that is people-centered and without borders.

The goal of the book is to provide a systematic examination of some of the challenges to human security that require a long view and, where possible, to suggest metrics that will allow us to measure short-term progress in addressing these challenges. Such a long view is often difficult for policy makers and political leaders—regardless of the political system in which they operate—because political realities would seem to require the delivery of short-term rewards. An example of such a metric, one that is applicable to development, is *infant mortality*, which can serve as a proxy for overall governmental effectiveness in executing policies and delivering services that improve social welfare in a country—high infant mortality rates are associated with inadequate social welfare provision. Another metric is *regime longevity* as a proxy for regime consistency—the risk of future instability is inversely related to whether the institutions comprising a country's political system are uniformly and consistently autocratic or democratic—systems that fall in between are notoriously unstable. Systems of metrics such as these will allow us to begin to identify those policy interventions that are appropriate to address human security in the multitude of circumstances in which it may be threatened.

The United Nations Development Programme's *Human Development Report* and the World Bank's *World Development Indicators*, among many other compilations, have helped to focus our attention on the greatest disparities between the promise of our era and its delivery to many of the poorest citizens of the globe. Through these annual publications, the need to address these challenges is entering the awareness of both the policy and research communities. But greater ability to access this vast array of global data does not translate immediately into an effective long-term policy agenda, either at the national or the international level. This book hopes to take a modest step in the direction of developing such an agenda for human security.

As noted, the point is to transition conventional thinking from national security to human security and in so doing to meet the needs of the most vulnerable and physically threatened populations. For example, in the area of conflict management and resolution, data on mediation styles show that those that have been successful in managing and resolving conflicts and crises between states have proven less effective in civil wars, particularly those involving massive civilian casualties and displacement resulting from direct fighting, as well as from resultant disease and malnutrition. The Democratic Republic of Congo is one among many examples of failed mediation attempts in a civil war that has claimed millions of lives over the past two decades. Current research shows that manipulative mediation styles can bring about agreements, but these agreements rarely address the root causes of the conflict and hence are not likely to result in tension reduction—an absolute requirement for conflict resolution. And recent research has provided us with at least one mechanism for achieving long-term conflict resolution in seemingly intractable intrastate conflict—the inclusion of domestic institutions in the process of mediation.

A Collective Action Agenda

The challenges briefly outlined above can be described as collective action problems. In the area of climate change, for example, it has become abundantly clear that collective action on the part of the community of nations is the only way to address it effectively. A coherent development policy to lift nations out of poverty and address the concomitant problems that underdevelopment spawns—conflict, terrorism, out-migration, disease—requires a collective approach. Conflict recurrence will require human capital and resources to move us from conflict management to conflict resolution.

Over the course of the last century, the members of the international community of nations have advanced a number of institutions and mechanisms to attempt to deal collectively with global challenges. Initially, such institutions were designed to address the severe collective security issues growing out of World Wars I and II, first through the flawed League of Nations and then through a more robust United Nations. Other institutions and mechanisms were designed to deal with regional security and development issues (Organization of American States, and African Union, AU) global financial arrangements (e.g. World Bank and International Monetary Fund), environmental factors (Framework Convention on Climate Change), and health issues (World Health Organization), often as arms of the United Nations and regional organizations. Yet, as we will see in the following discussions, the fundamental roadblocks facing all of these institutions and arrangements have been sovereignty and enforcement; and, while there have been notable successes, there have also been spectacular failures.

Notwithstanding the mandates of these collective action institutions and mechanisms, and the goodwill of their founders and administrators, the international community is stuck with a system of sovereign nation states, each of which exercises policies that meet its individual needs, often without regard to universal moral standards or the side effects that their policies will have on neighbors and the international community in general. Yet, as Ben Rhodes, US Deputy National Security Advisor to President Obama, has stated: "We want to galvanize collective action to underpin global norms. We don't want to do these things alone; we welcome others to be involved" (*The Economist* 2013, November 23). It is against this backdrop that this book calls for the renewal of collective action efforts, by highlighting several critical challenges and proposing measures that can embolden our leaders to engage in these collective action efforts. Global norms and institutions develop when nations and their leaders recognize that collective action is beneficial not only for the global system, but also to their own individual nations, as well as to themselves as leaders. As a poignant bumper sticker proclaims: "We all live downstream."

Global norms and institutions develop when nations and their leaders recognize that collective action is beneficial not only for the global system, but also to their own individual nations. We all live downstream.

Plan for the Book

In the following chapters, we will examine several key challenges to the security and well-being of people and nations in the 21st century. In Chapter 1, we explore the broad subject of conflict in general: its origins, current patterns, and prospects for addressing both short-term conflict management and long-term conflict resolution. We then follow with two chapters that deal with some of the principal threats to people and societies that have consequences for whether conflict will occur and spread. Chapter 2 tackles the complex role that ethnicity plays both within and between societies; and Chapter 3 addresses regime consistency and stability, focusing on the difficult transition from autocracy to democracy.

The next two chapters move from an approach that focuses primarily on internal factors to issues that are more global in nature. Chapter 4 addresses development, first from a historical perspective, then transitioning to an examination of sustainable development goals that are likely to make a difference in addressing inequalities resulting from poverty, poor health delivery, and poor educational systems, among others. Chapter 5 addresses climate change, perhaps the greatest challenge facing human security today, and how opportunities for collective action to address this challenge are being squandered as sovereign states debate questions of blame and burden sharing.

In the Conclusion, we summarize the key recommendations for the measurement of progress toward achieving the goal of enhancing human security through collective action. An action agenda for collective responsibility is presented, as a means for emboldening our leaders to support policies that will address some of the long-term challenges facing our own and future generations.

Chapter 1

Conflict

The Myth and Reality of Conflict: Setting the Scene

Ask anyone on the street pretty much anywhere in the world, and they will tell you with certainty that conflict around the world is up; in fact, way up. Just look at Iraq, Syria, Afghanistan, the Central African Republic, South Sudan, and Ukraine. Yet the statistics tell a different story—less active conflicts than any time in the last three decades, less casualties, less lethal terrorism, etc. As of December 2012, there were 26 armed conflicts ongoing in 22 countries (Wilkenfeld 2014), down from 38 armed conflicts involving more than 40 countries at the end of the Cold War in 1989–90. So why is there this widespread misperception? What is it that people are sensing that is somehow at odds—drastically—with the evidence?

As with most misperceptions, there is some truth to the matter, so let us delve more deeply. Here's what we know: Figure 1.1 presents the number of active interstate and intrastate conflicts from 1946 to 2012, relying on data from the Uppsala Conflict Data Program and the Peace Research Institute Oslo. Of particular note is that the phenomenon of **interstate conflict**, involving two or more states, has all but disappeared from the international system. Conflict in the system today is made up almost entirely of **intrastate conflict**, or conflicts within states. And after peaking in 1990 with 38 active conflicts, the system has reached something of a steady state of between 25 and 30 active conflicts per year.

Most observers projected that the end of the Cold War in 1990 would usher in an era of unprecedented peace: no more threat of nuclear war; the end of East–West tensions; peaceful democratic transitions in Eastern Europe and the former Soviet Union; economic development and no more proxy wars and alliances in Africa and Latin America; and continuance of 1980s economic growth in Asia, which would lead to peace. But a number of high-profile and deadly conflicts exploded or continued

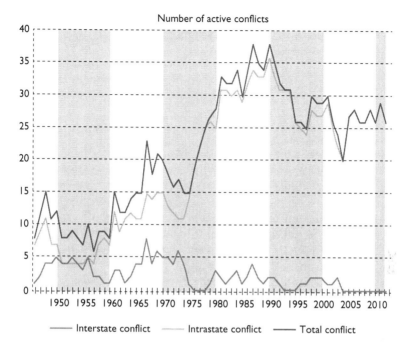

Number of active conflicts

Interstate conflict ——— Intrastate conflict ——— Total conflict

Figure 1.1 Number of active conflicts, 1946–2012.

Source: Backer and Huth 2014b, p. 19, Figure 3.1.

over the next few years: the former Yugoslavia, Rwanda, Chechnya, Ethiopia, Tajikistan, Haiti, etc. (Crocker et al. 2001). Nevertheless, in many respects a less conflictual era has followed the Cold War.

Myth 1 The international community has played an increasingly important role in the settlement of armed conflicts.

Conflict Recurrence

But here's what we also know:

Those conflicts that are around have been around for a while—they are what the experts call intractable. That is, "conflicts that have persisted over time and refused to yield to efforts to arrive at a political settlement—through either direct negotiations by the parties or mediation with third-party assistance" (Crocker et al. 2005). A list of intractable conflicts today usually includes Sudan, Kashmir, the Korean Peninsula, Israel–Palestine, Somalia, the Democratic Republic of Congo (DRC), and Afghanistan. And when they erupt again, we—well, we with the aid of the press—tend to dredge up the context, and of course that context comes with reference to how many have been killed overall in the conflict, not just in the present instance. Two million killed in the DRC over the past 20 years, so now when there is a massacre of 100 or even 1,000 civilians along the border with Rwanda—relatively small numbers—it reminds us of the two million, and therefore the present instance may sound worse than it actually is. Conflicts that have been in our perceptions for a while tend to get overblown.

Reality Of the 39 armed conflicts that became active in the last 10 years, 31 were conflict recurrences—instances of resurgent, armed violence in societies where conflict had been largely dormant for at least a year.

So, during this current period, the greatest threat of armed conflict has come from countries that recently managed a serious armed conflict. The current rate of **conflict recurrence** is at its highest level since World War II. One of the greatest challenges facing the international community involves achieving real and lasting resolution of these recurring and seemingly intractable conflicts.

The current rate of conflict recurrence is at its highest level since World War II. One of the greatest challenges facing the international community involves achieving real and lasting resolution of these recurring and intractable conflicts.

In the post-Cold War era, civil wars last almost four times longer, are less likely to terminate in agreement, and are more likely to recur than interstate wars. Fifty-seven percent of states that experienced a civil war since the end of the Second World War also experienced a civil war recurrence. And some civil wars have recurred *multiple* times. Walter (2013) lists the following cases: Iraq, Afghanistan, Burundi, Rwanda, Angola, Chad, DRC, Indonesia, Laos, Myanmar, Philippines, Somalia, Sudan, and Sri Lanka.

Figure 1.2 shows the evolution over time of the mix between new and recurring conflicts in the system. As can be seen quite vividly, there has been a clear shift in the balance between new and recurring conflicts over time, dramatically bringing into focus the general failure of the system to deal effectively with conflicts in order to prevent their recurrence. Another perspective on this issue is that the pool of recently terminated conflicts contains more conflicts with a history of recurrence than ever before (Hewitt 2012b). Simply put, despite the proliferation of institutions, we are not getting it right in terms of conflict resolution.

Figure 1.2 New and recurring conflict, 1946–2007.

Source: Wilkenfeld 2011, p. 232, Figure 14.2.

The Shifting Nature of Conflict

As the distribution of conflicts has shifted in the post-Cold War era from a predominantly interstate phenomenon to one dominated by intrastate rivalries (Figure 1.1), and as conflict recurrences have become fixtures of this environment (Figure 1.2), scholars and practitioners of international politics have scrambled to adapt conflict management and conflict resolution tools to meet this shifting challenge. This shift toward an increased need for the international community to become involved in intrastate conflicts is especially challenging, as intrastate conflicts can prove to be more difficult to address than interstate ones, for a variety of reasons. For example, due to their nature, intrastate conflicts tend to include "significant power asymmetries," with one side being more powerful and better prepared than its adversary (Gartner 2011). This can become especially problematic when, as often happens, one side is a non-state actor, and hence has fewer constraints on their behavior as a result of being less institutionalized and less accountable to a domestic constituency. This also means that they may not feel themselves as bound by the same international norms regarding the use of violence as are their state adversaries (Gartner 2011: 382).

The "invasion" of Iraq by the Sunni-dominated Islamic State in Iraq and Syria (ISIS) in June 2014 follows this non-state actor pattern. Furthermore, state governments are often hesitant to allow third parties to intervene, because "conflict management provides status, [especially as] negotiating as equals attributes credibility to civil war leaders" (Gartner 2011: 382). The presence of apparently zero-sum issues in intrastate conflicts makes them particularly difficult to resolve. Finally, commitment problems are more likely to occur in mediation attempts at the intrastate level, because parties can have insincere motives. Instead of using mediation to arrive at a durable solution, parties may use it to justify approaches to nationalism, to achieve legitimacy, or simply to buy time to mobilize resources as they regroup (Beardsley 2011).

Causes of Intrastate Conflict: Grievance, Greed, And Opportunity

What are the primary causes of intrastate or civil conflict, and what makes their resolution so much more difficult than the resolution of conflict between nation states? Regarding causes, the academic literature is split in terms of its support for two competing theories pertaining to motivation—*grievances* and *greed*. **Grievances** arise from dissatisfaction with the status quo. This can result from group-specific disadvantages that derive from specific discriminatory or repressive policies, or from common historical practise or status (Gurr 2000) (see also the discussion of ethnicity in Chapter 2 of this volume). Grievances can also arise from society-wide restricted access to political power or different economic conditions such as poor performance and low levels of development (Hegre and Sambanis 2006; Collier et al. 2008b; Goldstone et al. 2010), or less integration into world markets (Hegre et al. 2003). Relative deprivation can also play a role (Gurr 1970).

On the other hand, **greed**-based explanations focus on profit seeking on the part of rebelling groups. In the midst of intrastate conflict, such profits can be generated from lootable resources (diamonds, oil, etc.) (Walter 2013). Examples include the Revolutionary Armed Forces of Columbia (FARC; coca), the National Union for the Total Independence of Angola (UNITA; diamonds), and the Revolutionary United Front (RUF) in Sierra Leone (diamonds, timber). And often, what starts as a grievance-based conflict evolves over time into one that exhibits aspects of greed as well, as opportunists work alongside or even take over from ideologues.

In addition to motivation, groups can only fight when they can organize and mobilize, that is, recruit and reward supporters. **Opportunities** for organization can result from establishing ties with sympathetic elites, living under an anocratic system[1] that allows groups to organize, or weakened states that lack capacity to effectively repress (e.g., Sudan, DRC) (McAdam 1996; Buhaug et al. 2009; Fearon and Laitin 2003; Gates et al. 2006; Hegre et al. 2001). A weakened state increases the opposition's perception that a war is winnable, making it a less risky choice (Walter 2013). A weakened state also contributes to the *grievance* factor by having less capacity to meet group demands. Groups also need to *mobilize* human and material resources to operate their rebellion, create safe havens (McCarthy and Zald 1977; Tilly 1978; Weinstein 2005; Collier et al. 2003), and provide selective incentives to supporters and fighters in exchange for their loyalty and participation (Lichbach 1995; Humphreys and Weinstein 2008). These resources can come from elite allies, external patrons, lootable resources, or agricultural production (Humphreys 2005; Walter 2013). Defensible territory also helps (Fearon and Laitin 2003), as does residing in a society where military training and equipment are abundant and diffusely distributed (Collier and Hoeffler 2004; Backer and Huth 2014a). An increase in resources in the aftermath of conflict—e.g., new sources of funding or patronage—can spur recurrence by lowering opportunity costs of renewed violence. From this perspective, spaces between wars are simply lulls in fighting due to resource depletion, not actual settlements (Walter 2013).

Also somewhat related to the opportunity factor is the role of diffusion and contagion in spurring conflict. Evidence shows that a state that lives in a "bad neighborhood" has an increased chance of experiencing civil conflict itself, typically because either a conflict in a neighboring state spills across international borders or there are cross-border ethnic or communal ties that provide a resource base for a rebel group (Backer and Huth 2014a; Hegre and Sambanis 2006; Goldstone et al. 2010).

Obstacles to Negotiated Settlement

Notwithstanding the circumstances that may motivate armed conflict, violence is risky and costly, and thus there should be a potential settlement that both parties would prefer over the resort to violence (Fearon 1995). But even when such a potential settlement exists (in game-theoretic terms, a zone of agreement), bargaining problems can often prevent the two parties from reaching a settlement prior to violence, or from reaching an agreement once violence has occurred. At least four factors get in the way of successful bargaining that could lead to conflict avoidance or resolution.

Notwithstanding the circumstances that may motivate armed conflict, violence is risky and costly, and thus there should be a potential settlement that both parties would prefer over the resort to violence.

Issue Divisibility Problems The sides can't agree on how to divide the pie—each wants to control the government, or they want control over territory, or the rectification of perceived damage or discrimination. While all of these things should in theory be divisible (Fearon 1995)—via some type of concessions like power sharing, autonomy, special privileges, or side payments in exchange for dropping demands (Walter 2013)—they wind up being perceived as more zero-sum in character.

Information Problems One or both sides refuse to divulge—either by withholding or deliberately misrepresenting—their actual capabilities and intentions and/or resolve in order to gain a strategic advantage or get more concessions from their opponent (Fearon 1995). This situation of uncertainty and incomplete information negatively affects their ability to identify mutually acceptable alternatives to violence (Fearon 1995; Powell 1999), to assess fairness of agreements, and to predict probabilities of winning a war.

Commitment Problems One or both sides cannot commit to honoring an agreement (Fearon 2004; Powell 2006). Commitment problems are most likely to occur when:

A. One or both sides have strong incentives to renege on an agreement, such as when the terms of the agreement are barely above their reservation points or do not distribute benefits in line with their capabilities;
B. The reneging side gains a significant strategic advantage by doing so;
C. The state is authoritarian or political institutions are weak, since the state can renege on a deal it cuts and its opponents have little or no political or legal recourse (Fearon and Laitin 2003; Bates 2008);
D. Ethnicity is involved (see separate discussion of ethnicity in Chapter 2 of this volume);
E. The parties are unable to reach an agreement or are unwilling to enforce compliance with the agreement;
F. A third party is unavailable, unable, or unwilling to intervene and guarantee or enforce compliance with an agreement or provide security guarantees during sensitive demobilization processes (Walter 2013).

Factionalism Problems (e.g., Iraq, Burundi, DRC) Factionalism exacerbates the other three types of bargaining problems noted above, particularly when it affects the rebel side. More factions mean that some are going to be more radicalized and are going to seek less divisible goals. Hence, conflict is more common when there are more groups with more divergent interests (Walter 2013). Shifting and competing factions also means that bargaining positions, zones of agreement, and alliances are more uncertain and in flux. This makes it more difficult to understand what will be an acceptable settlement for all (an information problem) (Cunningham 2006) and relatedly increases the chance of an agreement breaking down due to dissatisfaction (a commitment problem). Spoiler factions cause commitment problems and increase chances of conflict recurrence (Stedman 1997). Factionalism tends to increase the length of the conflict.

Management Versus Resolution

There is an important distinction between "conflict management" and "conflict resolution." This distinction will be particularly important as we introduce and then evaluate the effectiveness of management and resolution techniques and instruments.

Conflict management has been defined as "a set of actions designed to *limit or control the level and scope of violence in a given conflict* [italics added], while striving to accomplish a set of objectives at the national…or international level" (Maoz 2004: 13). Conflict management involves finding a balance between winning by maximizing one's interests, or avoiding risk by defusing the situation. George's early work (1984, 1991) can be seen as enhancing this definition by introducing an attempt to balance coercive diplomacy and strategic military moves with risk control in order to avoid war.

"Conflict management" has been defined as a set of actions designed to limit or control the level and scope of violence in a given conflict. "Conflict resolution" attempts to move the parties toward the elimination of the root causes of the conflict.

For present purposes, the primary and distinct mission of conflict management is termination of the conflict before it escalates or spreads. Some scholars note that this type of effort is aimed at settlement of the immediate issues under dispute or the stopping of violent interactions between the parties. For Kolb and Babbitt, management implies a "temporary respite in an otherwise ongoing conflict" (1995: 80), while Kleiboer (1998) describes management as an effort to neutralize the destructive consequences of a conflict. Thought of in this way, conflict management can include any of the following activities: deterrence moves and reactions to them, arbitration, repression of the conflict, containment of the conflict, arms reductions, or any solution that involves the disputants simply arriving at a consensus based on compromise. As we will see in the discussion below, third parties can play a crucial role in conflict management by slowing down the pace of events occurring between the conflicting parties (Kleiboer 1998), ensuring constant communications between the parties, and trying to get them to be more flexible regarding their thoughts and actions (Mitchell 1981).

Conflict resolution differs from conflict management in the scope of objectives pursued. The goal of conflict resolution is *to move beyond temporary settlements and toward elimination of the roots of the conflict between the parties*. The challenge is to get the parties to redefine or restructure their relations in such a way that their respective goals no longer conflict, or to get them to believe that they can each achieve their goals despite one another, not at the cost of the other (Susskind and Babbitt 1992). In this sense, temporary settlements should only be viewed as intermediate stages en route to an eradication of the roots of the conflict (Kleiboer 1998). The success of attempts to resolve conflicts may be judged in terms of how effectively the outcome terms can be implemented (Bercovitch 1992), how satisfied the parties are with the outcome, and how durable the peace was in terms of preventing a return to violence (Beardsley 2011). In many long-term protracted conflict situations, a succession of crises may be managed, followed by a final successful instance of conflict resolution.

Often, the conceptions of short- and long-term peace in these situations are at odds with one another. Immediate humanitarian concerns or heightened tensions between the disputants demand a focus on more short-term outcomes (Quinn et al. 2013a; Beardsley 2011). In this case, it is valuable and necessary for the parties to make basic concessions and forge agreements that curb hostilities and de-escalate the situation. However, the ultimate goal is long-term peace, and outcomes that simply provide short-term relief from strain may be insufficient to achieve that larger goal.

Compromise is an inseparable component of peaceful crisis management and conflict resolution. Concessions help disputing parties move further toward or into their shared bargaining space. Formal negotiated agreement is a type of compromise-based outcome of particular interest. Formal agreements are more binding and contain higher costs for defaulting than informal, tacit, or unilateral compromise outcomes. Creating and implementing formal agreements requires at least a moderate amount of resources, so disputants will try to avoid the sunk costs brought on by signing an agreement that they project will collapse. Formal agreements also contain punishments for noncompliance, and contractual norms and audience costs legitimize retaliation should the agreement be violated (Fortna 2003). Owing to this cost structure, formal agreements are more likely to be reached when their provisions lie within the parties' overlapping range of preferable outcomes. This array of factors means that formal agreements are typically more sustainable relative to other nonviolent outcomes.

Even though achieving formal agreement at the termination of the conflict is important, the best-case scenario would involve a sustained reduction in tensions between the parties following the crisis. However, there are significant threats to durable peace.

In the immediate aftermath of intrastate conflict events, parties often continue to experience higher-than-normal **stress** as they emerge from periods of intense hostility. This stress is likely to devolve into a resumption of crisis-level tensions when one or more actors: (a) sign an agreement whose terms are barely above their reservation points; (b) have devious objectives and use the break in tensions to rearm; (c) experience a change in capabilities after conflict termination; or (d) reassess how the distribution of capabilities between themselves and their opponent(s) matches with the distribution of benefits provided by an agreement (Powell 1999; Richmond 1998; Werner 1999). In each of these cases, if the actor is unsatisfied with the terms of the outcome and believes that its utility will be maximized by returning to the battlefield or brinkmanship, it is likely that peace agreements will break down.

Conversely, agreements are more durable when they lie well above each side's reservation point and when the parties receive benefits in accordance with their distribution of capabilities. Peace is also more stable when each side credibly commits to ensuring each other's security (Quinn et al. 2013a; Fortna 2003; Hartzell et al. 2001).

Matching Conflict Management to Conflict Dynamics

Figure 1.3 (adapted from Crocker et al. 2001, and from Lund 1996) moves beyond the sources of conflict to focus on the dynamics of conflict and the timing of appropriate responses by the international community. The diagram indicates the points in the life cycle of a conflict at which various conflict management techniques are appropriate. Also useful is its focus on four phases of peace: **peace-making**—mediation, negotiation, and coercive diplomacy; **peace enforcement**—threat or use of force, sanctions, and arms embargoes; **peacekeeping**—lightly armed, outside military forces, security forces bolstered, refugees repatriated, and other humanitarian assistance; and postconflict **peace-building**—foreign aid and humanitarian assistance, judicial measures, rule of law, creation of functional government, economic development, and education and training. These four phases of peace correspond to the four collective-action agenda items discussed in the section below titled Collective Action Plan: From Management to Resolution: monitoring and early warning, mediation, intervention, and postconflict reconstruction.

We must keep in mind that conflicts rarely follow this idealized path from outbreak through management to resolution. In the sections below, we will address several mechanisms for short-term conflict management and longer-term conflict resolution. The focus is on collective action on the part of the international community and how its effectiveness might be measured.

Conflict and International Collective Action: Traditional Instruments

Before turning to thoughts on an action plan for addressing the management and resolution of conflict and crisis in the international system today, let us pause to briefly review some of the collective mechanisms

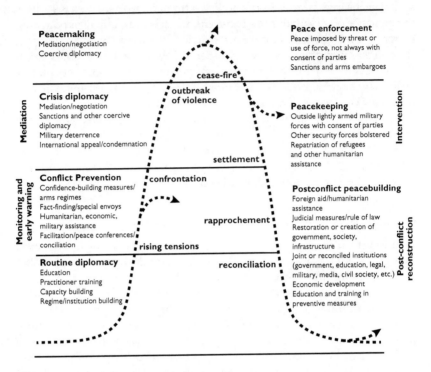

Figure 1.3 The life cycle of international conflict management.

Source: Adapted from Lund 1996, and Crocker et al. 2001.

that are currently in place to address this issue. Both the UN and a range of regional and subregional organizations have formal mandates to take action to address conflicts and crises. It is easy to dismiss these organizations because of some spectacular failures in recent years—the memories of international organizations' missteps in Rwanda, Bosnia, and Somalia in the 1990s still haunt the UN, AU, and NATO among others, as well as the leading nations that played major roles in these events.

But this is to some degree unfair. At the interstate level, the UN, for example, tends to get involved in conflicts and crises that are longer, more violent, and more complex in terms of numbers of involved actors, and where the gravity of threat is high (DeRouen 2003; Beardsley and Schmidt 2012). Touval (1994) argues that the UN gets involved in conflicts that are risky and intractable, and that often involve several prior failed mediation attempts. Its involvement is dictated by its organizational missions, but also the national as well as collective self-interest of the five permanent members of the Security Council. Notwithstanding these limitations, in the area of well-financed, multidimensional peacekeeping missions, the UN has had a strong effect in reducing the likelihood of recurrent violence (Collier et al. 2008b). This effect is even stronger when the UN has had more resources in the form of more troops to conduct these tasks (Doyle and Sambanis 2006). And UN peace-building also increases the likelihood of democratization after civil war, particularly in the short term (Doyle and Sambanis 2000).

At the interstate level, the UN tends to get involved in conflicts and crises that are longer, more violent, and more complex in terms of numbers of involved actors, and where the gravity of threat is high.

The number of regional organizations has increased significantly in recent years, and their involvement in regional conflict management has increased (Pevehouse 2002; Gartner 2011). Regional organizations can be more successful than the UN by employing region-specific skills, knowledge, and understanding that extraregional and/or global actors often cannot (Crocker et al. 2011). They also tend to have more interest and stakes in conflicts, and more commitment to their resolution (Fearon and Laitin 2003). While each region has engaged in some sort of collective peace-building, there is significant variation across regions. The Economic Community of West African States (ECOWAS), the Organization of American States (OAS), and the Organization for Security and Cooperation in Europe (OSCE) have been particularly active in regional conflict management. According to Gartner, these characteristics result in regional governmental organizations (RGOs) being viewed as more trustworthy than extraregional actors. But they also may get the tougher cases, and it is more difficult for RGOs to be neutral or to be viewed as unbiased, because members may be supporters of one or the other side in the conflict (Gartner 2011; Crocker et al. 2011).

NGOs and other civil society actors have become more involved in conflict management efforts in recent times, related to both global decentralization of conflict management and problems related to regional management, discussed above. NGO efforts are usually lower-profile and typically involve facilitating problem-solving sessions or providing good offices. Such NGOs can play an important role in improving relationships, building trust, facilitating communication, and building broad "supportive constituencies" (Crocker et al. 2011: 537) for dialogue and peace-building. Non-state actors typically work alongside states, IGOs, the private sector, and/or private individuals.

Two recent examples underscore the significant role that NGOs have played in conflict management and resolution. In the Liberian Civil War (1999–2003), mediated by an array of regional, extraregional, and global actors, an important mediation role was played by a series of Liberian civil society organizations—religious, women's, human rights, and legal groups—that pressured the parties to reach agreement. The Women of Liberia Mass Action for Peace Group went so far as to prevent the sides from leaving the negotiating room until they reached agreement (Crocker et al. 2011). In the North Malian conflict of 1990–5 between the Malian government and Tuareg rebels from the Popular Front for the Liberation of Azawad, the traditional community took the lead role as a mediator alongside Norwegian Church Aid, an international NGO focused on conflict resolution and other issues. This effort included provision of security guarantees by the traditional leaders. It successfully achieved both a semi-formal agreement in 1994 and a durable peace between the group, the government, and the Songhai, an ethnic group that has long experienced tensions with the Tuareg.[2]

The record is obviously mixed, given the earlier discussion of the current state of conflict resolution versus conflict recurrence. Nevertheless, it would be a mistake to omit from discussion those mechanisms that have been traditionally applied by IGOs, RGOs, and NGOs, as they have attempted to fulfill their peace-making, peacekeeping, and peace-building functions. And in many cases, the UN, RGOs, and NGOs can play an important role in the implementation of the collective action plan outlined below.

Collective Action Plan: From Management to Resolution

The sections below present an agenda for the development of a comprehensive set of interacting tools that the international community either has available to it or must develop and hone in order to cope with the challenges brought on by unresolved or recurrent conflict, particularly at the subnational level. They address these threats at all phases of the life cycle of international conflict management (see Figure 1.3): conflict prevention through monitoring and early warning, peace-making and peace enforcement through mediation and intervention, and finally peace-building in the area of postconflict reconstruction. Taken together, these tools can be the basis for a forward-looking approach to international stability and economic development and growth. They can form the basis of a comprehensive global approach to unresolved and recurrent conflict, and provide entry points to impact long-term global trends toward the provision of greater human security.

Monitoring and Early Warning

The rationale behind the development of early warning systems for instability in general and conflict and crises in particular lies in the recognition that it is easier to influence global events in their earliest stages, before they become more threatening and less manageable

(O'Brien 2010). Such systems, although in their infancy, hold the promise of providing early enough warning so that policy makers can set, calibrate, and adjust their strategies so as to be out ahead of instability events.

The rationale behind early warning systems for instability in general and conflict and crises in particular lies in the recognition that it is easier to influence global events in their earliest stages, before they become more threatening and less manageable.

The Center for International Development and Conflict Management (CIDCM) at the University of Maryland has been at the forefront of efforts to develop systematic approaches to early warning, particularly as they pertain to the identification of those countries at greatest risk for future civil conflict and instability (Hewitt 2012a; Backer and Huth 2014a). Other efforts have been undertaken by the Political Instability Task Force of the US Government (see Goldstone et al. 2010), by the U.S. Agency for International Development (2005), and by research efforts such as those led by Hegre and Sambanis (2006), Collier and Hoeffler (2004), and Fearon and Laitin (2003).

CIDCM's approach has resulted in the production of the *Peace and Conflict Instability Ledger*, a biannual assessment of the risk of future conflict and instability for 162 countries. The ledger is based on a structural model developed from data on a set of factors representing four broad categories of state features and functions drawn from the political, economic, security, and social domains. The specific indicators are institutional consistency, economic openness, infant mortality rate, militarization, and neighborhood security. Based on the model, a risk ratio is produced, which for 2012–14 ranked the following countries in the top 10 in terms of risk of instability: Afghanistan, Guinea-Bissau, Djibouti, Guinea, Burundi, DRC, Somalia, Niger, Mali, and Pakistan (Backer and Huth 2014a). While other approaches to early warning produce some differences in the rank ordering of specific countries, there is a good deal of convergence on membership in the top 25.

Such assessments, particularly where they converge despite differences in data sources and analytic methodologies, have already begun to serve as a basis for policy decisions regarding countries and regions most in need of both development aid and regime-stabilization programs. The US Agency for International Development, through its Alert List Reports (USAID 2013), has employed these rankings in making decisions about critical target countries, as well as on the types of aid packages that would be most appropriate for the specific circumstances of those societies. The Obama Administration's decision to base such aid on the dual objectives of development and stabilization, rather than solely on the basis of progress toward democratization and strict support for US objectives, has the potential down the road to get us closer to a need-based foreign assistance program. Early warning monitoring is the key to such decisions.

A new frontier in conflict early warning and peace-building has opened up with the increasingly widespread use of crowdsourcing and other social media for collecting data on and understanding violence, monitoring crises in real time, providing alternatives to government and media narratives on events, and identifying which areas and populations are most in need of humanitarian assistance. Using individuals and the public as source material, it involves monitoring their use of or actively asking them to use social media (Facebook, Twitter, YouTube, etc.) and electronic communication (email, text, etc.) to report acts of violence, and then mapping those acts electronically (Google Maps, Lonely Planet, etc.). Examples include the nonprofit organization Ushahidi's documentation of violence surrounding Kenya's December 2007 elections, Standby Volunteer Task Force's documentation of the Libyan civil war that began in March 2011, and The Syria Crisis Tracker Map's documentation of ongoing human rights violations in Syria since early 2011. These new methods address some of the drawbacks of traditional methods to monitor crises that rely on weekly completion of structured surveys by field monitors who are limited in number, cannot be eyewitnesses to most events, and cannot generate data in real time (Meier 2014). Not to be minimized, however, are challenges to crowdsourcing as well, which include government-imposed communications blackouts, the need for filters to check for reliability and accuracy, need for public–private philanthropy to increase access, sampling to account for low usage of social media, and need for geographic identifiers (Meier 2014).

Conflict Management Mechanisms

The international community has available to it a number of mechanisms for the management and resolution of conflict. *Management here involves eliminating the violent and violence-related means of pursuing the conflict, so that the issues can be worked out at the political level* (Zartman 1997). Conflict management can include any of the following activities: deterrence moves and reactions to them, arbitration, repression of the conflict, containment of the conflict, arms reductions, or any solution that involves the disputants simply arriving at a consensus based on compromise, with or without the assistance of a mediator (Burton 1990).

Building upon the discussion above concerning the construction of early warning mechanisms for conflict, it is important to understand how people are mobilized into violence and conflict in order to bring more effective tools to bear on the management and resolution processes.

For example, GDP per capita has been cited by scholars as a critical determinant of civil war onset (Collier and Hoeffler 2004; Fearon and Laitin 2003). Several models of individual behavior can be at play in explaining the behavior of individuals who become involved in such conflicts (Justino et al. 2013). "Which of these is in play at any given time—low opportunity costs for fighting, greed and grievance, self-protection, and perception of weak government—is critical in determining how policy interventions should be designed to effectively prevent or mitigate violent conflict" (Justino et al. 2013: 12–13). For example, if individuals are motivated to join rebel groups because of individual security concerns, then large-scale counterinsurgency actions on the part of the government will be counterproductive, because they are liable to lead individuals to feel even less secure.

"Which of these is in play at any given time—low opportunity costs for fighting, greed and grievance, self-protection, and perception of weak government—is critical in determining how policy interventions should be designed to effectively prevent or mitigate violent conflict."

Conflict management nearly always involves the division of power and commonly takes place in a power-bargaining situation. Third parties acting as crisis managers often seek to slow the pace of events occurring between the conflicting parties (Kleiboer 1998), to be in constant communication with these parties, and to encourage them to be more flexible regarding their thoughts and actions (Mitchell 1981). In this section, we will review key empirical findings on successful mediation in crisis management and conflict resolution, and then make some policy recommendations on how to translate these successes into collective action policy. In particular, our interest is in short-term outcomes that are referred to as *crisis management*—and post-crisis tension reduction among parties—a long-term outcome that are referred to as *conflict resolution*. We will examine broad mechanisms through which the international community has taken collective action in the management of conflict. Our focus, as it has been through most of this chapter, will be on collective security mechanisms that are particularly relevant to subnational conflict—the locus of most conflict in the system today.

Intervention Through Peacekeeping Missions

While intervention can take a number of forms, peacekeeping missions are perhaps the most critical in addressing conflict at the subnational level. In the post-Cold War era, peacekeeping has been focused on helping to bring about long-term peace between disputants and to "prevent the resumption of civil conflict" (Fortna 2004: 271). Peacekeeping also expanded to include enforcement missions. This latter shift has proven problematic, with high-profile early failures in Bosnia and Somalia causing rethinking of where and when to send troops (Doyle and Sambanis 2006). Peacekeeping has evolved to take on four primary forms.

Observer missions are usually small and nonmilitarized. The purpose is to serve as a buffer or to monitor ceasefires, troop withdrawals, etc., while peacemaking proceeds. The United Nations Disengagement Observer Force (UNDOF) was established in 1974 following the agreed disengagement of Israeli and Syrian forces in the Golan Heights, and has remained in the area to monitor the ceasefire and to supervise the implementation of the agreement. Monitoring committees fit here as well, although they are generally less well armed.

Traditional peacekeeping missions are usually larger than observer missions and typically involve an observer component plus lightly armed military units that can only act in self-defense. The purpose is similar to that of observer missions, but they are better armed. In 2007, the AU and the UN created the AU/UN Hybrid Operation in Darfur (UNAMID). With a core mission of protecting civilians, it is also tasked with policing, security for humanitarian assistance, monitoring and verifying implementation of agreements, assisting in an inclusive political process, and contributing to the promotion of human rights and the rule of law.

Multidimensional peacekeeping missions are typically traditional peacekeeping missions plus a large civilian peace-building component (Fortna 2004). "Civilian functions" include "economic reconstruction, institutional reform...election oversight" (Doyle and Sambanis 2000: 791), reintegration of former combatants, security sector reform (e.g., police training and monitoring), human rights monitoring, and in some cases administration (Fortna 2004). UNAMID in Darfur has elements of both traditional peacekeeping and multidimensional missions.

Enforcement missions are the most militarized type of mission. They can "impose peace by force" (Fortna 2004: 270). Their purpose can range from creating safe conditions for humanitarian assistance to military operations to counter aggression. Military operations have taken three forms: 1. Peacekeepers fight against one or more parties with little to no consent, which have usually been ineffective; 2. Peacekeepers impose security measures (e.g., humanitarian corridors, no-fly zones, etc.) without unanimous consent; and 3. Peacekeepers punish defection from accords (Doyle and Sambanis 2006).

In 2013 the UN Security Council established an intervention brigade based in Goma of three infantry battalions and auxiliary forces under the command of the UN Organization Stabilization Mission to the DRC (MONUSCO), charged with carrying out offensive operations to neutralize armed groups that threaten state authority and civilian security. Also in 2013, the Security Council created the UN Multidimensional

Integrated Stabilization Mission in Mali (MINUSMA), authorized to use all necessary measures to stabilize the key population centers and to prevent the return of armed elements to those areas.

At the intrastate level, the UN is more likely to intervene in cases that are violent, that have ended in stalemate rather than clear-cut military victories, that lack formal agreements that have ended the conflict, have high death rates, have been deemed intractable, that may have involved several failed mediation attempts, and that involve weak states (Fortna 2004; Gilligan and Stedman 2003; Doyle and Sambanis 2006). While a general concern for humanitarian crises often motivates UN intervention, the self-interests of the member states, particularly the permanent members of the Security Council, are an important complicating factor.

But global organizations often lack the consensus, resources, and cultural sensitivity to deal effectively in local conflicts. It is here where regional organizations can and do play a significant role in conflict management and resolution. Some regions have a relatively large number of institutions and mechanisms for conflict management (e.g., OSCE, NATO, EU, and the Council of Europe among European institutions; and the AU, ECOWAS, and the African Peer Review Mechanism in Africa). Other regions and their institutions have been more constrained in building effective mechanisms. In Asia for example, sovereignty norms have remained strong and ASEAN's role regarding security has not broadened to include peace-building (Crocker et al. 2011).

Global organizations often lack the consensus, resources, and cultural sensitivity to deal effectively in local conflicts. It is here where regional organizations can and do play a significant role in conflict management and resolution.

Mediation

Mediation is "a process of conflict management where disputants seek the assistance of, or accept an offer of help from, an individual, group, state, or organization to settle their conflict or resolve their differences without resorting to physical force or invoking the authority of the law" (Bercovitch et al. 1991: 8). In this section, we will identify the key international actors and institutions that can provide mediation in conflict situations, and discuss the various styles of mediation that they can apply. Ultimately we will let research guide us to the most effective combinations of actors and styles that can have the greatest impact on crisis management and conflict resolution. In this discussion, we will include global, regional, and domestic mediators.

> Mediation is a process of conflict management where disputants seek to settle their conflict or resolve their differences without resorting to physical force or invoking the authority of the law.

Mediation styles are classified as follows:

Facilitation: The focus here is on ensuring communication and information sharing among parties, but with no substantive contribution. At the very least, facilitators help to open or maintain lines of communication between parties. Actions may be as simple as providing good offices and a forum so that they can talk. But they also may be more active: encouraging compromise and redefinition of problems into non-zero-sum terms, conducting trust-building activities (Fisher 1972; Aggestam 2002), structuring the negotiation agenda to ensure discussion of important issues, serving as a conduit through which parties pass messages when they cannot meet face-to-face, or supplying and clarifying information (Touval and Zartman 1985; Bercovitch and Houston 1996).

Formulation: Here the focus is on proposing, promoting, or coordinating parties on specific solutions, without pressure or incentives. Formulators work to identify the set of outcomes that are acceptable to both sides—i.e., the zone of agreement—and then use persuasion and suggestion to coordinate the parties' focus on specific ones. They may also propose outcomes of their own. If a zone of agreement does not exist or is narrow, formulators may work to redefine the issues so that the parties come to view certain outcomes as acceptable (Touval and Zartman 1985; Bercovitch and Houston 1996). Formulators may be especially important during bargaining stalemates (Schelling 1960).

Manipulation. The focus is on using pressure and leverage, and controling information (Bercovitch 1997). Mediators using this set of techniques employ positive and negative incentives (i.e., "carrots" and "sticks") to change parties' cost-benefit calculi regarding fighting versus peace: sticks are used to raise costs or decrease benefits of continued fighting, and carrots are used to increase benefits or decrease costs of cooperation (Carnevale 1986; Richmond 1998; Schrodt and Gerner 2004).[3] In doing so, manipulators can expand the zone of agreement or perhaps create one that does not yet exist (Hopmann 1996; Wilkenfeld et al. 2003). They can also help the parties to save face when making unpopular and difficult concessions to a greater extent than less directive mediators, since they have more control over the process (Rubin 1980). Manipulators are typically powerful or have prominent positions, as leverage stems from resources and status. Manipulators may also provide *agreement or security guarantees*; help the parties to implement agreements, maintain ceasefires, and demobilize troops; or enforce compliance with agreements. Security guarantees can take the form of monitoring/oversight committees or peacekeepers (e.g., UN in Cambodia, El Salvador, Sudan, and DRC; NATO in Bosnia) (Hartzell et al. 2001; Walter 2002; Fortna 2003; 2004; Smith and Stam 2003).

Mediation at the Interstate Level

At the *interstate* level, mediation has a significant positive effect on *conflict management* (formal agreement) in **international crises**. Manipulation is significantly more effective at managing crises than the less-directive mediation styles of facilitation and formulation. But mediation has a mixed effect on *conflict resolution* after international crises. It is effective at preventing crises from recurring in the short and medium terms—1 and 5 years, respectively—but has a negative effect on durable peace in the long term. And here, less-directive mediation styles are more effective than manipulation at achieving durable peace. Under pressure to stop the fighting as quickly as possible, manipulators may use their leverage expediently without addressing the serious underlying problems between the conflict adversaries (Beardsley 2011; Beardsley et al. 2006; Wilkenfeld et al. 2003, 2005; Quinn et al. 2006; Morgan 1994; Bercovitch and Houston 1996).

Mediation at the Intrastate Level

Among *intrastate* conflicts and crises, mediation also has a significant positive effect on conflict management. Here too, manipulation is significantly more effective at managing crises than less-directive mediation styles (Quinn et al. 2013a, 2013b; Zartman 1989; Rothchild 1997). Mediator-arranged security guarantees are the most effective form of manipulative mediation at achieving agreements (Doyle and Sambanis 2006; Quinn et al. 2013a). But mediation has a mixed effect on conflict resolution at the intrastate level, with empirical findings unable to give very clear guidance on how best to use mediation to facilitate conflict resolution at this level. This finding is of considerable concern, given the earlier discussion of conflict recurrence as a dominant phenomenon in the post-Cold War era.

A particularly challenging set of intrastate cases involves violent conflicts and crises that are rooted in ethnic divisions and are part of protracted conflicts; and this phenomenon characterizes an unusually large portion of conflicts and crises in Africa. What are the best means for promoting short-term crisis management and long-term conflict resolution among these cases? Are conflict management and conflict resolution fundamentally different tasks, for which certain approaches to intervention may be more or less effective? Here we grapple with these issues by focusing on Africa, although the intent is to generalize and thus build a set of indicators and recommended strategies beyond that troubled continent.

Ethnic violence across many regions of Africa presents the international community with wrenching dilemmas and difficult decisions. While the images coming out of the Central African Republic and South Sudan today are perhaps freshest in our minds, many other African countries have experienced outbreaks in recent years—Kenya, Ethiopia, Somalia, Nigeria, Rwanda, and Burundi. Eight of the twenty-six currently active conflicts in the world are in Africa (Asal and Wilkenfeld 2013) and 17 of the top 25 countries most at risk of future instability are on that troubled continent (Backer and Huth 2014a). Africa has experienced less external conflict management intervention than other regions, due in large part to its perceived peripheral status (Gilligan and Stedman 2003).

As we puzzle over the problem of conflict recurrence at the intrastate level, a set of recent research findings specific to the mediation of African ethnic crises sheds some light and also points toward mechanisms that are likely to make a difference to moving forward. The key finding has been that, despite an admirable record for mediation of creating conditions for reaching agreements to end intrastate crises, particularly when more manipulative forms of mediation are employed, such agreements have only limited durability. But in all the mix of different mediation styles and mediator types, the involvement of domestic mediators seems to be a factor in moving some of these crises toward conflict resolution.

Long-term tension reduction among adversaries is a much rarer event and more impervious to mediator influence than formal agreement (see Quinn et al. 2013a). Nevertheless, if the goal of mediation is to bring about long-term peace, findings for African conflicts suggest emerging evidence for the role for domestic mediation toward that end. The case of Angola provides a clear example of the connection between domestic mediation and post-crisis tension reduction. Successful domestic mediation efforts were preceded by the failure of purely regional or extraregional mediators to achieve long-term peace, illustrating the differential effects of domestic and external mediation on this outcome.

The civil war between Angola and the National Union for the Total Independence of Angola (UNITA) ended in 1994 with the Lusaka Protocol, but implementation of the agreement was sluggish. A new crisis emerged in May 1998, triggered by UNITA engaging in large residual troop movements, reoccupation of several districts that it had previously relinquished to state rule, and several low-level clashes with Angolan troops. The crisis simmered for several months, unable to be resolved

by several outside efforts, including the conflict's long-running mediation team consisting of the UN and a troika of extraregional observer
countries—the US, Portugal, and Russia. In July 1998, the crisis escalated
into the third civil war between the two sides.

Under pressure from the UN and US to end the conflict, Angola asked
the UN to push hard-line UNITA leader Jonas Savimbi to accept peace
in December 2001. The UN used the Inter-Ecclesiastical Committee for
Peace in Angola (COIEPA), a domestic religious organization, to establish
contacts with Savimbi. The Community of Sant'Egidio, a Rome-based
Catholic lay organization, also worked alongside the UN and COIEPA.
The mediation team facilitated talks between the two sides, exchanged
and analyzed the parties' proposals, and offered its own proposals.
The UN also used a manipulative approach: a combination of pressure,
sanctions against UNITA, and security guarantees. It is likely that the
domestic religious mediators played a less-intrusive, albeit important, role
alongside UN manipulation.

The mediation effort increased and in 2002 military delegations from
Angola and UNITA signed the Luena Memorandum of Understanding.
The nearly comprehensive agreement terminated the crisis, resolved all
military matters between the two sides, and called for a resumption
of the Lusaka Protocol's political process. No further crises occurred
between UNITA and Angola. Although exhaustion, factionalization, and
declining power on the rebel side, as well as UNITA-leader Savimbi's
death, contributed to bringing the crisis to termination, the mediation
effort played a key role, speeding up the process by acting as the crucial conduit through which long-dormant negotiations were reestablished
between the two sides, offering peace proposals, and agreeing to provide security guarantees during the postwar peace-building process. For
years, the UN had unsuccessfully led mediation efforts aimed at secur-
ing long-term peace in Angola, endeavors including a bevy of regional
actors and extraregional and former colonial powers. But it was not
until the UN worked alongside domestic mediators that a final peace
was achieved, bringing a 4-year civil war and a decades-old conflict to
conclusion.

The Angola case makes clear that a successful collective action
plan for addressing recurring conflict and crisis should include domestic
actors in the mix of strategies and institutions involved in these efforts.
While domestic actors may lack the manipulative clout and resources to
bring about conflict resolution on their own, their presence in the process,
particularly when mediation partners can employ a more manipulative
style of mediation, assures that the parties in the conflict will have peace
partners who are both culturally sensitive to their needs and are likely
to stay involved in the process of peace-making and peace-building that

is important for sustaining agreements. International and regional mediators of necessity move on to the next hotspot, but the domestic actors remain on the scene and have a direct stake in a positive outcome.

A successful collective action plan for addressing recurring intrastate conflict and crisis should include domestic actors in the mix of strategies and institutions involved in these efforts.

Postconflict Reconstruction

Given the frequency of conflict recurrence that has been discussed throughout this chapter, one of the most important steps that the international community can take to address this issue is to target postconflict situations and to try to prevent recurrence. That translates to a focus on "recovery…prevention and mitigation" during the stages of "reconciliation, reconstruction, and stabilization" (Backer and Huth 2014b: 22). In the sections below, we will identify several actions that can be undertaken both collectively and locally to provide a better atmosphere for sustained peace-making. We will focus on four areas where actions taken during the period immediately following active conflict can have the greatest impact.

Sustained Conflict Management Processes

Poverty, lootable resources, and low economic development have been linked to higher likelihood of civil war recurrence (Doyle and Sambanis 2000; Collier and Hoeffler 2004; Walter 2004; Fortna 2004). A lack of postwar economic development may be especially crucial for causing recurrence (Collier et al. 2008b; Doyle and Sambanis 2006).[4] As noted earlier, it behooves us to think in terms of human security and the linkage between economic and social development, respect for human rights, and peace. We will discuss in Chapter 4 the inability of wealthy nations and international and regional organizations to adequately meet the development needs of many nations. But even when we do attempt to address these needs, our efforts have not been sufficiently sustained over the long haul. Put simply, our attention wanders as we are bombarded with new needs that vie for the attention of the international community and the limited resources that have been available. As a consequence, we have been unable to devote the attention and resources that are needed at various stages of recovery from conflict. We know now that targeted international aid programs should be increased, or at least sustained, for 5 to 10 years after the end of war and should aim at promoting social programs as well as economic growth.

In recovery from conflict, we know now that targeted international aid programs should be increased, or at least sustained, for 5 to 10 years after the end of war and should aim at promoting social programs as well as economic growth.

The link between postconflict development aid and sustainability of peace is quite clear. Research has shown that the pattern of postconflict aid disbursements should probably gradually rise during the first four post-conflict years, and gradually taper back to normal levels by the end of the first postconflict decade. There is evidence to suggest that the period immediately following the end of conflict is a temporary phase during which aid is particularly effective in promoting economic growth. But historical evidence shows that aid flows/allocations usually taper off just when they should be ramping up (Collier and Hoeffler 2004; Hoeffler 2010).

Peace-building in general needs to account for civilians to a greater extent, in terms of both allowing for their contribution to the process and understanding how they are affected by violence. Peace-building is typically a top-down process, and the civilian population is rarely consulted or given a vote when peace-building policies are drafted and implemented.[5] Certain types of civilians receive some attention: women (see discussion below), because they "disproportionately experience sexual violence, coercion, and enslavement at the hand of armed groups...(and) may also be more likely to suffer from indirect consequences of the conflict" (Vinck and Pham 2014: 111), as well as traditional and religious leaders, and civil society representatives due to their high status. When a wider range of civilians is considered, simplistic assumptions are often made about their postconflict concerns: "security, satisfying basic needs for food and shelter, returning to a normal life, and obtaining reparation and justice" (ibid.: 105). But they can have strong feelings about peace-building and actively facilitate or thwart it (Vinck and Pham 2014).

Transitional Justice Processes

Tribunals, truth commissions, and other **track II processes**, commonly referred to as transitional justice processes, have been employed with increasing success in the post-Cold War era as part of an approach to rebuilding societies and nations that are emerging from conflict. A truth commission is:

> an ad hoc, autonomous, and victim-centered commission of inquiry set up in and authorized by a state for the primary purpose of (1) investigating and reporting on the principal causes and consequences of broad and relatively recent patterns of severe

violence or repression that occurred in the state during determinate periods of abusive rule or conflict, and (2) making recommendations for their redress and future prevention.

(Freeman 2006: 18)

A criminal tribunal is a "judicial body created to investigate and prosecute individuals accused of violations of human rights or humanitarian law in the wake of violent conflict" (International Institute for Democracy and Electoral Assistance 2003).

As Meernik et al. (2010) point out, nations that adopt transitional justice tend to begin the postconflict phase in better political health than those that don't. Long-running civil wars seem particularly likely to result in truth commissions. The comparatively higher daily death rate for civil wars that were not followed by either a truth commission or a tribunal suggests that intense and destructive wars are not likely to result in the adoption of transitional justice. Nations whose civil wars end in settlement are more likely to adopt transitional justice. Nations involved in intensely violent wars that result in outright victory by one side or conclusion short of a settlement are the least likely candidates for transitional justice.

Nations that adopt transitional justice tend to begin the postconflict phase in better political health than those that don't.

Nations adopting transitional justice tend to begin the postconflict phase in better political health. Their scores on indicators of political and civil rights, and level of democracy are significantly higher than for all other post-civil war states. Per capita gross domestic products of truth commission and tribunal states rise significantly at a fairly steady pace over the course of the postconflict years. In contrast, the group of states that do not experience any form of transitional justice—a group with a slightly higher average GDP per capita—experiences stagnant economic growth during the postconflict period (Meernik et al. 2010).

A Crucial Role for Women in the Postconflict Environment

Although women are profoundly affected by armed conflict, subject to an array of gender-based abuses both during the violence and in its aftermath, they are often excluded from formal peace-building efforts (Caprioli et al. 2010). Yet women are critically important for the process of creating a more just, sustainable, and durable peace. In many cases, women may be the only remaining vestiges of civil society left after intense conflict.

Women's participation in the peace-building process, whether by formal involvement in negotiations or engagement through grassroots political mobilization, is integral to the success of the negotiations themselves. Rather than imposing a unilateral solution, research indicates that women tend to take a more cooperative approach to dispute resolution and are less likely to support the use of violence. Perhaps due to a holistic view of security that includes social and economic issues, incorporating women in political negotiations tends to solidify conflict resolution (Caprioli et al. 2010).

While no country has implemented a fully gender-sensitive peace process, even limited attention to women's issues appears to correlate with positive outcomes. Close examination of various cases confirms that women generally effect positive outcomes for peace duration and social indicators, and that peace agreements are more durable when women formally participate in their negotiation. An ideal peace process would include both grassroots mobilization and formal representation of women.

Women generally effect positive outcomes for peace duration and social indicators, and peace agreements are more durable when women formally participate in their negotiation.

There is also empirical data on how women's participation relates to the duration of agreements to end conflict (Uppsala Conflict Data Program 2008). Most of the agreements studied are still in force today and all but two effectively ended major violent conflict within the country. In contrast, the majority of the agreements where women were not involved have come to an end through rejection or defection by one or more of the parties.

The Obama administration announced on Oct 26, 2010 a commitment of *$44 million to "Women's Empowerment Initiatives,"* $17 million of which was to be spent in Afghanistan. The funding was in direct response to UN Security Council Resolution 1325, which was adopted in October 2000, and "marked the first time the Security Council required people in conflict areas to respect women's rights and to support the essential role that women play in peacemaking and ending sexual violence in conflicts." *United Nations Development Fund for Women (UNIFEM)* is calling for National Action Plans to be enacted in support of 1325. The United States has not yet developed an action plan, but according to then US Secretary of State Hillary Clinton, this funding is an important step (Clinton 2010).

Paced Democratization

As we will see in Chapter 3, the building of sustainable democracy is a long-term process. One of the grave dangers of imposing democratic institutions before a full societal comprehension of democratic norms and values is that certain trappings of democracy can actually make the situation worse. For example, in multiethnic societies, there have often been historical cultural norms that have kept various ethnic groups in rough balance and some sort of sustainable equilibrium. Imposition of elections in a society not ready for them can mean extreme ethnic voting patterns, which in turn can lead to a more forced division of society along ethnic lines than had heretofore existed, creating tensions and perhaps ultimately conflict.

In Figure 1.4, we see evidence from the past several decades suggesting that, prior to 1995, there were no significant differences among democracies, semi-democracies, and autocracies in terms of impact on conflict recurrence. In the past 15 years, democracies have shown the lowest risk of conflict recurrence, while autocratic regimes have exhibited the highest risk (Hegre and Fjelde 2010). We will see in Chapter 3 that democratic reversals that result in anocracy have the highest rate of instability, and it is not a far reach to make the connection between this instability and conflict. Hence, we argue here for what we have termed paced democratization, which would include a focus on the building of a culture of democracy and some of its institutions, before too much emphasis is placed on elections.

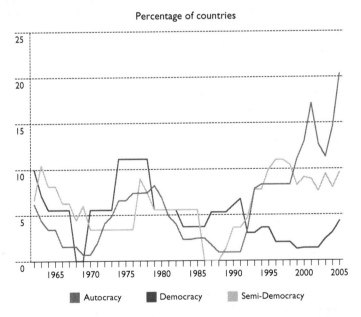

Percentage of countries

Figure 1.4 Post-conflict countries that revert to conflict, 1960–2007.

Source: Hegre and Fjelde 2010, p. 83, Figure 8.2.

Paced democratization would include a focus on the building of a culture of democracy and some of its institutions before too much emphasis is placed on elections.

The mechanisms and actions outlined in this section—monitoring and early warning, intervention and peace-building, postconflict reconstruction, and paced democratization—constitute an action plan for the international community as it addresses head-on the critical post-Cold War phenomenon of intrastate conflict recurrence. Other mechanisms are available, but are not discussed in detail, including power sharing, third-party security and agreement guarantors, autonomy or partition, waiting for a stalemate, more emphasis on peace-building, and a serious revision of the UN's role in addressing conflict.

Conclusion

We began this chapter with the key observation that almost all conflict in the international system today is occurring within countries, termed "intrastate conflict." That is coupled with the fact that the number of active conflicts has been in steady decline since the end of the Cold War. We then note, however, that conflict recurrence is a major current concern—during the past two decades, the greatest threat of armed conflict has come from countries that recently resolved a serious armed internal conflict. The current rate of conflict recurrence among these intrastate conflicts is at its highest level since World War II.

Against this backdrop, we have examined a number of mechanisms available to the international, regional, NGO, and local communities to deal with the recurrent threat of conflict. We have examined mechanisms that can help the international community move from short-term conflict management to long-term conflict resolution. These mechanisms include monitoring and early warning systems, intervention in the form of mediation, postconflict reconstruction and reconciliation processes, and paced democratization. Key findings include:

- Understanding how people mobilize into violence and conflict is critical for the development of proper conflict management and resolution mechanisms.
- Matching the dynamics or the life cycle of conflicts with available conflict management and resolution processes is critical for success.
- Coordination among international, regional, and domestic institutions and organs enhances the chances of sustained conflict resolution.

- Domestic actors with a direct stake in positive conflict outcomes can play critical roles in sustaining peace-making and peace-building.
- In rebuilding civil society in a postconflict environment, transitional justice processes such as tribunals, truth commissions, and other Track II processes can be critical in creating and sustaining peace.
- The active inclusion of women in the process of postconflict rebuilding of civil society is crucial in creating and sustaining the peace.

While each conflict arena presents its own set of unique circumstances, decades of peace-making, peace-building, and peacekeeping experience can now provide the international community with elements of an action plan which can then be adapted to fit individual cases.

Notes

1 "Anocracies are hybrid political systems with both authoritarian and democratic features" (Frantz 2014). See Chapter 3 for a more extended discussion of the characteristics of anocratic systems.
2 This agreement broke down in 2012 with a renewed Tuareg insurgency, with both France and ECOWAS becoming involved in managing that conflict.
3 Carrots include such things as providing side payments and agreeing to pay costs to set up agreement (Carnevale 1986; Smith and Stam 2003; Schrodt and Gerner 2004; Rauchhaus 2006).
4 Doyle and Sambanis (2006) find that states with higher levels of GDP per capita and energy resources in the aftermath of civil wars are less likely to experience war recurrence.
5 Part of the problem is how to assess civilian perspectives. Progress has been made in recent years via surveys, interviews, and focus groups with civilians affected by violence (Vinck and Pham 2014).

Chapter 2

Ethnic Diversity

The Myth and Reality of Ethnic Diversity: Setting the Scene

If we have any hope of addressing global challenges through the institution of the nation-state, we must first attend to the conditions conducive to its continued stability. Several of the topics covered in this book touch on the issue of security—from the individual, to the group, and finally to national security. In this chapter, we focus on the individual and group levels, and unpack the complex set of relationships and interactions that accompany ethnicity. Ethnic, religious, cultural, and racial diversity are facts of life in most countries. Such identity for many is important to their self-concept, expressed both in the home and in community and political life.

Myth 2 Diverse societies are culturally dynamic, facilitating individual and collective identity, and fostering creativity, imagination, and invention.

Ted Gurr, one of the leading scholars on ethnonationalism, has defined an **ethnic group** as follows:

> people who share a distinctive and enduring collective identity based on common descent, shared experiences and cultural traits. They may define themselves, and be defined by others, in terms of any or all of a bundle of traits: customary behavior and dress, religious beliefs, language, physical appearance ("race"), region of residence, traditional occupations, and a history of conquest and repression by culturally different people.
>
> (Gurr 2000: 3–4)

An ethnic group has been defined as people who share a distinctive and enduring collective identity based on common descent, shared experiences and cultural traits.

Current ethnic diversity of states

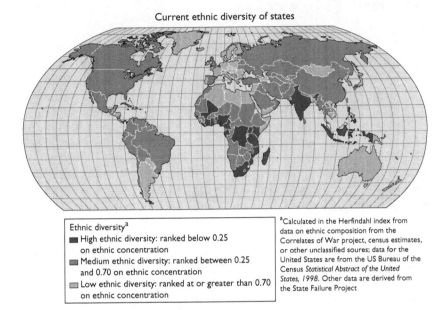

Ethnic diversity[a]

■ High ethnic diversity: ranked below 0.25
on ethnic concentration

■ Medium ethnic diversity: ranked between 0.25
and 0.70 on ethnic concentration

▨ Low ethnic diversity: ranked at or greater than 0.70
on ethnic concentration

[a]Calculated in the Herfindahl index from
data on ethnic composition from the
Correlates of War project, census estimates,
or other unclassified soures; data for the
United States are from the US Bureau of the
Census *Statistical Abstract of the United
States, 1998*. Other data are derived from
the State Failure Project

Figure 2.1   World ethnic diversity.

Source: Adapted from World Ethnic Diversity Map 2000, www.mappery.com/map-of/world-ethnic-diversity-map.

Figure 2.1 presents a world map showing how wide the variation is in ethnic diversity among the world's 190+ countries. Perhaps the most striking feature is the amazing concentration of ethnically diverse societies in Africa. In fact, according to one set of measures, the top 20 ethnically diverse countries are in Africa. Japan, North Korea, and South Korea are the least diverse countries on the globe. Interestingly, with some key exceptions like the Balkans, European countries demonstrate very low levels of ethnic diversity; and some of the individual country statistics are staggering. Fearon (2003) has produced a ranking of countries based on ethnic fractionalization scores. These scores calculate the probability that two persons from the same country meeting on the street will be from different ethnic groups. These probabilities range from highs of 0.93 for the DRC, 0.93 for Uganda, 0.81 for India, and 0.75 for Afghanistan, to 0.012 for Japan, 0.004 for South Korea, and 0.002 for North Korea (Fearon 2003).

Reality One in every seven people on the globe is a citizen of a diverse society in which ethnic minorities suffer some form of discrimination—political, economic, social or cultural (United Nations Development Programme 2004; Minorities at Risk Project 2009).

Although that in and of itself is disturbing enough, even more disturbing is that seven of the ten most lethal terrorist acts in the past decade have been perpetrated by organizations with strong ethnic links (Asal et al. 2008). What are the contributing factors in moving an ethnicity-based organization from the adoption of legitimate means of political and social mobilization and action to violence and in some cases terrorism? In the Middle East and North Africa, for example, current research shows that these factors include a nondemocratic ideology, advocacy of self-determination, foreign and diaspora support, rhetoric justifying violence, and significant repression by the governments of the countries in which they reside. If all five factors are present, there is an 89 percent probability that the organization will engage in violence, often in the form of terrorism (Wilkenfeld et al. 2009).

Seven of the ten most lethal terrorist acts in the past decade have been perpetrated by organizations with strong ethnic links.

A decade ago, the United Nations Development Programme's *Human Development Report 2004* (United Nations Development Programme 2004) focused in on "Cultural Liberty in Today's Diverse World." In it, they argued that a multicultural approach to building more inclusive societies is not only desirable, but also possible. In the report, they then go on to debunk leading misperceptions associated with the supposed difficulty in achieving pluralism in a world dominated by cultural and ethnic diversity.

- People's ethnic identities compete with their attachment to the state, so there is a trade-off between recognizing diversity and unifying the state (United Nations Development Programme 2004: 2). Individuals can have multiple identities—ethnicity, religion, race, as well as citizenship. *There is no inevitable need to choose between state unity and recognition of cultural differences.* India, for example, with its 2,000+ ethnic groups and a vast diversity of cultures, has been reasonably cohesive, although a number of separatist groups are active in various parts of the country (Quinn 2008). The constant challenge is in reinvigorating India's commitment to practises of pluralism, institutional accommodations, and conflict resolution through democratic means (United Nations Development Programme 2004: 49).
- Ethnic groups are prone to violent conflict with each other in clashes of values, so there is a trade-off between respecting diversity and sustaining peace (United Nations Development Programme 2004: 3). While we have noted in Chapter 1 that conflict in the international system is now predominantly subnational in nature, *ethnic and*

cultural factors in and of themselves are not the single or simple cause of conflict. Better explanations focus on economic inequalities between the groups and conflict over political power, land ownership, and other economic assets.

- Cultural liberty requires defending traditional practices, so there could be a trade-off between recognizing cultural diversity and other human development priorities such as progress in development, democracy, and human rights (United Nations Development Programme 2004: 4). *Culture is not an immovable set of values and practises, but rather is constantly revised and reinvigorated as adaptation occurs and values and practises are redefined, adapting to changing realities and the exchange of ideas* (United Nations Development Programme 2004: 4).

- Ethnically diverse countries are less able to develop, so there is a trade-off between respecting diversity and promoting development (United Nations Development Programme 2004: 4). *While it is the case that many ethnically diverse societies also have low levels of development, there is no clear evidence of a cause-and-effect relationship.* Malaysia, for example, which ranks in the top quartile on the ethnic fractionalization index (Fearon 2003), has been one of the world's fastest growing economies for the past two decades (United Nations Development Programme 2004: 4).

- Some cultures are more likely to make developmental progress than others, and some cultures have inherent democratic values while others do not, so there is a trade-off between accommodating certain cultures and promoting development and democracy (United Nations Development Programme 2004: 4). Sometimes called "cultural determinism," *the idea that a group's culture explains its economic performance and its ability to incorporate democratic principles has not been supported by either statistical analysis or historical case studies.* These unfounded theories can lead to support for nationalistic policies that denigrate and even suppress so-called inferior cultures, and stand in the way of national unity, democracy, and development. At the extreme, they can lead to tensions both within and between countries (United Nations Development Programme 2004: 5).

Ethnic diversity in and of itself is not particularly problematic, and as indicated can be a force for innovation and creativity in society. But when ethnicity is politically mobilized in a divisive manner—as it has been in the past in countries as far flung as Rwanda and the former Yugoslavia, or as it is today in Iraq, Afghanistan, Pakistan, and in many parts of Africa, it can become a very powerful means of motivating and organizing individuals for violence.

Ethnic diversity can be a force for innovation and creativity in society. But when ethnicity is politically mobilized in a divisive manner, it can become a very powerful means of motivating and organizing individuals for violence.

Figure 2.2 shows the countries in the world that, according to 2006 data from the Minorities at Risk (MAR) project, have at least one militant, ethnically based minority organization (Wilkenfeld 2011). So the reality is that, when the ethnic blend does not work, it does not work in spectacularly negative fashion.

In Chapter 1 we noted a general decline in conflict in the international system after a peak in the late 1980s and early 1990s. This shifting pattern is almost entirely attributable to a decline in ethnic wars, which Gurr (2000) feels is the result of three converging factors. Windows of opportunity for political activism in the former Soviet sphere and Eastern Europe have now largely closed (although recent events in the Ukraine stand out as an obvious exception). Civil capacity for addressing **ethnopolitical** challenges has increased, especially in democratic societies. And international efforts to publicize and prevent violations of group rights increased markedly after the Cold War (Gurr 2000: xiv). With all of this, however, we have reached something of a steady state in the number of domestic (including ethnic) conflicts ongoing in any particular year, averaging about 28 per year for the past decade. In Chapter 1, we discussed this phenomenon in the context of conflict recurrence, that is, our inability to resolve these conflicts in a way that would bring about a lasting settlement among the parties. Are ethnic conflicts unique in the types of issues they raise and therefore the types of techniques needed for their resolution?

According to Gurr, there are three main explanations for the extreme difficulty in bringing ethnopolitical conflicts to successful conclusion. First, the assertion of ethnic and other communal identities will continue, because it is based on persistent grievances about inequalities and past wrong, and because movements based on identity have succeeded often enough in the past and justify emulation and repetition. Second, the ethnic conflict management strategies that have been favored by Western states and international organizations in the past have not been uniformly effective. For example, the encouragement of democratic institutions and elections in weak, heterogeneous states often increases the chances of ethnopolitical conflict. Internationally brokered settlements, cease-fires, amnesties, and signing ceremonies often mask the remaining conditions that lead to the next spasm of fighting. And third, states, international, and regional organizations that promote negotiated settlements often declare victory and depart after the first round of multiparty elections and

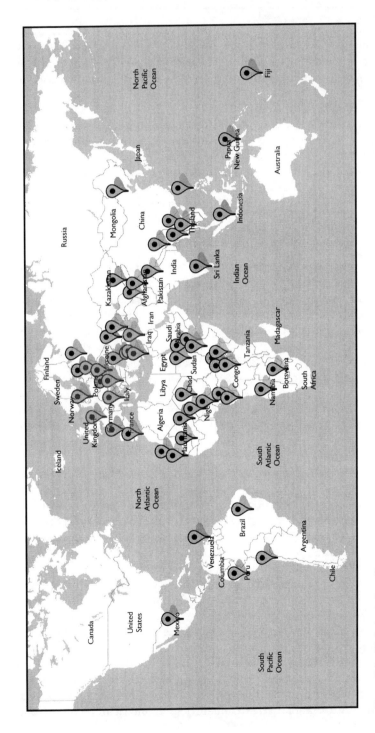

Figure 2.2   Global ethnic militancy.

Source: Wilkenfeld 2011, p. 230, Figure 14.1.

settlements, rather than remaining around to provide sustained political and material resources in post conflict situations (Gurr 2000: xiv–xv).

Ethnicity, Conflict, and Violence

In this section, we will delve more deeply into what may be an increasingly fraught relationship between ethnicity and conflict. Invariably, ethnic diversity has come to be closely associated with violence and conflict. While examples of harmonious multiethnic societies are numerous— Canada, Singapore, Malaysia, Belgium, Switzerland—so too are cases in which an ethnic divide has brought on civil strife, government repression, spillover into multiethnic neighboring states, and, in the extreme, foreign intervention on the side of one or another of the contesting ethnic groups—the Balkans (Winston Churchill famously said that "the Balkans produce more history than they can consume," to which Ambassador Samuel Lewis added "locally"), Rwanda, Sudan, Somalia, etc. The incorporation of the Sudetenland into Nazi Germany in 1938, ostensibly to protect ethnic Germans in the region, left the rest of Czechoslovakia weak and powerless to resist subsequent occupation of the rest of Czechoslovakia in March 1939. At the time of this writing, Russia is engaged in an intervention in Ukraine in support of ethnic Russians in the eastern regions of that multiethnic nation, having already annexed Crimea in 2014.

Ethnic diversity has come to be closely associated with violence and conflict in the form of civil strife, government repression, spillover into multiethnic neighboring states, and in the extreme, foreign intervention.

Despite the fact that not all individual ethnic group members or organizations that claim to represent them use violence, ethnicity can be a powerful tool for organizing violence, and incidents of ethnic violence are high profile and can be highly destructive. For example, as we see in Figure 2.3, in any given year, a large proportion (roughly 20–30 percent) of ethnic organizations in the Middle East and North Africa use violence (Asal and Wilkenfeld 2013).

The Impact of Nationalism

Perhaps the most long-standing explanation for why ethnic conflict occurs is one based on competing nationalisms. **Nationalism** can take a civic form, which is typically inclusionary and centered around shared principles and institutions. Or it can take an ethnic form, which is typically exclusionary and centered around more restricted shared culture or ancestry. Some argue that nationalism is a "given" due to humans

Percent of organizations using strategy

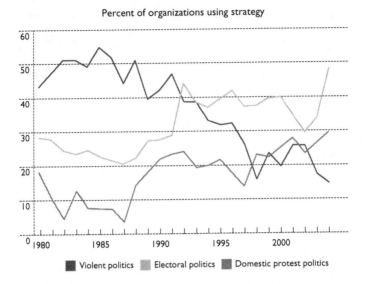

Figure 2.3 Strategies of ethnic organizations in the Middle East and North Africa.

Source: Asal and Wilkenfeld 2013, p. 106, Figure 7.1.

having a natural affinity for those sharing the same language, culture, ancestry, etc., and that the intent of nationalism is to protect and preserve the nation and its uniqueness. From this perspective, ethnic conflict is rooted in deep-seated, ancient, immutable, and in some cases irreconcilable national and/or ethnic differences (Geertz 1973; Horowitz 1985; Huntington 1996; Vanhanen 1999). Others argue that nationalism is not a given, but is instead situational and that conflict is a result of group differentials and disadvantages that stem from processes of modernization, particularly uneven development or state policies and institutions that restrict a group's access to political or economic power, or cause competition among different groups (Kedourie 1960; Hobsbawm 1990; Fearon and Laitin 2000).

Grievance, Power, and Inclusion

Along with the argument that competing nationalisms explain ethnic conflict, **grievances** were also used to explain this conflict, with early studies by Davies (1962) and Gurr (1970). Although overshadowed by other arguments in succeeding years, more recently the grievance argument has come back into vogue. Gurr's (1993, 2000) work, based on MAR data, continued to explicitly incorporate grievances as an explanatory factor of ethnic conflict. More recently, evidence from a number of studies using the newer Ethnic Power Relations (EPR) dataset has pointed to ethnic grievances and competition for state power as key drivers of ethnic conflict since the end of the Second World War (Cederman et al. 2010b; Wimmer et al. 2009a). In both cases, the analysts find that a combination of grievance and opportunity/mobilization factors are important for understanding why ethnic conflict occurs. Grievances/goals can take several forms: access to more political power within the current state, rectification of discriminatory policies, partial (i.e., sub-state) or full (secessionism, irredentism) autonomy, or complete control of political power within the current state.

A combination of grievance and opportunity/mobilization factors are important for understanding why ethnic conflict occurs.

Discrimination and disadvantages are linked to grievances. In countries where state power is determined or exercised on the basis of ethnicity, ethnic groups that are excluded from the ruling power coalition will be aggrieved because they will lack the same access to public goods and services, economic opportunities, "legal advantages such as the benefits of full citizenship rights, a fair trial...protection from arbitrary violence, and symbolic advantages such as...prestige" (Cederman et al. 2010b: 95). As a result, the excluded group will experience resentment and will be more likely to support rebellion (Petersen 2002). Cederman et al. contend that frequently "the state is not an ethnically neutral institution but is an active agent of political exclusion that generates (ethnic) conflicts in the first place" (2010b: 89). In other words, ethnic competition for power and the inclusion/exclusion dynamic that accompanies it are more important drivers of ethnic conflict than ethnic mistreatment in a broader or more diffuse sense or other types of ethnic grievances aimed at lessening discrimination (Wimmer et al. 2009a). Recent losses of status/power (Gurr 1970; Petersen 2002; Cederman et al. 2010b) and majority exclusion/underrepresentation are found to be especially salient and facilitate rebellion more strongly than general disadvantages.

An important, potentially intervening factor in the ethnicity–violence relationship concerns the nature of the political ideology that typifies an ethnic organization. For example, there is strong evidence that ethnic organizations in the Middle East and North Africa are less likely to rebel if they are espousing a democratic ideology and more likely to rebel if they are espousing a nondemocratic ideology (Wilkenfeld et al. 2009; Asal et al. 2008).

Another important relationship links *ethnicity, territory, and conflict*, although it has been difficult to pin down. Some find that ethnic groups with a territorial base, particularly those for which that territory is strongly salient as a symbolic "homeland," are more likely to rebel than those that are more widely dispersed or that are concentrated in urban areas (Dudley and Miller 1998; Cleary 2000; Fearon and Laitin 1999; 2003; Gurr 2000; Toft 2003; Hannum 1990; Weidmann 2009; Lichbach 1995). The reasons why a strong territorial base may lead to more violence are many of the same as those associated with stronger identity and ties: lower coordination costs for collective action, group cohesion, internalized norms and sanctions for participation (Oberschall 1973; McCarthy 1996; Hechter and Okamoto 2001). But other research finds that decentralization and autonomy lessen the probability of ethnic rebellion by giving groups more control over their affairs while providing them some opportunities for participation and lessening the effects of ethnic security dilemmas[1] (Hechter 2004; Gurr 2000; Lijphart 1977; Kaufmann 1996). And others find that autonomy increases ethnic rebellion by reinforcing and emboldening regional identities and parties; strengthening regional institutions, making the region more capable of challenging the state with violence; and leading to legislation that discriminates against or disadvantages minorities in those regions (Kymlicka 1998; Snyder 2000; Cederman et al. 2010b). Related to this, there is evidence that territorial control facilitates ethnic rebellion among ethnic organizations in the Middle East and North Africa (Wilkenfeld et al. 2009). Such control helps groups to mobilize and take command of their own resources. All told, the evidence from many studies points to the complexity of the interrelationships among ethnicity, territory, and conflict.

Groups with greater access to resources and greater ability to mobilize them are more likely to rebel (Collier et al. 2003; Tilly 1978), and for a longer time (Fearon 2004). Sources include people power, lootable resources, smuggling and other criminal activity, elite allies, external patrons, and agricultural production (Collier and Hoeffler 2004; Fearon 2004; Walter 2013; Wilkenfeld et al. 2009). *External support*, often in the form of a strong diaspora community, is especially important. Ethnic groups with such external support will have more resources with which to pursue violence. This helps to lessen power disparities that typically favor the state, thereby increasing the group's bargaining strength and hence emboldening the group and causing it to perceive a higher probability of winning a fight with the state (Gurr and Harff 1994; Tilly 1973; Gurr 2000; Fearon and Laitin 2003; Tambiah 1996; Lichbach 1995; Jenne 2004, 2007; Olzak 2006; Salehyan 2009; Walter 2013; Wilkenfeld et al. 2009).

Larger states are particularly prone to separatist violence. In such states, cohesion is lower (Wimmer et al. 2009a). Also, central state control is less likely to reach all groups in an even manner, but the central state still extracts resources from everyone. Those on the geographic periphery are most likely to launch a secessionist rebellion, because they simultaneously see fewer returns in terms of central state resources and less saturation of state control and/or law enforcement. This makes them aggrieved, decreases their identification with the state, and provides them with lower costs for launching rebellion, particularly one in which guerilla tactics play a central role, as is often the case in separatist rebellions (Buhaug 2006).

Repression has a complex and highly inconsistent relationship with rebellion (Davenport 2007), both ethnic and nonethnic. There is evidence that repression: raises the costs of and therefore hinders rebellion (Tilly 1978; Jenne 2007); increases the likelihood of rebellion (Francisco 1996; Juergensmeyer 2003); has an inverted-U relationship with rebellion (Lichbach and Gurr 1981; Muller and Seligson 1987); lacks an inverted-U relationship with rebellion (Lee et al. 2000); has varied effects on rebellion depending on contextual factors such as who is being targeted, regime type, and timing (Lichbach 1987; Gupta et al. 1993; Moore 1998); and has no effect on rebellion (Gurr and Moore 1997). This wide variation in results is one of the most significant puzzles in understanding the repression–dissent nexus, particularly since there is near-universal evidence that the opposite relationship flows in one direction only: rebellion consistently leads to repression (Davenport 2007).

Ethnicity and Terrorism

While definitions of **terrorism** abound, scholars have identified several common characteristics: threat or actual use of violence; civilian targeting as part of the act itself; aimed at a wide audience; intentions are to coerce, instill fear, and/or recruit for the cause; designed for maximum publicity; and designed to achieve long-term rather than short-term tactical victory.

One of the most disturbing and most negative outgrowths of contestation in ethnically diverse societies has been the adoption of terrorism by some ethnicity-based organizations. In fact, "eight of the ten most lethal [terrorist] groups (and fifteen of the top twenty)...are all classified as religious or religious and ethnonationalist in orientation" (Asal and Rethemeyer 2008: 446). This includes Al Qaeda, the Taliban, Hamas, and the Lord's Resistance Army (LRA). In the Middle East and North Africa, for example, a little more than a third of the 104 ethnic-based organizations active in the period 1980–2004 have engaged in terrorism (Asal et al. 2008).

One of the most disturbing and most negative outgrowths of contestation in ethnically diverse societies has been the adoption of terrorism by some ethnicity-based organizations.

A distinguishing feature of terrorism associated with ethnic organizations is that violence against the state often goes hand in hand with provision of social services by these organizations, for example in the area of education. Hamas in Gaza and Hezbollah in Lebanon have also participated in electoral politics. This cloak of partial legitimacy by virtue of these nonviolent organizational activities has created great ambiguity in dealing with these organizations as strictly terrorist in nature. Organizations can revert to not using terrorism when it is no longer strategically beneficial. This happened with Amal, which claims to represent Lebanese Shi'ites: it regularly used terrorism but then stopped doing so in 1989. Other organizations switch back and forth from using terrorism to not doing so, such as the Fatah Revolutionary Council, which claims to represent Palestinians (and which has switched back and forth from violence to nonviolence over time) (Asal and Wilkenfeld 2013).

Organizations driven by religious or ethnic ideology are more likely to be involved in terrorism (Crenshaw 1988; Laqueur 1999). What is the nature of the linkage between ethnicity and terrorism? Asal and Rethemeyer argue that "ethnonationalists caught in long-lasting struggles can be just as indiscriminately violent as organizations motivated by religious fervor" (2008: 438; see also Bloom 2005; Pape 2003; Pedahzur et al. 2003). They argue that a significant ideological component is the "othering" of the general population: "If there is a clear dividing line between members and 'others'—as there is in ethnic and some religious conflicts—then ideologically there is no reason to discriminate when killing" (Asal and Rethemeyer 2008: 438; see also Juergensmeyer 2003)—clearly a hallmark of terrorism as opposed to other forms of political violence.

Dehumanizing the "Other"

Furthermore, this boundary with the "other" (Tilly 2003: 21) allows for viewing all "on the other side" as legitimate targets. Such attacks may generate publicity that in turn facilitates recruitment and demonstrates organizational effectiveness, seriousness, and resolve. As Tilly points out, mass killing can be a boundary-activating mechanism for the terrorists' constituency (Tilly 2003). If this view is correct, then organizations that have religious or ethnonationalist motivations are likely to be more lethal than organizations that lack a religious or ethnic component in their ideology (Asal and Rethemeyer 2008).

The concept of "othering" is relevant here. For religious terrorists, God or some other divine being is a large part of their intended audience, which can justify violence against groups and individuals (Hoffman 1999). Ethnic terrorists are intent on targeting an "other" ethnic group and have been found to be as violent as those with a religious motivation

(Pape 2003; Bloom 2005). In both religious and ethnic terrorism, anyone that is immoral or of the opposite ethnicity is a target, regardless of whether they are a state actor or civilian, and the chances of dehumanization of the other are high (Crenshaw 1988). Religious terrorists in particular are often driven by a powerful motive to alienate (and eliminate) the others (i.e., nonbelievers) due to an absolutist, good-versus-evil (i.e., cosmic war) narrative (Juergensmeyer 2003; Asal et al. 2008). In contrast, political terrorists hope to rule the population or transform the political system at some point, and therefore face higher audience costs for using terrorism (Simon and Benjamin 2001).

Nevertheless, there is evidence that most terrorists—regardless of their ideology, and even in the case of religious terrorists—have nationalist goals that align well with public beliefs and/or grievances, or at least the successful ones do. A current example of this phenomenon is ISIS—its fundamentalist brand of Islam is closely tied to its territorial ambitions in Syria and Iraq in the form of the reestablishment of the Caliphate. This undercuts the argument that terrorists are driven primarily by goals that are unrealistic or not attuned to public sentiment. From this perspective, the main differences between terrorists and moderates may be disagreement about the utility, legitimacy, or morality of the type of violence being used (Pape 2003).

Ethnic Diversity and International Collective Action: Traditional Instruments

What are the actions that can and should be taken by the international community to address those factors that in the past have led to ethnic violence and that have prevented the parties from reaching strong and lasting conflict resolution in ethnically diverse societies?

One strategy for dealing with ethnic, religious, and linguistic diversity has involved policies of **assimilation and integration**. According to the United Nations Development Report 2004, such policies have involved the following elements:

> Centralization of political power; construction of a unified legal and judicial system based on the dominant group's language and legal traditions; adoption of official language laws; construction of a nationalized system of compulsory education based on the dominant group's language, literature, and history; diffusion of the dominant group's language and culture through national cultural institutions; adoption of state symbols celebrating the dominant group's history, heroes and culture; seizure of land from minority and indigenous groups; adoption of settlement policies in minority groups historical areas; and adoption of immigration policies giving

preference to those sharing the dominant group's language, religion, or ethnicity.

(United Nations Development Report 2004: 48)

In this book, we advocate a very different approach. As Gurr argues, a central element of successful collective protection for group rights is the principle that disputes between communal groups and states are best settled by **negotiation and mutual accommodation.** This principle is then backed up by the active engagement of major powers, the UN, and regional organizations, where they apply various mixes of diplomacy, mediation, inducements, and threats to encourage negotiated settlements of ethnic conflicts (Gurr 2000: 279). Accommodation is facilitated by four interrelated forces: the active promotion of democracy, proactive action on the part of national peoples and minorities, the reestablishment and maintenance of global and regional order, and the recognition that the costs of violent ethnopolitical conflict have become evident both to governing elites and to the leaders of the ethnopolitical movements themselves (Gurr 2000: 280).

A central element of successful collective protection for group rights is the principle that disputes between communal groups and states are best settled by negotiation and mutual accommodation.

Collective Action Plan: A Global Doctrine for Embracing Ethnic Diversity

In recent years, what Gurr has termed a "global doctrine for managing conflicts in heterogeneous societies" (2002: 27) has begun to take form:

It is based on premises that *communal contention about access to the state's power and resources should be restrained by recognizing minority rights and negotiating power-sharing arrangements; that threats to divide a country should be managed by the devolution of state power; and that the international community has proactive responsibility for promoting these outcomes* [italics added].... The most influential international actors now assert the normative and practical superiority of pluralism, power-sharing, and regional autonomy within existing states.

(Gurr 2002: 28)

In the sections below, we will discuss this evolving doctrine for managing ethnic conflict around its five central elements. The elements of this global doctrine will be used to develop policy recommendations and indicators to address the consequences of ethnic diversity within and across political systems.

Discrimination and Differentials

"The individual and collective rights of racial, ethnic, and religious minorities require international recognition and protection" (Gurr 2002: 44). There is a need to channel ethnic conflicts over state power and resources into conventional politics and for the establishment of institutional guarantees for participation and the collective redress of grievances.

The individual and collective rights of racial, ethnic, and religious minorities require international recognition and protection.

While discrimination is often pointed to as a clear manifestation of racial, ethnic, and religious differentials, it is the broader political and economic disadvantages and/or differentials facing a group that pose the overarching fundamental problem (Wimmer et al. 2009a). So a first task is to develop a reliable indicator that will help us identify those societies in which such differentials exist and therefore are at risk for discrimination, grievance, and ultimately violence.

The **Minorities at Risk (MAR)** project, created by Ted Gurr, contains annual indicators on the levels of political and economic discrimination faced by ethnocommunal groups throughout the globe from 1950 to 2006 (Minorities at Risk 2009). Data on these two indicators are collected according to the following rubric:

Measuring Political Discrimination

0: No discrimination.
1: Discrimination due to historical neglect, with remedial or protective policies in place.
2: Discrimination due to historical neglect, with no remedial or protective policies in place.
3: Discrimination due to prevailing social practise, with no formal exclusion.
4: Discrimination due to official public policy, with formal exclusion or repression or both.

Measuring Economic Discrimination

0: No discrimination.
1: Discrimination due to historical neglect, with remedial or protective policies in place.
2: Discrimination due to historical neglect, with no remedial or protective policies in place.

3: Discrimination due to prevailing social practise, with no formal exclusion.

4: Discrimination due to official public policy, with formal exclusion or repression or both.

MAR focuses on discrimination that affects a group's collective rights rather than group members' individual rights. It includes a wider list of collectively held characteristics on which a group can be discriminated against (culture and religion), rather than focusing solely on descent (race, nationality, and ethnicity), thus emphasizing differential group treatment. MAR groups are classified as suffering discrimination in a relative and contextual sense, in comparison to the dominant group in society and on the basis of substantive issues that are locally meaningful. This helps to avoid bias in favor of Western standards of human rights. A group can also be included if it is an advantaged, powerful minority. The logic here is that such groups are either politically powerful, but at "risk" of being "displaced by rival groups" and becoming "subject to retaliatory restrictions" (Gurr 2000, 108), or economically powerful and already actively discriminated against politically or culturally (Gurr 2000).

Figure 2.4 below traces the trends in political discrimination over the past five decades and shows a general decline in discrimination, particularly in its overall severity, with greatest declines occurring in the post-1990 period. This despite the fact that the number of groups that are discriminated against has not changed. "The [graph]...shows the positive consequences of the human rights regime" (Gurr 2002: 32). Despite discrimination against rebellious groups, the past half-century has shown

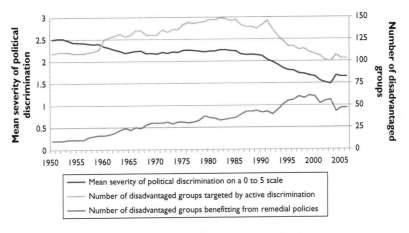

Figure 2.4 Political discrimination against minorities, 1950–2006.

Source: Updated from Gurr 2002, using 2006 Minorities at Risk data.

a steady increase in the number of minorities "benefiting from substantial public efforts to compensate for discriminatory inequalities" (ibid.).[2]

Figures 2.5 and 2.6 show considerable regional variation. Western democracies (including Japan) and sub-Saharan Africa have shown dramatic decreases over the relevant time period, albeit under radically different circumstances. Latin America, with the highest political discrimination scores of all regions, has been stubbornly resistant to change—its discrimination score in 1950 was the highest in the international system, and its score in 2006 was still the highest. Asia's score has also remained relatively high and unchanged.

Another related measure of this phenomenon is included in the **Ethnic Power Relations** (EPR) dataset, which features an annual indicator of levels of ethnic group inclusion or exclusion from central executive power (Wimmer et al. 2009a, 2009b). To some degree, this measure

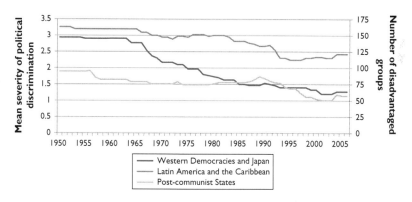

Figure 2.5 Political discrimination against minorities in Europe and Latin America, 1950–2006.

Source: Updated from Gurr 2002, using 2006 Minorities at Risk data.

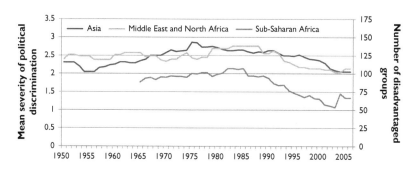

Figure 2.6 Political discrimination against minorities in the Global South, 1950–2006.

Source: Updated from Gurr 2002, using 2006 Minorities at Risk data.

captures political differentials more broadly speaking, rather than focusing solely on discrimination. Groups are classified according to three categories:

1. Exclusion from Central Power—group has no access to central power. This could mean no access to power but some regional autonomy, no access to power but not discriminated against, or no power and discriminated against.
2. Power-sharing Regimes—group has access to central power in the form of arrangements that divide power among various ethnic groups. The group can be either a senior or junior partner in such an arrangement.
3. Absolute Power—group is the principal central power-holder and does not "share power with other political leaders" (Wimmer et al. 2009b: 3). The group either has a monopoly of power or is the dominant power holder with "some limited inclusion" of some other groups.

A program for the active updating and monitoring of the MAR political and economic discrimination variables and the EPR dataset on a real-time basis can be a component in providing both individual societies and international and regional organizations with early warning of situations that may be on the verge of ethnicity-based violence.

Democracy and Power Sharing

"Democratic institutions are the preferred domestic means for guaranteeing group rights in heterogeneous societies and for pursuing political programs to redress inequalities that have resulted from discrimination.... Mutual accommodation is the optimal strategy for managing conflicts between challenging groups and states" (Gurr 2002: 34–5). Evidence suggests that democracies see greater ethnic protests but lower ethnic rebellion.

Democratic institutions are the preferred domestic means for guaranteeing group rights in heterogeneous societies and for pursuing political programs to redress inequalities that have resulted from discrimination.

Researchers have established a close link between **democracy and democratic participation** on the one hand, and lower probabilities of ethnic violence on the other (Sambanis 2001; Wilkenfeld et al. 2009). Admittedly, instability associated with incipient democratization and movement into anocracy from autocracy has also been linked to increased chances of violence, especially when set against a backdrop of protracted ethnic tension (Gurr 2000, 2002; Snyder 2000; see also Chapter 3 of this book). But group rights are best guaranteed through domestic democratic institutions that facilitate the redress of inequalities resulting from discrimination (Gurr 2002: 34–5).

How do we measure whether openness and democratic participation are present? Chapter 3, on democracy and regime consistency, discusses in greater detail the **Polity Score** as a yearly measure of the extent of regime competitiveness and openness, and the degree to which political participation is enhanced by the regime. Measured on a scale from -10, denoting extreme authoritarianism, to $+10$, denoting a well-functioning democracy, movement along this scale has been helpful in tracking yearly changes in regimes. Sudden and large shifts in this score, coupled with preexisting repression of ethnic minorities, can provide early warning of a deteriorating security situation for the citizens of a particular country.

Power sharing is an additional mechanism for ensuring the rights of ethnic groups. Power-sharing arrangements are most closely linked to democracy, and these two features form the second pillar of Gurr's (2002) evolving doctrine for preventing and resolving ethnic rebellion and conflict. "Within the context of democratic institutions, mutual accommodation is the optimal strategy for managing conflicts between challenging groups and states, rather than suppression or forced assimilation of groups that claim separate identities and interests" (Gurr 2002: 35). There is evidence of a positive relationship between power sharing and peace, particularly in the aftermath of civil war (Walter 2002; Hartzell and Hoddie 2003; 2007; DeRouen et al. 2009). Such arrangements can be particularly effective at managing ethnic conflict if they are implemented before the situation deteriorates into violence (Gurr 2002). Perhaps the most analyzed and recognizable form of power sharing is political power-sharing, which has to do with whether the group is guaranteed representation in the central government. The MAR project contains an indicator of such power sharing and classifies groups as participating in power-sharing arrangements if they have arrangements such as "appointed positions in [the] cabinet, appointed positions in [the] legislature, [or] guaranteed elected positions in [the] legislature (Minorities at Risk 2009: 13).

A strong argument can be made for having the broadest form of power sharing, measured on political, economic, territorial, and military dimensions. Databases such as MAR and EPR have reliable indicators of political and territorial power-sharing, but not the others.

Hartzell and Hoddie (2003: 320) developed a highly robust indicator of power sharing, conceived of as arrangements that attempt to "balance power among groups" not only on the basis of whether groups share power, but also in terms of how that power is divided. In particular, the measure focuses on whether that division makes it "exceedingly difficult for any group to threaten the lives and interests of others" (ibid.: 320). Their indicator accounts for four different forms of power sharing: 1.) Political, which focuses on legislative, executive, and administrative proportional representation; 2.) territorial, which focuses on either federalism or distinctively assigned regional autonomy status; 3.) military, which focuses on distribution of power within "the state's coercive power;"[3] and 4.) economic, which focuses on distribution of access to "economic resources controlled or mandated by the state" (ibid.: 320). Hartzell and Hoddie created a five-point composite scale that added together how many of these four different forms of power sharing were present, with the zero category being the absence of any form of power sharing. In their current form, these indicators are only relevant for a select group of ethnic conflicts: those that escalated to violence, reached the level of civil war, and were contained in agreements that ended those wars. Extension of these indicators to the analysis of situations that have both escalated and not escalated to violence, as well as power-sharing arrangements between groups in general, regardless of whether or not they were negotiated as part of agreements that terminated violent episodes, would be particularly useful.

Regional Autonomy

"Conflicts over self-determination are best settled through negotiations that provide regional autonomy and institutional means for pursuing collective interests within existing states" (Gurr 2002: 44). The actual formation of new states is rare—two recent examples are East Timor in 2002 and South Sudan in 2011.[4] The more common outcome is negotiated settlement granting autonomy.

Conflicts over self-determination are best settled through negotiations that provide regional autonomy and institutional means for pursuing collective interests within existing states.

The third element of Gurr's (2002) evolving doctrine for preventing and resolving ethnic rebellion and conflict pertains to territorial power-sharing. As noted earlier, some research has found that regional autonomy increases the likelihood of ethnic rebellion, while other studies find that it prevents ethnic rebellion. Still others have found that autonomy facilitates the resolution of ethnic self-determination movements (Gurr 2002), and increases the durability of peace in the aftermath of civil war (Rothchild and Hartzell 2000; DeRouen et al. 2009; Hoddie and Hartzell 2005).

Most armed self-determination conflicts are settled via agreements in which territorial power-sharing plays a central role. Spoiler problems do tend to plague self-determination conflicts, but when such conflicts finally end, it is most often through groups dropping their exit demands and agreeing to some form and degree of sub-state autonomy (Gurr 2002).[5] DeRouen et al. (2009) argue that, like military power-sharing, territorial power-sharing is a less costly concession for a government to make at the end of armed conflict than political power-sharing, since it is able to retain control of central state institutions.

Several research groups have proposed indicators of territorial autonomy, including MAR, EPR, and Hartzell and Hoddie. The MAR indicator is judged superior for our purposes, since it is a dichotomous indicator of whether or not the group has administrative autonomy, defined as "control of political and bureaucratic structures in an autonomous region" that is "legally recognized by" the "home government" (Minorities at Risk 2009: 13). The legal recognition qualification makes the indicator a good measure of territorial power-sharing. Groups that only have de facto autonomy—typically due to circumstances such as living in a failed or weak state whose administrative reach does not extend to all regions, or due to the state abandoning its administrative control of a region during an armed conflict—and those that only claim autonomy without negotiating it with the government are not classified as having autonomy.[6]

Promoting Stability and Settlement in Multiethnic Societies

"International and regional organizations have responsibilities for protecting and promoting minority rights, anticipating and deterring the onset of ethnic wars, and promoting and enforcing negotiated settlements in wars once they are underway" (Gurr 2002: 44). Such international engagement is often necessary to provide sufficient incentives to parties to stop fighting.

International and regional organizations have responsibilities for protecting and promoting minority rights, anticipating and deterring the onset of ethnic wars, and promoting and enforcing negotiated settlements in wars once they are underway.

As we have seen, the vast majority of people live in multiethnic societies, and about one in seven people are members of a repressed minority. Movements for self-determination among many of these minorities inevitably run into various degrees of opposition from the larger majorities in which they are situated and under which they often suffer severe repression. It is widely, although not universally, recognized that the international community has an obligation to act to promote and protect the rights of these minorities. Yet often this obligation runs into stiff opposition from states that view international action as a threat to their sovereignty. What principles should govern the role of the international community as it contemplates intervention in order to protect minority rights?

The United Nations Agenda for Peace, adopted by the General Assembly in 1992, propounded the following principle:

> The absence of war and military conflicts amongst States does not in itself ensure international peace and security. The non-military sources of instability in the economic, social, humanitarian and ecological fields have become threats to peace and security. The United Nations membership as a whole, working through the appropriate bodies, needs to give the highest priority to the solution of these matters.
>
> (United Nations Agenda for Peace 1992)

In outlining the kinds of collective responses to communal conflict—preventive diplomacy, peace-making, peacekeeping, and postconflict peacebuilding—the UN accepted the norm that international and regional organizations, and individual states, have the responsibility to promote peaceful settlement of emerging ethnic conflicts (Harff and Gurr 2004). One particular aspect of international and regional responsibility for intervention in ethnic conflicts pertains to civil wars in general, and mass killing of civilians in particular. It is widely accepted now that international organizations have both the right and the responsibility to respond with military means and with peace enforcement operations (Harff and Gurr 2004: 190).

Particularly effective recently have been partnerships between the UN, member states, host countries, and regional organizations in **peacekeeping operations**. This unique partnership draws on the legal and political authority of the Security Council, personnel and financial contributions of member states, and the accumulated experience of the UN Secretariat in managing operations in the field. Member states establish mandates and adjust deployments to meet emerging and changing conditions on the ground, and contribute troops and equipment. For example, creative partnerships with international and regional organizations are becoming a regular feature in UN peacekeeping. Some recent examples include the UN working with the AU in Darfur, alongside NATO in Kosovo and Afghanistan, as well as succeeding an EU military operation in Chad and handing over policing operations to the EU in Kosovo (United Nations 2012).

There are currently 15 peacekeeping operations and one special political mission—the United Nations Assistance Mission in Afghanistan (UNAMA)—led by the Department of Peacekeeping Operations. These are, in Africa: Western Sahara, Mali, DRC, Darfur, Abyei (Sudan), Liberia, South Sudan, Cote d'Ivoire; and other: Haiti, Afghanistan, Golan (Israel and Syria), Cyprus, Lebanon, Kosovo, India and Pakistan, Middle East.

A different organizational arrangement for peacemaking involves both the UN and regional organizations. A current example of such UN and regional organization coordination is the African-led International Support Mission to Mali (AFISMA). This mission is led by the Economic Community of West African States (ECOWAS), which organized a military mission to support the government of one of its members—Mali—which was attempting to cope with an insurrection by Islamic rebels in the northern part of the country. The mission was authorized by UN Security Council Resolution 2085, passed on December 20, 2012, which "authorizes the deployment of an African-led International Support Mission in Mali (AFISMA) for an initial period of one year" (United Nations Security Council Resolution 2085, 2012). The map in Figure 2.7 dramatically demonstrates the regional nature of this type of peacemaking mission.

In response to UN peacemaking failures in ethnic conflicts in Rwanda and Bosnia-Herzegovina, we have only recently seen an expansion of the UN's mandate for peacemaking with the development of the concept of a robust response. Recent implementations have included Sierra Leone, the DRC, and Haiti. In the DRC in 2013, the UN Security Council authorized an intervention brigade within the existing operations in the country "to help neutralize armed groups" (United Nations 2013). This was the first time in its 68-year history that peacekeeping forces were deployed offensively against a particular group, in this case the March 23 Movement (M23) (Kishi 2014).

Membership in International and Regional Organizations with Minority Rights Agendas

When preventive means fail to deter ethnic and other conflicts that threaten regional security or gross violations of human rights, the U.N. and individual states acting with international authorization have the right and obligation to respond with military sanctions and peace enforcement operations (Gurr 2002: 44).

Jentleson (2000) has termed this *coercive prevention*, arguing that while it is rarely sufficient, it is often necessary. This means "credible threats of military action" (Gurr 2002: 42).

When preventive means fail to deter ethnic and other conflicts that threaten regional security or gross violations of human rights, the U.N. and individual states acting with international authorization have the right and obligation to respond with military sanctions and peace enforcement operations.

Membership in organizations and signing on to framework conventions devoted to the protection of minority and ethnic community rights

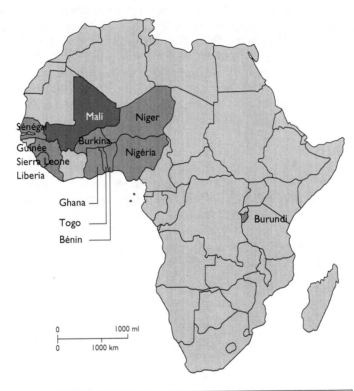

Mali, the country for which the International Support Mission was set up
Countries that are members of the African-led International Support Mission in Mali (AFISMA)

Figure 2.7 Members of the International Support Mission in Mali.

Source: Adapted from http://en.wikipedia.org/wiki/African_led_International_Support_Mission_to_Mali.

does not in and of itself assure compliance and proactive vigilance. But there is nevertheless considerable international collective pressure to sign on and adhere to the fundamental human rights principles that are enshrined in these organizations and documents.

The NGO Minority Rights Group International maintains a list of states that have signed and ratified "major international instruments relevant to minority and indigenous rights" (2012: 224). It not only covers the major global agreements such as the UN's International Convention on the Elimination of All Forms of Racial Discrimination (1966), but also some key regional instruments such as the Council of Europe's Framework Convention for the Protection of National Minorities (1995) and the African Charter on Human and Peoples' Rights (2003). Most states are signatories to and have ratified these treaties, particularly the UN's International Convention on Racial Discrimination.

There is greater variation in the signing of regional agreements, and although most states are still party to these in their respective regions as well, regional variations highlight areas where more work is needed. Of the regional agreements, those for Europe and Africa go furthest in ensuring group rights. The African Commission on Human and Peoples' Rights can hear cases and make decisions on complaints brought to it by minority groups, while the European Court of Human Rights has handed down rulings regarding minority rights in the context of interpreting Europe's Framework Convention. By contrast, the Americas have relatively weak agreements covering ethnic, racial, and cultural rights. Asia currently has no regional group rights agreement and is significantly lacking in regional mechanisms that ensure or promote protection of group rights (Gurr 2002; Crocker et al. 2011; Minority Rights Group International 2012).

International Prevention of Ethnic Violence

There is a significant lack of global data on international *prevention* of ethnic violence. A prototype dataset is the Managing Intrastate Low-Intensity Conflict (MILC) dataset housed at Uppsala University's Conflict Data Program (UCDP) (Managing Intrastate Low-level Conflict 2007). MILC contains indicators measuring conflict-management efforts conducted by intermediaries in conflicts in which there were more than 25 but less than 1,000 battle deaths. Certain types of military interventions are included if the interveners act as neutrals or even on the side of one of the parties when the prevention of further violence is the objective, as long as the interveners do not become a warring party to the conflict itself (Melander et al. 2009).

MILC contains individual indicators measuring several different types of intervention activities: "indirect, direct, unclear, and bilateral talks; good offices; arbitration; fact-finding missions; permanent observers; and peacekeeping operations" (Melander et al. 2009: 61). MILC also identifies the third party by name (via an actor ID number) and type: single state, group of states, neighboring state, single IGO, group of IGOs, UN, permanent UN Security Council member, and an "other" category, which captures things such as "NGOs, prominent persons (i.e., independent individuals), religious denominations, etc." (Managing Intrastate Low-level Conflict 2007: 7).

All of the intrastate conflict management efforts identified by MILC have escalated to violence, and MILC by and large contains data on efforts in low-level conflicts or those that are short of war. Hence, while MILC indicators are a good source for assessing the effectiveness of third-party efforts to prevent escalation to *war*, it cannot be used to assess the prevention of *violence*.[7] In order to assess the ability of international actors to prevent violence, we recommend that the prototype provided by MILC be expanded to cover situations where ethnic tensions may be simmering—protests, political or intramilitary crises split along ethnic lines, instances where ethnic actors are arming themselves independently of the state, etc.—but have not yet escalated to armed conflict.

Conclusion

As we argued early in this chapter, ethnic diversity is a source of both great creativity and innovation, while at the same time a source of potential tension resulting from real or perceived discrimination. We have reviewed the parameters of ethnic conflict on the world stage, and emphasized in particular how ethnic tensions and competition have led in extreme cases to terrorism directed against other ethnic groups or the state in general. And we've recommended an action agenda to address the negative outgrowths of ethnic diversity.

This action agenda has been based in large part on Ted Gurr's work on an emerging global doctrine for managing conflicts in multiethnic societies. This doctrine addresses the protection of racial, ethnic, and religious minorities, and calls for the development of democratic institutions as the best means for guaranteeing group rights and addressing inequalities. It calls for regional autonomy arrangements within existing states; and it calls for increased attention to the roles that international and regional organizations can and should play in anticipating and deterring the onset of ethnic wars. In the extreme, the doctrine makes the case for military responses in the form of sanctions and peace-enforcement operations, sometimes referred to as "robust international intervention." While many problems persist, Gurr argues that the trends are unmistakable:

> [We can already discern] a long-run and near-global improvement in the status of minorities, a sharp decline in new ethnic wars, the settlement of many protracted wars, and proactive efforts by states and international organizations to recognize group rights and channel ethnic disputes into conventional politics.
>
> (Gurr 2002: 29)[8]

Notes

1 An ethnic security dilemma can occur when states fail (quasi-anarchy) and ethnic groups arm themselves to provide for their own security, because they cannot rely on the state to do so (self-help) (see Posen 1993).

2 A slight uptick in the mean severity of discrimination beginning in 2004 may be explained in part by MAR having dropped roughly 30 groups from the dataset as part of its most recent update, and all but two of these had experienced no discrimination in recent years. Africa was most affected, with roughly two-thirds of those dropped being located in this region.

3 DeRouen et al. (2009) find that military power-sharing has a positive effect on durable peace after civil wars. They argue that this form is less costly than political power-sharing, because the state's probable losses are not as large: the state is likely to retain control of the armed forces, even when rebels are integrated.

4 Kosovo's independence in 2008 has not been recognized yet by the United Nations.

5 In some cases, negotiated agreements that end self-determination conflicts may grant the group political power-sharing, or some combination of political and territorial power-sharing (Gurr 2002).

6 MAR also contains indicators of the year that the group gained regional autonomy and the percentage of the group that lives in the autonomous region.

7 MILC also does not have an indicator to select out ethnic conflicts specifically, even though the data covers these types of conflicts (along with all others).

8 In personal correspondence with Wilkenfeld in March 2014, Ted Gurr was asked about his 2002 assertion that the international community had the mechanisms in place to deal more effectively with ethnonational conflict. He replied: "I am as cautiously optimistic now as I was a decade ago—the principles and mechanisms are in place. A lot of the 'new' ethno-political conflicts are flare-ups of old ones—the Crimea situation, for example, has deep historical roots, and I expect that one way or another Crimea will become again part of Russia. So far as I can tell, all the trends either have continued, or at worst flat-lined."

Chapter 3

Instability, Democracy, and Regime Consistency

The Myth and Reality of Regime Consistency and Democracy: Setting the Scene

There has been a significant increase in the number of democracies among the states of the international system, coupled with a decrease in the number of autocracies. As the data in Figure 3.1 show, about 1990 was the point in time when democracies began to outnumber autocracies among the nations of the world. Despite some very recent reverses such as Bahrain, Venezuela, and Cote D'Ivoire, the trends appear to be stable. As of 2011, there were 95 democracies (58 percent of all states) and only 20 autocracies (12 percent) (Frantz 2014). The Middle East is the only region of the world still dominated by autocracies (Gleditsch and Ward 2006).

There has been a significant increase in the number of democracies among the states of the international system, coupled with a decrease in the number of autocracies. The Middle East is the only region of the world still dominated by autocracies.

There is also strong empirical evidence showing that democracies experience less internal violence and are less repressive than autocracies. This latter phenomenon, sometimes known as the "domestic democratic peace" (Davenport 2007), has often been linked to the democratic peace concept in international politics, wherein we find fully democratic states rarely if ever using violence against each other to settle disputes.

Myth 3 The significant increase in the number of democracies among the states of the international system, coupled with a decrease in the number of autocracies, bodes well for a more tranquil international system—the democratic peace.

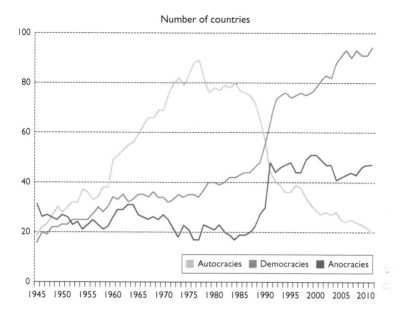

Figure 3.1 Distribution of countries by regime type.

Source: Frantz 2014: 25.

Dangerous Transitions

Regimes are resilient. In any given year, the chance of a transition from one type of regime to another is only 4 percent (Frantz 2014). Nevertheless, Huntington argues that the proportion of democracies has not increased gradually, but rather in three waves—the early 1800s, at the end of the Second World War, and at the end of the Cold War (Huntington 1991). But most changes that occur do not end in democracy: most are from autocracy to anocracy or vice versa (Frantz 2014). Despite the declining number of autocracies, only half that have ended since 1974—Huntington's beginning of the "third wave of democratization" (Huntington 1991)— have resulted in surviving, stable democracies (Geddes 1999). But regardless of type of autocratic regime, autocracies are much more likely to break down and transition to democracy when they are situated in a "democratic neighborhood" (Gleditsch and Ward 2006).

Reality The transition from autocracy to democracy is the period most fraught with potential instability and conflict.

What is disturbing about Figure 3.1 is the third line, which plots the number of "anocracies" in the system over time (red line). Much of the decline in the number of autocracies since the mid-1980s has fed the ranks of anocracies, which have held constant at about 50 or 30 percent of all states in the system for the past two decades (Frantz 2014). Anocracies are hybrid regimes, exhibiting some of the characteristics of democracy while retaining some autocratic institutions and practices. Regan and Bell define anocratic regimes as those that

> have the institutional capacity for some broader participation in the governing process,...some institutional ability to facilitate candidate recruitment beyond the selection by a small cadre of anointed leaders, and...exhibit some political behaviors consistent with a budding civil society.
>
> (2010: 748)

But these regimes also typically "have incomplete development of the mechanisms to redress grievances" (ibid.). In many cases these are regimes in transition from autocracy to democracy, while in a few cases, these regimes are slipping from democracy back toward autocracy via anocracy—the so-called democratic reversal (see Goldstone et al. 2010).

The decline in the number of autocracies since the mid-1980s has resulted in an increase in anocracies—hybrid regimes exhibiting some of the characteristics of democracy while retaining some autocratic institutions and practices.

Research shows that is it these anocratic, transitional regimes which are at the greatest risk for instability. Goldstone et al. (2010) find that the factor most highly associated with instability events is a form of anocracy termed "partial democracy with factionalism" (see also Ulfelder and Lustik 2007). "A certain kind of relationship among political elites— a polarized politics of exclusive identities or ideologies, in conjunction with partially democratic institutions—most powerfully presages instability" (Goldstone et al. 2010: 198). Zakaria points to what he calls an increase in "illiberal democracies" since the 1990s—states that have electoral democracy but significant civil liberties restrictions (e.g., Russia, Philippines, Sierra Leone, Pakistan, Peru). Zakaria notes that few of these democracies have become more liberal and in fact most have tended to increase their illiberalness over time (Zakaria 1997; see also Zakaria 2014).

While strong democracies and strong autocracies are best able, obviously through differing means, to control tendencies within their societies to devolve into conflict and violence, anocracies are less able to do this. In fact, an argument can be made that anocracy is not a regime type at all, but rather a type of instability (see, for example, Fearon and Laitin 2003). The transitional aspect of anocracy may be more important for causing instability and insecurity than the regime type itself. Some current examples of anocratic states are Cambodia, Iraq, Jordan, Rwanda, Algeria, and Chad (Polity, 2014).

Because anocracies are also more likely to experience greater real or perceived threats to their longevity from opposition groups than either autocracies or democracies, this increases the likelihood of repression in anocracies and hence constitutes an even greater threat to human security (Davenport 1995). Unlike autocracies, anocracies allow more room for opposition demand-making and organizing, and have weaker state security apparatuses to deter dissent (Hegre et al. 2001). But, unlike democracies, anocracies also have few and tenuous institutional means to respond to demands or to channel them into nonviolent participation, which also feeds back and increases both dissatisfaction and the likelihood of more dissent (Regan and Bell 2010); this goes for demands of all types, both more and less extreme. Furthermore, anocracies have lower levels of legitimacy than both democracies and autocracies. As a result, anocracies will view threats as magnified—even if they are less extreme—and with few alternative means of responding, they will repress more (Regan and Henderson 2002). Finally, anocratic states provide fewer credible commitments to honor participation, to uphold citizen rights, and to limit repression, largely because the system is in flux. Therefore, citizens have little basis for expectations about how the state will treat them and what behavior it will tolerate, because they have less-consistent and more unknown signals to go on (Findley and Young 2011).

So the dilemma for the international community is how to promote democratic values in societies emerging from long histories of authoritarian rule, while at the same time keeping these states from slipping into instability and conflict in precisely this anocratic transition period. The Peace and Conflict Instability Ledger (Hewitt 2012a; Backer and Huth 2014a) indicates that, during the decade ending in 2012, of the 15 states most at risk for instability, the vast majority can trace that increased risk to a transition to more democratic governance that led to a classification of partial democracy. This is particularly true of postconflict societies, because they are vulnerable to the same forces that drive conflict recurrence (see Chapter 1)—poor economic growth, lingering disagreements about power-sharing arrangements, and continued opportunities for insurgencies to organize (Hegre and Fjelde 2010).

So the dilemma for the international community is how to promote democratic values in societies emerging from long histories of authoritarian rule, while at the same time keeping these states from slipping into an anocratic phase of instability and conflict.

There are, however, some positive aspects of transitions from a regional perspective. Democratic transitions are spatially clustered, and regional rather than global factors are more important. "Since 1815, the probability that a randomly chosen country will be a democracy is about 0.75 if the majority of its neighbors are democratic, but only 0.14 if the majority of its neighbors are nondemocratic" (Gleditsch and Ward 2006: 916). Autocracies are much more likely to break down and transition to democracy when more of their neighbors are democratic and when their neighbors have experienced a transition to democracy. Here we find diffusion effects at play: external support for democratic movements from democratic neighbors, nearby examples of outgoing autocratic elites doing well in the posttransition democracy, and the threat of isolation by neighbors for not democratizing. In addition, if the overall neighborhood is less conflictual—the democratic peace—this increases the likelihood of a democratic transition. When situated in a peaceful neighborhood, autocrats are less able to use external threat as a justification for maintaining the status quo (Gleditsch and Ward 2006).

Unstable states, whether full-blown failed states that are unable to provide basic human security to their populations or fragile states that appear to be on the road to this status, constitute a threat not only to their own citizens, but also to the broader regional and international systems. Underdevelopment in the form of underperforming economies impacts the economies of neighboring states by robbing them of the advantages of regional markets. Unresolved domestic tensions—ethnic, class, or religious in origin—can spill over into the international system in the form of terrorism and outmigration. Political instability can encourage the incursion of third-party forces to enhance the power of respective groups—witness the recent tragic histories of the Democratic Republic of Congo, Syria, and most recently Iraq.

Developed states, predominantly democratic regimes, have long promoted democratic reform as the surest way to domestic stability. Other political systems have argued for the strong state, often accompanied by various degrees of repression—essentially autocracy—as the best way to promote stability. What all seem to agree on is that the middle of the spectrum between democracy and autocracy is perhaps the least stable of all systems (Hegre et al. 2001; Fearon and Laitin 2003; Findley and Young 2011), so movement out of this status in one direction or another is a desirable goal (Regan and Bell 2010). But given these sharp divergences in goals and means, collective action on the part of the international community to address the common threat to human security arising from weak, unstable, and inconsistent regimes would appear elusive at best. In this chapter, competing approaches to addressing instability will be unpacked so that we can evaluate different paths and outcomes, as we move toward the recommendation of measures by which we can address progress toward regime stability in a collective action framework.

Measuring Instability

We begin by examining the elements of instability. Research on instability has uncovered important linkages with several of the challenges that this book has identified for further analysis—regime consistency, democratization, development. Two prominent research groups—the Political Instability Task Force (PITF) (Goldstone et al. 2010) and the Center for International Development and Conflict Management (CIDCM)—have developed measurement tools and forecasting models to better assess risk for instability and its attendant impact on the international community. Our focus here is on two major contributors to societal instability—regime type and consistency.

In their work on the Peace and Conflict Instability Ledger, Hewitt (2008, 2010, 2012a) and Backer and Huth (2014a) of CIDCM propose five variables that have been identified by researchers as correlating strongly with the onset of instability. These variables come from the political, economic, social, and security sectors.

From the realm of politics, regime or institutional consistency measures "the extent to which the institutions comprising a country's political system are uniformly and consistently autocratic or democratic. Political institutions with a mix of democratic and autocratic features are inconsistent" and are "more likely to experience political instability" (Backer and Huth 2014a: 6; see also Gurr 1974; Gates et al. 2006; Hegre et al. 2001). Economic openness is "the extent to which a country's economy is integrated in the global economy.... Countries that are more tightly connected to global markets have been found to experience less instability" (Backer and Huth 2014a: 6; see also Hegre et al. 2003; Goldstone et al. 2000). Infant mortality rate is an indicator that serves as a proxy for a country's overall level of development "and its capacity to deliver core social services to its population" (Backer and Huth 2014a: 6). Research provides strong support for the relationship between infant mortality and the likelihood of instability (Backer and Huth 2014a; Esty et al. 1999; Goldstone et al. 2010). Militarization addresses the strong relationship between the degree to which "infrastructure and capital for organized armed conflict are more plentiful and accessible" (Backer and Huth 2014a: 6) and the likelihood of instability and armed conflict. "The likelihood of instability is greater in this setting because increased access to and availability of these resources increases the opportunities for organizing and mobilizing" (ibid.; see also Collier and Hoeffler 2004). Neighborhood security addresses the likelihood that "political instability...increases...when a neighboring state is currently experiencing armed conflict" (Backer and Huth 2014a: 6). This becomes particularly "acute when ethnic or other communal groups span across borders" (ibid.; see also Sambanis 2001; Hegre and Sambanis 2006; Goldstone et al. 2010).

Figure 3.2 shows how the countries in the CIDCM analysis were classified according to their estimated risk scores and provides a geographic landscape of the risk of instability (Backer and Huth 2014a: 8).

> Undoubtedly, Africa remains the most serious concern. Of the 47 African countries covered in the Ledger, 33 (70 percent) qualify for the high- or highest-risk categories. Of all the countries worldwide that qualify in those categories, African countries comprise 72 percent (33 of 46).
>
> (Backer and Huth 2014a: 8)

With regard to risk of instability, the countries of Africa are the most serious concern. Seventy percent of African countries are in the highest risk categories.

A similar though smaller concentration of states qualifying as high or highest risk exists in South Asia, in particular Afghanistan and Pakistan (Backer and Huth 2014a). Also highlighted in Figure 3.2 is the notion of "neighborhoods of instability." Particularly in Africa, but also in evidence in parts of South Asia, high risk of instability tends to spill from one

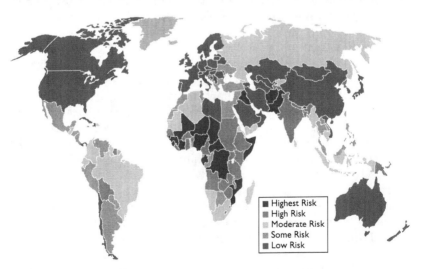

Figure 3.2 Risk of instability.

Source: David A. Backer and Paul K. Huth 2014a.

country to another. Sometimes referred to as a contagion effect, this phenomenon arises because of: out-migration of affected minority and other disadvantaged groups in unstable countries; violent conflicts between states and non-state actors that span or spill across international borders; rebellions that inspire actors in nearby states to take up arms; or instability that impacts the economies of surrounding countries and thus adversely affects the stability of these countries as well.

Vulnerability to Transition

Let us delve a little more deeply into the problems and challenges that regime transitions raise. *Periods of transition are periods of uncertainty and system vulnerability.* This results both from the destabilization of previous authority patterns and deconsolidation of institutions without substitution by new stable institutional arrangements. Transitions increase the likelihood of splits in the elite, domestic rebellion, or foreign intervention (Frantz 2014). At the extreme, this transition increases the probability of complete state collapse (Casper and Taylor 1996; Goldstone et al. 2010). While social movements and popular uprisings are often important mechanisms through which autocracy is ended, they do not form the basis of stable transitions and sustainable democracy (International Institute for Democracy and Electoral Assistance 2003).

While social movements and popular uprisings are often important mechanisms through which autocracy is ended, they do not form the basis of stable transitions and sustainable democracy.

Transitions from Autocracy

Transitions are often dangerous processes. They are often accompanied by, and even precipitated by, irregular leadership changes (see the discussion of leadership change in the section below on indicators of regime type and stability) (Frantz 2014). But regime transitions are not all equal in terms of their likelihood of increasing instability and threatening human security. Transitions from autocracy vary on threat to human security by the specific type of autocratic regime.

Military regimes are the least resilient and most unstable type of autocracy, but the transitions are also less violent than in personalist regimes. Military regimes usually break down via splits in the military elite, but the transitions are often self-induced and as a result less likely to reach the point of a violent crisis (Geddes 1999).

Single-party regimes are the most resilient and most stable type of autocracy, and least likely to experience civil conflict. When faced with threats, single-party regimes typically have more institutional capacity to co-opt the opposition and retain the support of critical backers than other types of autocratic regimes, since the regime's ruling mechanisms—in this case, party structures—reach into a broader scope of socioeconomic life than those of other types of autocratic regimes (Fjelde 2010; Geddes 1999).

Personalist regimes are in the middle in terms of resiliency, but the transitions are often the most violent and threatening for human security, and those transitions are least likely to lead to democracy. Personalist regimes are more resilient than military regimes, because they are more willing to fight back against threats or use material payoffs to negate such threats. But they are less resilient than single-party regimes, because they have narrower bases of support; are more susceptible to economic crises, since their support base is highly contingent upon material payoffs; and, in cases where the leader dies, they have fewer capable replacements waiting in the ranks, since dictators tend to eliminate those with ambition. Personalist regimes usually break down via violent overthrow or death of the leader. A typical outcome of the breakdown of a personalist regime is violent transition to a new autocratic regime (Geddes 1999).

Democratic Reversals

The system is also filled with examples of democratic reversals, that is, democratic states that have transitioned (back) toward autocracy. Among recent examples are Bahrain, Cote d'Ivoire, and Venezuela (Freedom House 2011). One set of factors links poverty, economic inequality, and declining levels of economic development to democratic reversals (Przeworski and Limongi 1997; Londregan and Poole 1996; Kapstein and Converse 2008; Epstein et al. 2006; Przeworski et al. 2000). Others argue that it is weak institutions and especially weak constraints on executive power and fewer checks and balances that are most closely associated with democratic reversals (Kapstein and Converse 2008; Fish 2001, 2006). And ethnic fragmentation and inadequate provision of public goods such as health care and education (Kapstein and Converse 2008) can also be factors. Regardless of cause, transitions from democracy back to anocracy are the most likely transition to lead to repression (Zanger 2000) and civil war, much more so than transitions from autocracy to anocracy (Regan and Bell 2010). In democracies, citizens have high expectations for future returns, so a democratic reversal will be viewed extremely negatively, as closing opportunities for future returns, and the repression that is typically applied by new autocrats increases the incentive to rebel (Regan and Bell 2010; Davenport 2007; Cederman et al. 2010a). Venezuela under Chavez was preceded by decades of democracy.

And democratic reversals increase the likelihood of further repression. In particular, a slide backwards from democracy into anocracy increases the likelihood of repression. Since citizens tend to be particularly resistant to democratic reversals, repression is viewed as more necessary and beneficial by elites that pursue a move toward autocracy. In addition, the instability associated with anocracy increases the likelihood of repression (Zanger 2000). This is a consistent theme: democratic reversals have a particularly pernicious effect on human security.

The Role of Elections in the Democratization Process

One of the most contentious issues growing out of the democratization versus stabilization debate has been the question of how and when open elections should be held. Writing about the Egyptian elections of 2012 and the ultimate overthrow of the democratically elected government by the military 1 year later, Leslie Gelb put it this way:

> There's one big, fat foreign-policy lesson that cuts against the American grain: elections, no matter how free and fair, are only the icing on the democratic cake, not the cake itself; and if the icing comes before the cake is baked, the result is rarely true democracy.
>
> (Gelb 2013)

According to Collier (2009: 8), the West has tended to promote "the wrong features of democracy: elections are the façade rather than the essential infrastructure" of democracy.

Elections, no matter how free and fair, are only the icing on the democratic cake, not the cake itself; and if the icing comes before the cake is baked, the result is rarely true democracy.

The conventional reasoning by those who argue in favor of rapid democratization and early elections is that they will reduce the power of autocrats; help the population become accustomed to the norms, habits, and practises of democracy; legitimize new leaders; speed up the withdrawal of foreign forces that may have been part of the transition from autocracy to democracy; give the population peaceful means of participation and thus provide incentives for nonviolence; and increase the likelihood of attracting foreign aid to support the process, since provision of such aid is often dependent upon the demonstration of good governance (Brancati and Snyder 2013).[1] Some who argue in favor of this approach contend that even if some election violence is to be expected and elections are imperfect, the end justifies the means.

But increasingly the evidence seems to be on the side of those who argue against early elections. There is evidence that an elections-first approach to democracy tends to exacerbate rather than curb civil conflict. This is especially the case in developing states, and particularly in Africa (Collier 2009). There is also evidence that the introduction of multiparty elections in autocratic states increases the likelihood of civil conflict at a much quicker pace than other types of autocratic transitions such as coups (Fjelde 2010). In cases where mass participation demands are strong, political entrepreneurs—those who seek to further their political careers and popularity by pursuing the creation of policy that pleases the populace—will appeal to traditional cleavages (ethnicity, religion, economic populism), and competitive elections will tend to accentuate traditional differences rather than promote cross-cleavage coalitions. In cases where mass participation demands are weaker, smaller factions (often armed) will jockey for power in the new democracy (Snyder 2010). Elections represent the potential for large shifts in power or strengthening of incumbent power, so actors on both sides can view them as threatening (Powell 2004). As a result of all of this, electoral losers are more likely to resort to violence (Collier 2009; Mansfield and Snyder 2007; Brancati and Snyder 2013). Often-cited examples of failure of early elections include: Bosnia, Burundi, Iraq, DRC, Cyprus in the 1960s and 1970s, and Argentina in the 1950s, 1960s, and 1970s (Brancati and Snyder 2013). Certainly the Egyptian election of 2012 during the Arab Spring can be classified as such.

There has been a good deal of discussion of essential preconditions for the implementation of elections in transitional democracies. Critical is the building of strong institutions that ensure a sufficient amount of legitimacy, accountability (Collier 2009; International Institute for Democracy and Electoral Assistance 2006), impartiality (Snyder 2010), and effective participation (Machado et al. 2011). These institutions should include the rule of law, a free press, capable institutions for the equitable distribution of public goods, independent and capable electoral authorities, independent courts/judiciary, bureaucracies with sufficient capacity, and protection for the outgoing regime (Collier 2009; Flores and Nooruddin 2009; Mansfield and Snyder 2007; Paris 2004; Ball 1996; Regan and Henderson 2002; International Institute for Democracy and Electoral Assistance 2006). In particular, the importance of effective constraints on executive power is a recurring theme in the literature on democratization (Findley and Young 2011; Davenport 1996). And time for the development of political parties, particularly those that require broad support and that cut across old, or traditional, or existing societal cleavages (Paris 2004; Mansfield and Snyder 2007; Ball 1996; Regan and Henderson 2002). Finally, it is often suggested that elections should be delayed until a stronger and more dynamic civil society and democratic norms have had sufficient time to develop (Collier 2009; Flores and Nooruddin 2009;

Regan and Henderson 2002; International Institute for Democracy and Electoral Assistance 2006).

Regime Consistency and International Collective Action: Traditional Instruments

The international community shares some responsibility for democratic failures, since it often pushes for rapid democratization and early elections. Making matters worse, in postconflict situations, the international community will often push for early elections during untenable military stalemates based on unrealistic readings or insufficient consideration of actual balances of power between combatants. At the same time, the international community has had positive effects on the democratization processes by promoting power-sharing and helping to build stronger institutions, and, in the aftermath of conflicts, supporting demobilization and providing security guarantees so that elections can occur in a less threatening environment (Brancati and Snyder 2011). There is evidence that foreign aid aimed at democracy promotion can offset the negative effect that transitions to democracy have on security (Savun and Tirone 2011). Also effective is helping to design electoral systems with a focus on mechanisms that require broad support that cut across societal cleavages (Regan and Henderson 2002; Paris 2004; International Institute for Democracy and Electoral Assistance 2006).

Collective Action Plan: Indicators of Regime Type and Stability

We now turn to the crux of the issue—the development of a set of indicators that will allow us to assess the current state of affairs as regards both democratization and regime stability. And herein lies the collective action problem for the international system. While virtually all nations profess to value stability as a prerequisite for human security, the road to such stability can be tinged with ideological differences and realpolitik. *While one set of national systems promotes democracy first as a fundamental principle of human security, others promote stability first and political reform (perhaps) later.* It can even be argued that the need of Western developed states to support democracy as the surest way to ensure stability has seriously inhibited collective action by the international system as a whole to address instability and all of the problems that it engenders head on.

This book takes the unequivocal position that the road to stability must pass through a measured transition to democracy. And it is the collective responsibility of the international community to undertake measures that will help facilitate this democratic transition. Such aid can include technical and financial resources for state institution building and consolidation, strengthening judicial institutions and practises, strengthening political parties, and supporting and/or reforming pro-democracy civil-society organizations (Collier 2009; Ball 1996; Regan and Henderson 2002).

The road to stability must pass through a measured transition to democracy. It is the collective responsibility of the international community to undertake measures that will help facilitate this democratic transition.

While the road to stability is bumpy, as noted earlier in this chapter, the alternative route through repressive autocracy extracts too heavy a toll on human security and human rights in its quest for stable regimes. So the indicators and measures discussed below are designed to assess progress along this bumpy road.

A Static Indicator of Regime Type

Static measures of regime type are helpful for understanding the set of authority structures that characterize a regime at a given point in time. Central to most accepted static measures is the Polity IV Project and its work on political regime characteristics and transitions (Marshall et al. 2013).

Polity was created by Ted Robert Gurr and Harry Eckstein in the mid-1970s, and has long been the most widely used data source for analyzing and comparing regimes, authority patterns, and characteristics of states, covering the period 1800–2012. It focuses specifically on institutionalized regime and/or authority patterns and characteristics of central state authority. Polity identifies three dimensions of regime legitimacy and bases the coding of regime characteristics around these three dimensions: personal (competitiveness and openness of executive recruitment); substantive (decision constraints on the chief executive); and participation (regulation and competitiveness of political participation) (Marshall et al. 2013: 1). It treats these indicators as components of an overall regime score, referred to as the Polity Score.

For Democracy, states are assigned positive weights when they exhibit any of the following characteristics: executives are recruited via some type of elections; executive power is either subject to substantial limitations or holds a position of parity or subordination relative to an accountability group; or political participation is somewhat competitive. For the Autocracy scale, states are assigned positive weights when they exhibit any of the following characteristics: executives are recruited by either succession or designation; executive power is either unlimited or subject to only moderate limitations; or political participation is uncompetitive (restricted or suppressed) or excludes certain groups (regulated or unregulated). After calculating separate Democracy and Autocracy scores for a state, Polity then subtracts the latter from the former to calculate the state's overall Polity Score. This is a 21-point scale ranging from the most autocratic states on the lowest end (−10) to the most democratic states on the highest end (+10). Polity then classifies regimes according to their type, depending on how they fall on the Polity Score scale. It reduces the Polity Score to a three-point ordinal scale, using the most common regime typology and the following convention: Autocracy (−10 to −6 Polity score); Anocracy (−5 to +5 Polity score); Democracy (+6 to +10 Polity score) (Marshall et al. 2013).[2]

Although Polity is a static indicator and therefore one can expect only very subtle changes over time to the overall picture of the distribution of polity types, it is possible nevertheless to get an overall view of the general relationship between regime type and political instability. Figure 3.3 clearly shows the probability of political instability (y-axis) to be at its highest level during anocracy (Polity score between −5 and +5), with strong democracy and strong autocracy exhibiting much lower levels of instability.

By 2011, the beginning of what has come to be known as the Arab Spring, there was already a rather remarkable trend elsewhere in the world. In

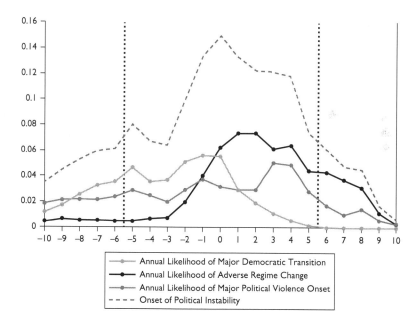

Figure 3.3 Polity score and the onset of political instability, 1955–2006.

Source: Monty Marshall, Polity IV website and Center for Systemic Peace, www.systemicpeace.org/polity/PTfig02.htm.

that year, Kyrgyzstan, Niger, and Thailand[3] transitioned from anocracy to democracy, while Myanmar transitioned from autocracy to anocracy. In the Middle East and North Africa, Tunisia, Libya, Egypt, Morocco, Bahrain, and Syria all began their transitional journeys, although to this point in only one— Morocco—did these changes mean greater levels of democracy through transitions from autocracy to anocracy (Frantz 2014).

Dynamic Indicators

While there is ample evidence that anocratic states are more likely to experience instability, conflict, and repression than full autocracies and democracies, there is also evidence that the dynamic aspects of regimes have a greater effect on violence and insecurity than do their static aspects. In other words, regime change affects instability more than institutional characteristics of regimes. In a detailed analysis, Regan and Bell (2010) show that this even holds for the least stable regime type: anocracy as a transitional stage has a greater effect on civil war than anocracy as a structural form.

Regime Durability

While there is no universal consensus as to what type of political regime—autocratic or democratic—is the best guarantor of human security through regime stability, *there is considerable evidence that highly democratic states use repressive measures far less than other types of regimes, and are therefore more supportive of human security* (Davenport and Armstrong 2004; Bueno de Mesquita et al. 2005). And there is considerable consensus about the unstable nature of regime transitions, and particularly those that pass through a stage of anocracy. Thus we might posit that regardless of regime type, there is something of a consensus on the desirability of regime durability.

Autocratic and democratic regimes will go about institution building to promote durability in different ways—democracies through the buildup and strengthening of institutions and processes through which the population can satisfy basic human needs and address grievances; and autocracies through the buildup of centralized state power and institutionalized control. Transitions out—through democratic regression in the case of democracies, and increased power to the people in the case of autocracies—will likely result in a period of anocracy, the least stable of all the regime types examined here.

Since change itself seems to increase the likelihood of insecurity, the natural presumption would be that regime stability is better for peace and security, and the evidence seems to bear this out (Hegre et al. 2001; Cederman et al. 2010a; Regan and Bell 2010). A promising indicator of regime durability assesses whether regime type is stable. This is defined as any period in which a regime does not fluctuate more than two points in either direction on the Polity score indicator. Any change that stays within this band is considered too small to be indicative of regime change, and therefore it is not likely that normal political processes are being severely disrupted (Cederman et al. 2010a). Analyzing the time period 1946–2004, (Cederman et al. 2010a) find that most states either experience more than one stable period, or stable period(s) do not cover the entire duration of that time frame, so there is variation in regime durability. Dramatic shifts away from long periods of durable regimes—a three-point band on Polity scores—are often associated with outbreaks of conflict. Generally, the shifts associated with conflict outbreaks are those from lower to higher Polity scores.

A second indicator of regime durability is the number of consecutive years that a state remains an anocracy. Recall that earlier we argued that anocracy is the most unstable of the regime types. There is much evidence pointing to anocracy as both the least durable and most conflict-prone regime type, and much discussion linking those two things together. But Regan and Bell (2010) use this indicator to demonstrate how anocracy itself can be stable, and, when it is, it has no effect on likelihood of civil war. They find instead that anocratic transitions are a much more powerful cause of instability than anocratic institutions (see Figure 3.4).

Putting these two indicators together, the combined message is that long periods of minimal regime fluctuation (Cederman et al. 2010a) and taking time in passing through anocracy on the way to democracy (Regan and Bell 2010) will be best for security, that is, don't rush the process.

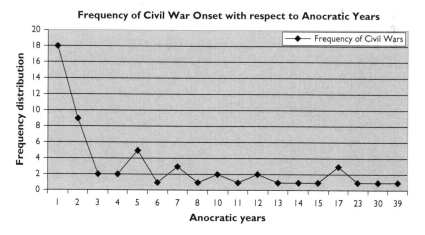

Figure 3.4 Frequency of civil war onset with respect to years of anocracy.

Source: Patrick M. Regan and Sam R. Bell 2010.

A further reason to adopt a slow and careful strategy is that regime changes into anocracy are most likely to give way to insecurity and instability in their early years, but that gives way to stability over time (Hegre et al. 2001; Regan and Bell 2010).

An important conclusion from this discussion of regime durability is that, when a country is in its earliest stages/years of the transition out of autocracy toward democracy, this is the moment for the international community to play a stabilizing role. Although circumstances will differ from case to case, overall the data show that the first 2 years are the most critical (Hegre et al. 2001; Regan and Bell 2010). Therefore, any rush to the outward trappings of democracy, such as early elections, is likely to be destabilizing and ultimately counterproductive. This is the period when stabilization measures should trump democratization measures, when imperfect regimes may need to be encouraged and supported, prior to a more robust march toward a more fully democratic society. As hard as it is to reconcile, it is often the case that the longer the state remains in the transitional stage of anocracy, the more likely it is to emerge with both a stable regime and a firm democratic foundation.

The first 2 years after a regime transition out of autocracy are the most critical—this is when stabilization measures should trump democratization measures, when imperfect regimes may need to be encouraged and supported, prior to a more robust march toward full democracy.

Magnitude of Regime Change

As discussed, transitioning to democracy is an inherent good for many reasons: The most democratic states are more durable, less repressive, and experience less violence than anocratic regimes; they ensure and protect human rights to a greater degree than autocracies, and protect freedoms of speech, association, and participation in the polity as fundamental goods in and of themselves. However, given the positive relationship between regime stability and societal stability, and the fact that transition processes have a larger inducing effect on violence than other factors, not all types of transitions are equally good for human security. Thus, states and societies should exercise caution if they embark on a transition process.

With this in mind, the magnitude of regime change is important during a transition process. Polity is often used as a source for calculating the magnitude of change in regime characteristics. Polity scores are largely stable, especially in the short and medium term, and "many changes in regime behavior take months and even years to fully manifest themselves;

this may be especially true for small or nuanced changes" (Marshall et al. 2013: 8; see also Regan and Bell 2010). However, significant changes are frequent enough to warrant examination. Given the fact that regime scores are relatively static over time, targeting time periods where there is actual change is likely the most effective approach to understanding the nature and assessing the effects of transitions. Marshall et al. (2013: 30) operationally define regime change as a three-point change in Polity score, "with each continuous, sequential change (in the same general direction)…occurring within three years or less of the previous change." This is intended to measure "a substantive, normative change in political authority considered sufficient to present real opportunities for regime opponents to challenge the, as yet, non-institutionalized authority of the polity" (Marshall et al. 2013: 30).

The approach recommended here is to consider the absolute value of the change in Polity score over the course of a period in which the state is identified as in the midst of a regime change. There is evidence that larger regime changes lead to greater likelihood of civil (Regan and Bell 2010) and international war (Gleditsch and Ward 2000). And there is some evidence that large changes—from autocracy to full democracy—that occur very quickly—in 1 year's time—decrease the likelihood of repression in the year of change, but repression increases again the following year, so improved conditions are not stable over time (Zanger 2000). Regardless, such large, fast changes may only be successful when other prerequisites for democracy are already in place (e.g., strong institutions, high levels of state capacity, rule of law, and strong judiciaries), as Brancati and Snyder (2013) found in their analysis of the timing of elections. An example of large, fast success due to favorable preconditions was South Africa's first postapartheid election. Thus, the general recommendation based on findings regarding regime durability and magnitude of change is that slow, small changes are the best for security.

Direction of Regime Change

As noted earlier in the discussion of regime transitions, the direction of regime change—toward autocracy or toward democracy—is critical in terms of assessing its impact on stability. And Polity is again the dataset most frequently used to measure this change.

Evidence exists that certain directions of regime change are more prone to instability than others. The strongest and most consistent evidence shows that shifts away from democracy, which are popularly termed "democratic reversals," have a strong negative effect on human security through an increase in the probability of both civil war and repression (Zanger 2000; Cederman et al. 2010a; Goldstone et al. 2010; Regan and

Bell 2010). In particular, a shift from democracy into anocracy is the most harmful scenario (Regan and Bell 2010; Zanger 2000).

Shifts away from democracy, which are popularly termed "democratic reversals," have a strong negative effect on human security through an increase in the probability of both civil war and repression.

The most common explanation for this set of findings is that movements into anocracy from democracy spur sharp resistance from an already organized population. This in turn creates a perfect storm for rebellion and repression when combined with newfound instability associated with anocracy and a regime trying to exert stricter controls over participation and political freedoms. Movements into autocracy on the other hand may signal the successful quashing of resistance, hence the lower likelihood of violence (Zanger 2000; Hegre et al. 2001; Davenport 2007; Cederman et al. 2010a; Regan and Bell 2010). The evidence regarding the effect of movements away from autocracy and toward democracy is mixed. Citizens tend to be more patient with systems in the process of opening than those in the process of closing (Regan and Bell 2010; Cederman et al. 2010a).

Overall, evidence exists that anocratic states that experience a succession of multiple transitions back and forth between more democracy and more autocracy are at an increased risk of experiencing instability and violence, and for extended periods (Gleditsch and Ward 2000; Hegre et al. 2001). Hence, the ideal scenario is movement out of autocracy and toward democracy, with steady, incremental progress in that direction over an extended period of time.

The ideal scenario is movement out of autocracy and toward democracy, with steady, incremental progress in that direction over an extended period of time.

For the international community, then, it is clear that there is no single script for enhancing stability and creating the conditions for a more open and democratic society. Rather, great care must be taken in assessing past instances of regime change and current local conditions in deciding upon a course of action likely to yield both stability in the short run and long-term democratization over time.

Leadership Change

We have already examined the impact of duration of regime on stability, and noted that regime transitions—through democratic regression in the case of democracies, and increased power to the people in the case of autocracies—will likely result in a period of anocracy, the least stable of all the regime types examined here. There is often a close connection between leadership change and regime durability.

A change in executive is not necessarily an equivalent of regime change, but it is often a precipitating factor. Assessing the relationship between the two, Frantz (2014) finds that countries experiencing leadership changes are eight times more likely to experience regime change than countries with no leadership change. Regime changes that end in democracy are especially likely to result from leadership changes: two-thirds of democratizations result from leadership changes compared with slightly more than half of transitions to autocracy and roughly 40 percent of transitions to anocracy.

The Archigos dataset contains information on leaders for 188 countries from 1875 to 2004, including a categorical indicator of leadership change that measures how a leader exits office. The classification is as follows:

1. Regular. These are changes that occur via established, existing sets of rules and norms (e.g., retirement, losing elections, and term limits);
2. Irregular. These are changes that occur illicitly or by force (e.g., assassinations, coups, and rebellions);
3. Death in office (ill health or suicide);
4. Foreign intervention (successful invasion).

(Goemans et al. 2009)

Because of the absence of institutional mechanisms to enforce regular leadership turnover, leaders in nondemocratic states are more likely to either hold on to power until they are physically unable to or be forcefully removed by the opposition. One-quarter of all leadership changes are irregular. Irregular leadership changes are much more likely to lead to regime change than regular leadership changes: 40 percent of irregular leadership changes lead to regime change compared with 10 percent of regular leadership changes.

Types of leadership change also vary by regime type. Leadership changes in democracies overwhelmingly occur via regular, established methods. Irregular changes are much more common in nondemocratic systems than in democratic ones. Hence, leadership changes in nondemocratic systems are also much more likely to increase instability than those in democracies (Frantz 2014).

Taking all of the above into account, it is clear that the external encouragement and facilitation of leadership change should not be undertaken lightly. Two recent examples from the Middle East bear unfortunate witness to lack of attention to this principle. In Egypt, the international community, with the US in the lead, was all too quick to encourage the replacement of the Mubarak regime through revolution and then pre-mature elections, with the resultant slip into violence, repression, and military takeover. In Syria, early international encouragement of leader-ship change has resulted in a massive civil war with an unknown outcome and human suffering on a scale seldom seen in recent years.

Conclusion

In this chapter we have tried to untangle the complex relationship between regime type and instability. We have come down strongly in favor of assisting those states that are moving from autocracy to democracy, and strengthening democracy-supporting institutions in transitional societies. While recognizing that transitional and/or anocratic regimes are often unstable, here are concrete steps that can be taken to promote the organic growth of democracy while minimizing instability.

Begin with political and institutional factors, because they may be more amenable to short-term change than economic and ethnic considerations (Goldstone et al. 2010; Snyder and Mahoney 1999).

Focus on building cross-cleavage ties (Paris 2004). Given the powerful effect that partial democracy with factionalism has on instability, policymakers should focus their efforts on crafting "policies and institutions that blunt or discourage factionalism when opening up political participation and competition" (Goldstone et al. 2010: 205).

Support building and strengthening of political parties (Flores and Nooruddin 2009; Regan and Henderson 2002). Political parties can impose a needed structure during chaotic transition periods (Savun and Tirone 2011). This is linked to building cross-cleavage ties; it is important to promote parties that cut across traditional cleavages.

Do not rush elections if democratic institutions and state capacity are weak. "Transition through a stage of semi-democracy should be managed with care, focusing more on the institutional frameworks and attention to opposition demands than simply on voting behavior" (Regan and Henderson 2002: 131).

Consider the role of a caretaker government to help provide stability and peace during an extended transition, while building institutions and capacity (Ball 1996). International actors can play a key role in supporting this process with democracy aid.

Be aware of resistance that anocratic regimes will likely put up to attempts to build stronger institutions. Institutional development gives the opposition a greater voice and more power, and it checks the bias that naturally favors incumbents in newly democratizing regimes. Hence, institutional development has the potential to decrease the anocratic regime's life span (Regan and Henderson 2002). While stability is most important during a transition, particularly in the early stages thereof, the end goal is democracy and not indefinite rule by an anocratic regime. Hence, institutional development helps to both keep the transition process slowly and steadily moving toward democracy and prevent the transitional regime from becoming semi-permanent.

Promote indigenous and local-level democratic practises, and strengthen civil society, rather than adopting a top-down model (Regan and Henderson 2002; International Institute for Democracy and Electoral Assistance 2006; Ball 1996).

Notes

1 On this latter point, see for example USAID's Millennium Challenge Corporation program, developed explicitly to encourage demonstrated progress in democratization through such institutions as elections (see Chapter 4 below).
2 Among the other leading sources of quantitative measures of regime type are the Democracy Index published by *The Economist Intelligence Unit* (2014) and *Freedom in the World* published by Freedom House (2011).
3 The year 2014 found Thailand transitioning once again from democracy to autocracy after a military coup.

Chapter 4

Development

The Myth and Reality of Development: Setting the Scene

The international community has long struggled with the tremendous inequalities of wealth and opportunity among the nations of the world. Both theories and programs abound, and as we will see below, progress has been made on a number of fronts. Yet with developed economies exhibiting great disparities in the distribution of wealth *within* their own societies and the accompanying differentials in opportunity that these disparities produce, it should not be a surprise to find that progress is slow in addressing these same disparities *across* nations as well. Nevertheless, there is little doubt that more than half a century of development programs have yielded significant progress.

Myth 4 The international community has been successful both in increasing the pot of international development aid funds and in directing those funds to the places where they are needed the most.

Figure 4.1 shows progress across four decades in reducing extreme poverty rates for various regions and groupings of states. The greatest progress has been recorded for China, where the **extreme poverty** rate went from 84 percent in 1981 to 12 percent in 2010. Sub-Saharan Africa, by contrast, showed the least progress, with extreme poverty still a fact of life for almost half the population.

International development became a significant global focus in the years immediately following the end of the Second World War, with the creation of the International Monetary Fund (IMF) and the Bank for Reconstruction and Development (now part of the World Bank). With the independence of Europe's colonies, what began largely as a program to provide support for postwar reconstruction for war-devastated Europe evolved into a more general development program. And for the US, emerging from the war as the dominant global economic power, this

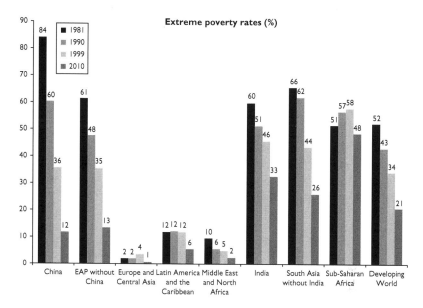

Figure 4.1 The evolution of extreme poverty rates by region, 1981–2010.

Source: P. Olinto and H. Uematsu 2013.

was an opportunity for it to draft "a new foreign policy of international involvement for the advancement of less economically developed areas" (Korchumova 2007: 2–3).

Development and Inequality

The particular approach that we will take in this chapter will argue that, while development aid has gone a long way in addressing some of the most fundamental problems facing developing countries, great disparities remain within and among these societies. And the poorest and most wretched of these societies impose enormous costs not only on their own people, but also on the societies around them, and even on the international community in general. Both the progress and the remaining challenges are captured in the World Bank report "The State of the Poor":

> Extreme poverty in the world has decreased considerably in the past three decades. In 1981, more than half of citizens in the developing world lived on less than $1.25 per day (formerly set at $1 per day). This rate has dropped dramatically to 21 percent in 2010. Moreover, despite a 59 percent increase in the developing world's population, there were significantly fewer people living on less than $1.25 a day

in 2010 (1.2 billion) than there were three decades ago (1.9 billion). But 1.2 billion people living in extreme poverty is still an extremely high figure, so the task ahead of us remains Herculean.

(Olinto and Uematsu 2013; bold added)

In 1981, more than half of citizens in the developing world lived on less than $1.25 a day (extreme poverty). This rate has dropped dramatically to 21 percent in 2010. But 1.2 billion people still live in extreme poverty today.

Reality But development aid is outpaced by the economic cost of state instability, fragility, and failure by a factor of almost four to one.

The aggregated data showing progress conceal the fact that Sub-Saharan Africa is the only region of the world for which the number of poor individuals has actually risen steadily—there are more than twice as many extremely poor people living in Sub-Saharan Africa today—414 million—than there were in 1990 (Olinto and Uematsu 2013). At the time of this writing, more than a third of the world's extremely poor live in Africa. As we see throughout this book, Africa is also the home of the majority of the world's most fragile and unstable states—is it any wonder?

This chapter takes on three related themes that help us think about development. First, it addresses the notion that aid is a critical driver of development. Second, it focuses in on issues of priorities, distribution, and assessment of impact. And finally, it provides a guide to development aid goals through brief examination of the Millennium Development Goals (MDGs) that the UN set for 2015, and a more detailed discussion of the emerging Sustainable Development Goals (SDGs), set for adoption by the United Nations General Assembly in 2014–2015 for achievement by 2030.

Approaches to Development: Modernization and Dependence

We begin this chapter with a review of development theory, and how that theory in its most recent form has been applied to a world of unequal wealth and opportunity. There is no doubt that early development theory had a somewhat condescending tone to it, along with strong advocacy for adopting Western cultural values and institutions. In an early work, Rostow argued that in order to achieve full **modernization**, which to him was typified by high mass-consumption, societies needed to shed their traditional attitudes and social institutions and replace them with Western equivalents (Rostow 1960). Even today, critics of development theory base their arguments in part on the implication of this early approach that called on developing countries to shed their own institutions and to adapt to those of the West. The early and sustained development of the so-called Asian Tigers—Hong Kong, Singapore, South Korea, and Taiwan—attested to the achievement of development gains without adapting institutions and culture to become more like the West.

Countering modernization theory, **dependency** theory has argued that developed states enjoy their current status as a result of exploiting the resources, cheap labor, and markets of poorer nations. Some early advocates of this theory, such as Frank (1966), have argued that developed nations explicitly keep peripheral nations in a state of perpetual underdevelopment. Development loans for long-term projects like dams and irrigation systems are slow to generate predicted income, while debt on these loans amasses. As a result, much of the aid money needs to be used for debt servicing, which can lead to pressure to accept multinational corporation investment that distorts these countries' economies, or in taking on support for Western strategic interests such as troop and equipment basing (Barrett and Whyte 1982). And there is evidence that substantial amounts of aid never leave the donor country: "for every British pound lent to LDCs, 70 pence is spent in the UK or spent on projects which primarily employ expertise from the donor country" (Chapman 2004: 67). Thus, as Frank argued, poor countries are locked into a system that is almost impossible for them to escape (Chapman 2004).

With the formation of the United Nations Development Programme (UNDP) in 1966, the international community signaled the beginning of a shift in focus to **human development**, a term attributed to Amartya Sen that highlights the importance of addressing human needs and capabilities. Among the issues addressed by UNDP as part of a development aid portfolio have been poverty reduction, crisis prevention and recovery, environment and energy, HIV/AIDS, urbanization, and climate change.

Two important global trends left their marks on the evolution of development aid programs. With the end of colonialism, former colonial governments have been the number one donors of aid to their former colonies. These include the UK, France, Belgium, the Netherlands, and Portugal. Although not a colonial power by standard definitions, the US has of course played a leading role as well in the evolution of development aid priorities. And as the colonies gained independence, the US initiated a shift in focus from postwar reconstruction to a focus on the non-Western world. "This was the beginning of international development based in foreign aid and assistance from the West to the rest of the world" (Hjertholm and White 2000).

Figures 4.2 and 4.3 are particularly instructive (UK Parliament 2012). In Figure 4.2, we track the main established Official Development Assistance (ODA) donors who are members of the Development

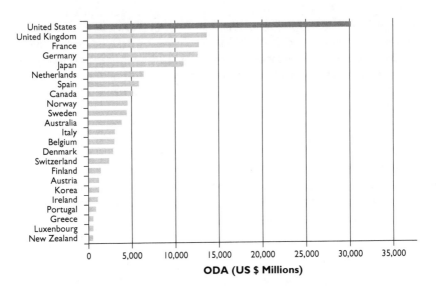

Figure 4.2 Official direct assistance (ODA) by members of the Development Assistance Cooperation Committee of the Organization for Economic Cooperation and Development.

Source: House of Lords – The Economic Impact and Effectiveness of Development Aid – Economic Affairs Committee. www.publications.parliament.uk/pa/idselect/ideconaf/278/27805.htm.

Assistance Committee (DAC) of the Organization for Economic Cooperation and Development (OECD) and how much they contribute in millions of dollars. The US leads all donors with a total of more than $31 billion in 2010, with the UK, France, Germany, and Japan grouped in the $15 billion range. From 1990 to 2010, ODA from DAC countries rose from about $40 billion to over $125 billion a year. However, as a proportion of gross national income (GNI), this figure fell over the same period from about 0.5 percent to 0.3 percent.

And Figure 4.3 tells an even more interesting story. Here we see that, as a percentage of gross national income, only five countries meet the UN-recommended standard of 0.7 percent of GNI: Norway, Luxembourg, Sweden, Denmark, and the Netherlands. The US comes in at 0.2 percent of GNI, ranking 19th![1]

As a percentage of gross national income (GNI), only five countries meet the UN-recommended standard of 0.7 percent of GNI: Norway, Luxembourg, Sweden, Denmark, and the Netherlands. The US comes in at 0.2 percent of GNI, ranking 19th!

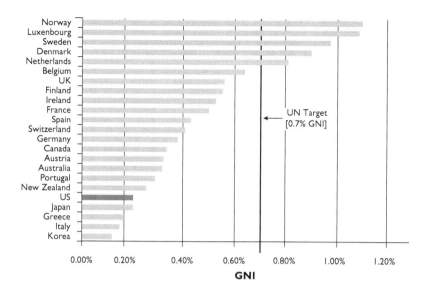

Figure 4.3 Official direct assistance (ODA) by members of the Development Assistance Committee as a proportion of gross national income (GNI).

Source: House of Lords – The Economic Impact and Effectiveness of Development Aid – Economic Affairs Committee. www.publications.parliament.uk/pa/idselect/ideconaf/278/27805.htm.

The second global trend with significant impact on aid patterns was the Cold War. In the competition for allies and proxies, the US gave much of its aid to countries it wanted to retain in its alliance, or, in other cases, simply to keep them from aligning with the USSR. And some of this aid was delivered to unsavory regimes. The US backed the Mobutu government in Zaire, based solely on his anticommunist stance, disregarding his many human rights abuses and his detrimental leadership of Zaire (Noble 1992). Some would argue that the Global War on Terrorism has had a similar recent effect on patterns of US aid.

With the end of the Cold War and with significant portions of the global population still languishing in what was termed "extreme poverty," defined then as living on less than $1 per day per capita, it was clear that a massive collective effort would be needed to address the issue. In 2000, UNDP played a central role in the promulgation and subsequent implementation of the **MDGs**, a set of eight ambitious development goals to be achieved by 2015. These goals include the eradication of poverty and hunger; achievement of universal primary education; gender equality and the empowerment of women; reduction of child mortality rates; improvement of maternal health; combating of HIV/AIDS, malaria, and other diseases; ensuring environmental sustainability; and the development of a global partnership for development (United Nations 2014). Progress on some of these goals by the target year 2015 has been impressive—eradication of extreme poverty, improvement in maternal health, combating of disease, and environmental sustainability in terms of greater access to clean drinking water; although it is important to point out that achievement of these goals has been uneven both among and within countries. Others goals will need to be addressed in coming years (see discussion below of the Sustainable Development Goals for 2030).

In 2000, UNDP played a central role in the promulgation and subsequent implementation of the MDGs, a set of eight ambitious development goals to be achieved by 2015.

Targeting Development Aid

In current practice, there are several ways in which development aid is allocated. The most widely used is **foreign aid**, which can be in the form of program-based aid that is given directly to the recipient government, and project-based aid, which is implemented with the help of the donor. **Humanitarian and/or disaster relief** is given specifically in response to a shock of some sort. **Remittances** are money sent directly to individuals, most often in the form of payments by migrants to their families in their home countries. **Foreign direct investment (FDI)** can help stimulate a state's economy, although some argue that FDI can lead to dependency.

One of the most persistent issues facing the international community as it strives to address development has been how to direct aid to the subnational areas and programs that need it the most. Despite a steady increase in total aid to developing countries over the past 50 years, donors have often been unsuccessful in directing the funds and programs to the areas with the greatest need. To illustrate this point, AidData Research Consortium collaborated with Malawi's Ministry of Finance to geocode aid locations for 30 donor agencies. Figure 4.4 shows the location for USAID health sector projects in circles, and the proportion of the population in each district with inadequate access to health services in shades of grey. This example illustrates that the location of USAID investments does not necessarily correspond to where there is the greatest need for services (Glassman 2014).

Aid Dependency and Economic Growth

One of the difficult unintended consequences of development aid is that it creates a syndrome similar to what has been termed the "resource curse."

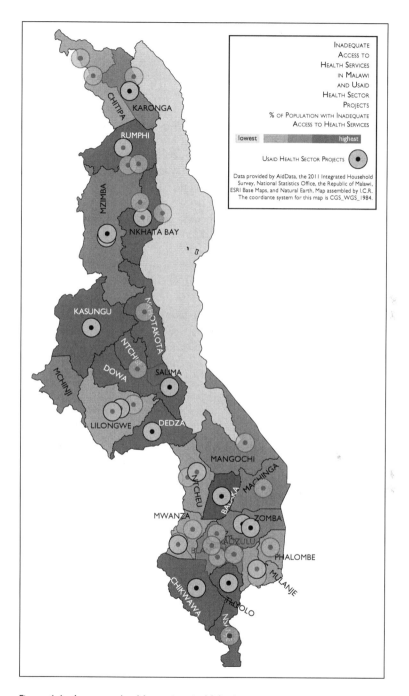

Figure 4.4 Access to health services in Malawi.

Source: A. Glassman 2014.

This condition arises when a country with an abundant natural resource with high international market value—oil or diamonds, for example—becomes reliant on the revenue generated from that single resource to the detriment of other sectors of the economy left un- or under-developed. Related to this is the so-called **Dutch Disease**, which refers to a condition under which the revenue from an abundant natural resource makes the nation's currency stronger and increases the exchange rate. This, in turn, results in the nation's other exports becoming more expensive for other countries to buy, and therefore renders their manufacturing sectors less competitive (Kishi 2014).[2]

Some argue that the concept of a resource curse could be applied to other types of non-tax revenue, such as international aid flows (see Brass 2008; Kishi 2014). When a significant portion of a state's income is derived from aid flows, this could have a dampening effect on investment in the development of important sectors of the economy. The state also becomes less dependent on domestic taxes and, paradoxically, the government becomes less accountable to its society (Therkildsen 2002). An equitable tax system can encourage constructive engagement between government and citizens, and can thus advance state building through a legitimate social contract between the citizens and the state (Gillies 2010). If a government does not need to levy taxes (i.e., if they are receiving enough revenue from non-tax resources such as development aid), then this accountability by the constituency may be lost; this can in turn make the population feel as though they do not have a sufficient say in democratic processes, which can in turn increase grievances that could later result in conflict (Kishi 2014).

When a significant portion of a state's income is derived from aid flows, this could have a dampening effect on investment in the development of important sectors of the economy. The state also becomes less dependent on domestic taxes and, paradoxically, the government becomes less accountable to its society.

This deterioration or weakening of state economic institutions as a result of aid flows is a recurring theme in the discussions of the pros and cons of development aid. State fragility and failure can result if state institutions are weak to begin with. Knack argues that "aid dependence can potentially undermine institutional quality, by weakening accountability, encouraging rent seeking and corruption, fomenting conflict over control of aid funds, siphoning off scarce talent from the bureaucracy, and alleviating pressures to reform inefficient policies and institutions" (Knack 2001: 310). Other possible adverse effects include a decline in the market for skilled labor, a decline in investor confidence because of potential volatility of past aid, and disincentives for domestic revenue generation (Birdsall 2007).

The Debate over the Financing Gap

The discussion surrounding whether and how to go about the granting of development aid has been enshrined in a debate of sorts between two prominent US development economists: Jeffrey Sachs of Columbia University and William Easterly of New York University. The financing gap emerges when there is a difference between the required investment needed in order to generate growth, and a country's own savings. Insofar as aid is concerned, the general idea is that capital will lead to investment that in turn will lead to economic growth. Since poor countries do not have the initial capital needed to begin this process, they can never reach full economic growth. Foreign aid comes in as a potential solution to underdevelopment, as aid can serve as the initial capital needed to get the process of development started. The bigger the financing gap, the greater the need for aid to fill this gap.

The financing gap emerges when there is a difference between the required investment needed in order to generate growth, and a country's own savings. Development aid can address this gap.

Sachs' argument is that the poorest countries have yet to develop, since most aid in these cases is generally given in the form of crisis response (Sachs 2005). Crisis response aid does not go into the economy for the most part, and therefore does not create investment. Crisis management in this sense does not lend itself to long-term planning, and so there has been minimal gain from aid thus far. Sachs argues for a "big push" of aid from the developed to the developing world in order to create capital, investment, and ultimately sustainable development.

Easterly (2006) argues that aid ultimately does more harm than good. His contention is that aid will not turn into investment. In his study, he examines 81 cases of specific aid programs and finds that in only 7 did aid lead to more investment. Further, he shows that Africa has been the biggest recipient of aid as a percentage of GDP, but has until very recently had the slowest economic growth rate of any region. He contends that aid overlooks the role of bad governance and corruption, and creates a negative incentive problem: the poorer the country remains, the more aid flows in, and the greater share corrupt politicians can pocket. And finally, the debt problem that some aid programs create leads to the phenomenon of new aid being used merely to pay off old loans. Aid changes hands at the highest level without doing much to help those it is meant to assist.

In recent years, this debate has been joined by private philanthropists, who have been more optimistic about the positive impact that aid has had on global poverty. In the widely read Annual Letter of the Gates Foundation for 2014, Bill and Melinda Gates have attempted to dispel three myths about the impact of development aid on global poverty. The first myth is that "poor countries are doomed to stay poor" (http://annualletter.gatesfoundation.org). Gates and Gates go on to point out:

> Don't let anyone tell you that Africa is worse off today than it was 50 years ago. Income per person has in fact risen in sub-Saharan Africa over that time, and quite a bit in a few countries. After plummeting during the debt crisis of the 1980s, it has climbed by two thirds since 1998, to nearly $2,200 from just over $1,300. Today, more and more countries are turning toward strong sustained development, and more will follow. Seven of the 10 fastest-growing economies of the past half-decade are in Africa.
>
> Africa has also made big strides in health and education. Since 1960, the life span for women in sub-Saharan Africa has gone up from 41 to 57 years, despite the HIV epidemic. Without HIV it would be 61 years. The percentage of children in school has gone from the low 40s to over 75 percent since 1970. Fewer people are hungry, and more people have good nutrition. If getting enough to eat, going to school, and living longer are measures of a good life, then life is definitely getting better there. These improvements are not the end of the story; they're the foundation for more progress.
>
> (Gates and Gates 2014)

Today, more and more countries are turning toward strong sustained development, and more will follow. Seven of the ten fastest-growing economies of the past half-decade are in Africa.

See Figure 4.5 for an illustration of the evolution of income distribution across the developing and developed world. In this diagram from the Gates Foundation Annual Letter for 2014, the darker shaded line represents the way income distribution looked 50 years ago, like a camel with two humps. The first hump represented the developing world, and the second lower hump represented the people in the wealthier nations. This has been dubbed the "camel world." The "dromedary world" better represents the situation today, with most of humanity now in the large hump in the middle.

Gates and Gates' second myth is that "foreign aid is a big waste." Here the argument rests on three mistaken notions. First, that the developed world spends entirely too much on aid, while neglecting domestic needs. The facts are quite different, as we have seen. Norway, the leading aid

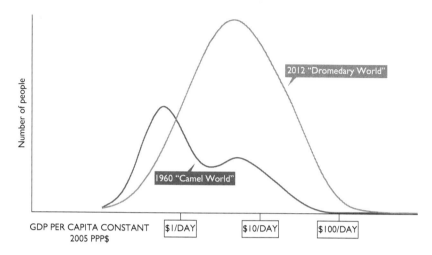

Figure 4.5 The poverty curve – from two humps to one.

Source: Adapted from B. Gates and M. Gates 2014. "2014 Gates Annual Letter: 3 Myths that Block Progress for the Poor." http://annualletter.gatesfoundation.org, which adapted its graph from Figure 2 on the following website: www.basvanleeuwen.net/bestanden/CGEH.WP_.No1_. Vanzandenetal.jan2011_0.pdf.

donor, gives somewhat less than 3 percent of its GDP to aid programs, while for the US the figure is less than 1 percent. Of this approximately $30 billion US contribution, roughly a third goes to health. The second critique is that aid recipient countries often house corrupt political systems, and so a good deal of the aid assistance is syphoned off before it reaches its intended target population. This is an argument for addressing corruption, rather than stopping these programs. And finally, there is the theory that aid creates dependence and harms natural growth of a multisector economy. Again to quote from the Gates Foundation report:

> We do know that aid drives improvements in health, agriculture, and infrastructure that correlate strongly with growth in the long run. Health aid saves lives and allows children to develop mentally and physically, which will pay off within a generation. Studies show that these children become healthier adults who work more productively. If you're arguing against that kind of aid, you've got to argue that saving lives doesn't matter to economic growth, or that saving lives simply doesn't matter.
>
> (Gates and Gates 2014)

Gates and Gates' third myth is that "saving lives leads to overpopulation." But the fact is that the countries with the highest death rates among children also have the highest population growth rates. In fact, as the graphic for Brazil in Figure 4.6 clearly shows, as the infant mortality rate declines due to better prenatal health care programs, fertility rates decline, as does the rate of population growth. Again to quote from the Gates' report:

> [T]he virtuous cycle that starts with basic health and empowerment ends not only with a better life for women and their families, but with significant economic growth at the country level. In fact, one reason for the so-called Asian economic miracle of the 1980s was the fact that fertility across Southeast Asia declined so rapidly. Experts call this phenomenon the demographic dividend. As fewer children die and fewer are born, the age structure of the population gradually changes.
>
> Eventually, there's a bulge of people in their prime working years. This means more of the population is in the workforce and generating economic growth. At the same time, since the number of young children is relatively smaller, the government and parents are able to invest more in each child's education and health care, which can lead to more economic growth over the long term.
>
> (Gates and Gates 2014)

The virtuous cycle that starts with basic health and empowerment ends not only with a better life for women and their families, but with significant economic growth at the country level.

Figure 4.6 illustrates the close positive link between reduction in child mortality rates (the probability per 1,000 that a newborn baby will die before reaching the age of five), fertility rate (the average number of

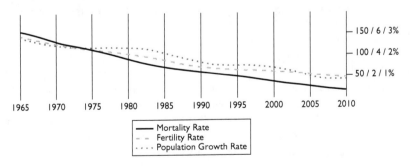

Figure 4.6   Child mortality, fertility, and population growth in Brazil, 1965–2010.

Source: Adapted from B. Gates and M. Gates. 2014. "2014 Gates Annual Letter: 3 Myths that Block Progress for the Poor." http://annualletter.gatesfoundation.org.

births per woman), and population growth rate (the percentage change of resident population compared to previous year), using Brazil as an example.

Development, Aid, and International Collective Action: Traditional Instruments

With the end of the Second World War in 1945 and the establishment of the UN, aid and development began to be thought of in terms of collective action issues for the international community. Beginning with the urgent need to provide humanitarian aid to a Europe devastated by the ravages of war, and the need to help repatriate up to six million displaced persons, the UN Relief and Rehabilitation Administration (UNRRA) came into being (Browne 1990: 3–5). With development and relief functions becoming increasingly globalized, the main functions of UNRRA were absorbed into two new organizations: the International Refugee Organization (later to become the UN High Commission for Refugees) and the United Nations International Children's Emergency Fund (UNICEF) (Browne 1990). As Browne points out, "it was the UN negotiations in the monetary, financial and trade areas that were perhaps of greatest significance in the ensuing aid story" (Browne 1990: 5). But this early collective action start on issues of reconstruction and development ran head on into the realities of postwar geopolitical divisions. "Ideology and the incompatibility of economic systems began to undermine the heady concepts of a unified world order and a system of multilateral consensus to administer it" (Browne 1990: 11).

In the mid-1960s, in the midst of the unparalleled independence movements particularly among former African colonies, the UN Development Programme was established. Its emphasis was on the basic notion of **human development**, a concept first enunciated by Amartya Sen, which highlights the importance of human needs and capabilities. In particular, UNDP took on the mission of capacity building, "helping people and their institutions perform better, sustain that performance over time and remain resilient during 'shocks'—to effectively contribute to the national human development goals" (United Nations Development Programme 2014). Thus, a significant shift took place from reconstruction aid in the immediate aftermath of the Second World War, to a pooling of resources to assist the poor. Efforts of the International Monetary Fund and the World Bank were geared toward loans to poor countries for economic and political development, and the UN offered humanitarian assistance along with food aid. "This was the beginning of international development based on foreign aid and assistance from the West to the rest of the world" (Korchumova 2007), led by the US and the former colonial powers—the UK, France, Belgium, the Netherlands, and Portugal.

Collective Action Plan: Development Goals

In keeping with the general theme of this book, development aid needs to be examined from the point of view of a collective action paradigm. Types of aid and types of donors differ greatly—the former in terms of direct assistance, investment, and disaster relief; the latter from international organizations, individual governments, NGOs, and private foundations and individuals. Motives, approaches, and outcome measures differ greatly across the types of aid and the types of donors, not to mention important differences in the characteristics of aid recipients. And each type of aid and type of donor is subject to different factors, causing potential fluctuation from year to year in total amounts of aid, where it is being directed, and how it is programmed for use. How, then, can we disentangle these factors in order to recommend a set of policies and measures that will result in a degree of uniformity and coordination?

Measuring Development

As was the case with previous chapters, we will now present a set of indicators that can be used to assess progress in development. The focus will be on those measures that take account of collective action on the part of members and institutions of the international community. And like in most other cases, this focus will be on indicators that will allow us to measure short- and medium-term progress.

A leading role in the creation of a collective action approach to development came with the founding of the *Human Development Report* in 1990. It began with the simple premise that "people are the real wealth of a nation" (United Nations Development Programme 2013a). Two of the leading thinkers at the time of the founding of the Report were Mahbub ul Haq and Amartya Sen. Here are their words on the subject:

'The basic purpose of development is to enlarge people's choices. In principle, these choices can be infinite and can change over time. People often value achievements that do not show up at all, or not immediately, in income or growth figures: greater access to knowledge, better nutrition and health services, more secure livelihoods, security against crime and physical violence, satisfying leisure hours, political and cultural freedoms and sense of participation in community activities. The objective of development is to create an enabling environment for people to enjoy long, healthy and creative lives.'—Mahbub ul Haq (1934–1998), founder of the Human Development Report:

'Human development, as an approach, is concerned with what I take to be the basic development idea: namely, advancing the richness of human life, rather than the richness of the economy in which human beings live, which is only a part of it.'—Amartya Sen, Professor of Economics, Harvard University Nobel Laureate in Economics, 1998.

(United Nations Development Programme 2013a)

The basic purpose of development is to enlarge people's choices (Mahbub ul Haq). Human development is concerned with advancing the richness of human life, rather than the richness of the economy in which human beings live (Amartya Sen).

Along with the founding of the Human Development Report came important empirical work, with one of the main results the creation of what has come to be the leading indicator of development, the **Human Development Index (HDI)**. HDI combines indicators of life expectancy, educational attainment and income.

The breakthrough for the HDI was the creation of a single statistic which was to serve as a frame of reference for both social and economic development. The HDI sets a minimum and a maximum for each dimension, called goalposts, and then shows where each country stands in relation to these goalposts, expressed as a value between 0 and 1.

(United Nations Development Programme 2013b)

In 2010, the **Inequality-adjusted Human Development Index** (IHDI) was introduced to take account of inequality; that is, a measure of what could be achieved if there were no inequality.

Earlier in this chapter we briefly addressed the **MDGs**, which were adopted by the UN in 2000. These eight goals, set to be achieved by 2015, were really the first attempt by the international community to spell out development goals in a format that included indicators of progress. MDGs include the following:

1. To eradicate extreme poverty and hunger
2. To achieve universal primary education
3. To promote gender equality and empower women
4. To reduce child mortality
5. To improve maternal health
6. To combat HIV/AIDS, malaria, and other diseases
7. To ensure environmental sustainability
8. To develop a global partnership for development.

Fifteen years on, and in light of experience with this first set of goals, development specialists from around the world met in Rio de Janeiro in June 2012 in the context of the United Nations Conference on Sustainable Development, Rio+20. The goal was to begin thinking through a revised round of development goals with an emphasis on sustainability. Subsequent to this meeting, a 30-member Open Working Group was tasked with preparing a proposal for **Sustainable Development Goals (SDGs)** for consideration by the General Assembly in September 2014.

Following the Millennium Development Goals (MDGs) for 2015, the Sustainable Development Goals (SDGs) for 2030 have been designed with an emphasis on sustainability.

In May 2014, the Leadership Council of the Sustainable Development Solutions Network, working under a mandate from the UN, issued a report entitled Indicators for Sustainable Development Goals (Sustainable Development Solutions Network 2014).[3] The report was presented to the 69th Session of the United National General Assembly in September 2014 for consideration and approval. The report presents operational priorities for the post-2015 development agenda, including 10 goals, over 30 targets, and more than 100 indicators.

The Sustainable Development Solutions Network has argued that setting development goals with an eye toward sustainability is important for a number of reasons. These include the following:

- They unite the global community and inspire coherent public and private action at local, national, regional, and global levels.
- They provide a coherent narrative of sustainable development and help guide the public's understanding of complex sustainable development challenges, including neglected ones.
- They promote integrated thinking and put to rest the futile debates that pit one dimension of sustainable development against another.
- They support long-term approaches toward sustainable development.
- They define responsibilities and foster accountability.
- They inspire active problem solving by all sectors of society.

In keeping with these overall reasons for proposing a new set of development goals for the international community, a preliminary list of these goals, first subjected to an extensive public comment process, was proposed for consideration by the United Nations General Assembly in September 2014. The SDGs are:

(1) End extreme poverty including hunger
(2) Promote economic growth and decent jobs within planetary boundaries
(3) Ensure effective learning for all children and youths for life and livelihood
(4) Achieve gender equality, social inclusion, and human rights
(5) Achieve health and well-being at all ages
(6) Improve agriculture systems and raise rural prosperity
(7) Empower inclusive, productive, and resilient cities
(8) Curb human induced climate change and ensure sustainable energy
(9) Secure ecosystem services and biodiversity, and ensure good management of water, oceans, forests, and natural resources
(10) Transform governance and technologies for sustainable development.[4]

The goals and indicators that will be discussed in this chapter will be based heavily on the work of the Open Working Group and its preliminary lists of SDGs, targets, and indicators. Some of these match up closely with some of the other issues and indicators that we discuss in detail in other chapters—particularly in the areas of environment, conflict, and stability (see Chapters 1, 3, and 5 of this book). In the sections below, we will discuss several of the remaining development goals, targets, and indicators.

Indicators of Development Through the SDGs for 2030

SDG #1: End Extreme Poverty, Including Hunger

As was the case with the MDGs adopted in 2000, extreme poverty tops the list of SDGs as well. In many parts of the world, poverty is closely associated with general fragility of society and regime, with such fragility often leading to conflict that can spill over into neighboring countries. Therefore, one of the goals here is to address in particular the least developed countries that are most vulnerable to fragility. The focus is on the proportion of the population living below the international poverty line. Extreme poverty has typically been measured by the **proportion of the population that lives below $1.25 PPP (purchasing power parity) per person per day.** The advantage of this measure is that it allows for comparisons to be made across countries. By holding the real value of the poverty line constant over time, it allows for an assessment of progress toward meeting the goal of ending extreme poverty.

But, as is often the case with such broad indicators, there are disadvantages to its use. The measure does not capture the *depth* of poverty—some people in a particular country may be living just below the poverty line, while others are living far below it. That is, it measures absolute rather than relative poverty. As Lenhardt has noted, it is the horizontal dimensions of poverty within a society that can point to the potential impoverishment of particular segments of society such as ethnic minorities, spatially disadvantaged communities, and disempowered women (Lenhardt 2013). Measuring the proportion of the population as a whole living below $1.25 per day does not account for these types of discrepancies.

In light of this shortcoming, an additional measure has been proposed, **depth of poverty**, sometimes referred to as the poverty gap. This measure addresses the issue of how far off households are from the poverty line. It gives the total resources needed to bring the poor in a particular country to the level of the poverty line, divided by the number of individuals in the population (World Bank 2011).

Additionally, the Sustainable Development Solutions Network (SDSN) has proposed the use of the UNDP's **Multi-dimensional Poverty Index** (MPI) which tracks deprivation across three dimensions: health (child mortality, nutrition), education (years in school, enrollment), and living standards (cooking fuel, toilet, water, electricity, floor assets—considered deprived if floor consists of dirt, sand, or dung). This is an effort to get away from a more narrow set of measures that depend solely on income disparities (SDSN 2014: 40).

Turning to the parallel goal of ending hunger and achieving food security, two measures have been proposed by SDSN to assess the prevalence of these problems in a society. The **prevalence of stunting in children under a certain age (2 or 5 years)** is a measure of the proportion of children whose height-for-age is far below the median height-for-age compared with a reference population. Stunting in children results from chronic malnutrition. It can have adverse effects on physical, mental, and emotional development, and may be impossible to reverse at a later age (SDSN 2014). Another measure associated with ending hunger and achieving food security is the **percentage of the population below the minimum level of dietary energy consumption**. This is a measure of the proportion of the population that suffers from hunger or caloric food deprivation (SDSN 2014: 44).

SDG #3: Ensure Effective Learning For All Children and Youths for Life and Livelihood

While the MDGs focused on universal primary education, the SDGs broaden the scope of its education objectives to include early child-development programs, quality primary and secondary education, and training to ensure that youths transition effectively into the labor market (SDSN 2014). This expansion of the goal recognizes the critical importance of all stages of education as the primary path to development.

In regard to early child development, the target is for all children under the age of five to reach their developmental potential through access to quality early child-development programs and policies. Extensive cross-national research has shown the important benefits of early investment in education. With developmental potential defined in terms of physical, cognitive, emotional, and social domains, we now know that early childhood education is a key factor, perhaps *the* key factor.

A common indicator to measure progress in this area is the **percentage of children receiving at least 1 year of quality preprimary education.** This exposure has consistent and positive effects on children's development. As the SDSN notes

> High-quality preschool can produce lifelong benefits for society, with positive effects observed on years of completed schooling, secondary school completion, reduced crime, reduced early pregnancy, and increased earnings.... As with many other [early childhood development] services, those from the most disadvantaged backgrounds benefit the most.
>
> (SDSN 2014: 61)

See also Berlinski et al. 2009 and van der Berg et al. 2011.

Regarding quality primary and secondary education, a wide range of positive outcomes has been cited, including improving health, higher wages and economic growth, and even its positive effect on democracy and political stability (Center for Global Development, n.d.). Specific measures include **completion rates** and **mastery of functional skills such as reading and mathematics.** Some advocate for various disaggregations according to gender, age, and region, arguing that the impact of these factors is often hidden in more aggregate statistics.

In terms of transitioning effectively into the labor force, one of the emerging ways for measuring this concept, originating in the UK but also now widely used in Japan, is the percentage of young people (usually aged 16–24) who are not in education, employment, or training—(NEET). A disadvantage of this indicator is that it does not account for other factors that can contribute to one's lack of access to the labor market, such as gender, ethnicity or patronage, and region.

SDG #4: Achieve Gender Equality, Social Inclusion, and Human Rights

Expanding upon the 2000 MDG "to promote gender equality and empower women," this broad SDG can be thought of in terms of three targets that SDSN has proposed for General Assembly consideration in 2014:

- Monitor and end discrimination and inequalities in public service delivery, the rule of law, access to justice, and participation in political and economic life on the basis of gender, ethnicity, religion, disability, national origin, and social or other status.
- Reduce by half the proportion of households with income less than half the national median income (relative poverty).
- Prevent and eliminate violence against individuals, especially women and children.

(SDSN 2014: 71–81)

In the area of discrimination, SDSN has proposed to build on measures developed by the International Labor Organization (ILO) to assess the **ratification and implementation of key ILO labor standards and compliance in law and practice.** This measure is particularly important because it addresses key labor standards that promote decent and productive work, where men and women can "work in conditions of equity, security, freedom, and dignity" (SDSN 2014: 73). Such a measure would track countries' ratification of and compliance with fundamental ILO conventions covering the following issues:

- Freedom of association and the effective recognition of the right to collective bargaining
- Elimination of all forms of forced compulsory labor
- The minimum age for labor and the immediate elimination of the worst forms of child labor
- Elimination of discrimination in respect of employment and occupation, including equal remuneration.

(SDSN 2014: 73–4)

An important indicator has been proposed in the World Economic Forum 2013 Report on the gender gap (World Economic Forum 2013). Specifically, the **Global Gender Gap Index** is comprised of four specific indicators: economic participation and opportunity, educational attainment, health and survival, and political empowerment. The report shows that 96 percent of the gap between men and women on health outcomes has been closed, as was almost 93 percent of the gap in educational attainment. "However, the gap between women and men on economic participation and political empowerment remains wide: only 60 percent of the economic outcomes gap and only 21 percent of the political outcomes gap have been closed" (World Economic Forum 2013: 16).

Earlier in this section, we addressed the issue of poverty in general, in terms of measures of extreme poverty. We now address the issue of inequality, with a focus on the notion of **relative poverty** within a society. For income distribution—the area where most of the work needs to be done in addressing equality of opportunity—the most common method for measuring relative poverty is the **Gini coefficient**, which measures the extent to which the distribution of income or consumption expenditure among individuals or households within an economy deviates from a perfectly equal distribution. The disadvantage of this measure is that the Gini coefficient measures individual-level inequality rather than group-level inequality; arguably, group-level inequality can lead to more subsequent issues within a state than individual-level inequality, as groups' common experiences of inequality can act as a mobilizing mechanism for conflict (Kishi 2014). When looking at state-wide rates of individual-level inequality, state-wide averages might imply that inequality is low; however this might be a result of inequality not being prevalent within a state save for inequality toward a small population. Importantly, however, the discrimination of a small minority is arguably what this target is most interested in capturing and/or measuring. As a result, disaggregation of the data here (by ethnicity, region, etc.) is important.

The third target noted by SDSN in this cluster addresses the **prevention and elimination of violence against individuals, especially women and children**. While a number of measures have been proposed, their accuracy has been notoriously suspect. It is widely agreed that domestic and/or sexual violence is underreported, and thus it is difficult to know whether changes in these reported averages are tangible changes or merely changes in reporting.

SDG #5: Achieve Health and Well-Being At All Ages

As with other SDGs, the process of formulating the health and well-being goal has involved input from individuals, governments, international organizations, and nongovernmental organizations. Many of these advocate broad development goals, while others are concerned with more narrow pieces of the entire development agenda. For example, in this latter group in connection with health issues, the US-based Campaign for Tobacco-Free Kids has taken a strong position on the health risks of smoking, and the impact of widespread use of tobacco products on the development goals of countries. In particular, as increased smoking rates will lead ultimately to an increase in diseases such as cancer and heart disease, this will necessitate the diversion of scarce financial resources from development programs in order to care for the impact of these diseases. A healthy society with increased life expectancy, coupled with low infant mortality, is not in fact a ticking population bomb as some have argued, but rather a society poised to move up the development ladder.

Three targets have been proposed for this goal by the SDSN for United Nations General Assembly consideration:

- Ensure universal coverage of quality healthcare, including the prevention and treatment of communicable and noncommunicable diseases, sexual and reproductive health, family planning, routine immunization, and mental health, according the highest priority to primary health care.
- End preventable deaths by reducing child mortality to 20 or fewer deaths per 1,000 births, maternal mortality to 40 or fewer deaths per 100,000 live births, and mortality under 70 years of age from noncommunicable diseases by at least 30 percent compared to the level in 2015.
- Implement policies to promote and monitor healthy diets, physical activity, and subjective wellbeing; reduce unhealthy behaviors such as tobacco use by 30%, and harmful use of alcohol by 20%.

(SDSN 2014: 82–92)

Among the indicators associated with this goal are those measuring the **percentage of the population with access to basic primary health services** and the **percentage of children receiving immunization according to the World Health Organization criteria**. Disaggregation by age, sex, and region will be particularly helpful in getting at patterns of discrimination and inequality within societies.

Neonatal, infant, and under-five mortality rates are not only helpful indicators in and of themselves, but they are strongly associated with the degree to which particular countries are able to deliver basic social and health services to their populations (Reidpath and Allotey 2003). And they are very susceptible to short-term fluctuations in the attention paid and financing allocated by home governments and outside parties. A steep decline in neonatal services, brought on by severe economic conditions within the country, or by changing priorities of international and non-governmental organizations, can lead to sudden and easily measurable increases in infant and maternal mortality rates.

The pursuit of healthy behaviors is closely linked to development goals. The **Household Dietary Diversity Score** measures the healthiness of diets and hence how well prepared a society is overall to climb the development ladder (Ruel 2003). Similarly, assessing the **percentage of the population that is overweight and/or obese** can provide us with information on the likelihood that societies will be able to develop (Food Research and Action Center 2010).

SDG #6: Improve Agriculture Systems and Raise Rural Prosperity

The targets identified for this SDG are:

- Ensure sustainable food production systems with high yields and high efficiency of water, soil nutrients, and energy, supporting nutritious diets with low feed losses and waste.
- Halt forest and wetland conversion to agriculture, protect soil resources, and ensure that farming systems are resilient to climate change and disasters.
- Ensure universal access in rural areas to basic resources and infrastructure services (land, water, sanitation, modern energy, transport, mobile and broadband communications, agricultural inputs, markets, and advisory services).

(SDSN 2014: 96–108)

With regard to ensuring sustainable food production systems, a key indicator is the **crop yield gap**, which is the actual yield as a percentage of the attainable yield. That is, the indicator helps account for productivity. "Future trajectories of food prices, food security, and cropland expansion are closely linked to future average crop yields in the major agricultural regions of the world;" as a result, measuring crop yield gaps is an important exercise in determining future productivity (Lobell et al. 2009). Similarly, **crop nitrogen use efficiency** is also a helpful indicator in measuring productivity (as well as sustainability and environmental impact), as nitrogen is an important component of fertilizer. High fertilizer efficiency is often a core component of measuring food security and environmental sustainability (SDSN 2014). Finally, **postharvest loss** as a percentage of food production is also an effective way to measure inefficiencies and waste. SDSN proposes to measure this through tracking the share of agricultural produce that is lost and/or wasted in a country with data from the FAO.

One of the most pervasive recent sources of environmental degradation has been the conversion of forests and wetlands to agriculture. While this trend has been going on for centuries, as we search for more agricultural land to feed the growing world population, we are intruding more and more into the last of the forests and wetlands on the planet, and thus inducing serious environmental degradation including, most prominently, those linked to climate change and accompanying extreme climate events. A key indicator here is the **annual change in forest area and land under cultivation**, a measure of the net change of forest area and the expansion of agriculture into natural ecosystems. A complementary indicator is the **annual change in degraded or desertified arable land**, which measures the condition of the land that affects its ability to provide ecosystem goods and services. This measure can include salinization, erosion, soil nutrient loss, and sand dune encroachment (SDSN 2014). For both of these indicators, the increased use of sophisticated remote sensing technology has provided methods for measuring these phenomena more accurately and in a more timely manner.

Finally, there are two measures that can help us assess the degree to which rural areas have access to basic resources and infrastructure services. The **percentage of the rural population using basic drinking water or basic sanitation** can help us assess access to basic infrastructure. Similarly, we can measure **mobile broadband subscriptions per 100 inhabitants in rural areas** (SDSN 2014). Access to broadband Internet is not only important as a tool for those involved in agriculture to increase the productivity of their land, but is also crucial to economic development, especially as corporate site selectors view this as vital, because they consider it as a critical piece of infrastructure (McQuade 2011).

SDG #7: Empower Inclusive, Productive, and Resilient Cities

The final SDG discussed in this section addresses aspects of a phenomenon that will be with us for the remainder of the century—the increasing urbanization of our planet. According to UN estimates, half of the world's population was living in urban areas at the end of 2008. By 2050 it is predicted that 64.1 percent of the developing world and 85.9 percent of the developed world will be urbanized. In many significant ways, the 2014 FIFA World Cup that took place in Brazil, with the accompanying numerous stories in the press on the favelas of Rio, have helped us focus on both the opportunities and also the severe challenges of the rapid growth in urbanization. China's future is now firmly urban, with 54 percent of its population now living in urban areas, among them more than 250 million migrants from rural areas (*The Economist* March 22, 2014). This fast-moving and revolutionary phenomenon will affect all aspects of our life on this planet for the foreseeable future.

The SDSN has identified three target goals in connection with the growth of cities:

- End extreme urban poverty, expand employment and productivity and raise living standards, especially in slums.
- Ensure universal access to a secure and affordable built environment and basic urban services including housing; water, sanitation and waste management; low-carbon energy and transport; and mobile and broadband communication.
- Ensure safe air and water quality for all, and integrate reductions in greenhouse gas emissions, efficient land and resource use, and climate and disaster resilience into investments and standards.

(SDSN 2014: 109–17)

Just as the SDGs have taken on extreme rural poverty, they also target extreme urban poverty by proposing a measure of the **percentage of the urban population with incomes below the national extreme poverty line**. Measurement is complex for the urban environment, because often goods and services that have relatively low cost in a rural environment, and/or can be obtained through labor without significant cash outlay, require higher incomes in urban areas. National poverty lines are therefore often poorly adapted to urban areas, where residents must often purchase basic amenities such as water, food, housing, and energy (SDSN 2014).

One of the outgrowths of rapid urbanization has been the tremendous growth in urban slums. The statistics are staggering: 1.4 million people live in the favelas of Rio, constituting 22 percent of the population of that city in 2010. In Nairobi, there are approximately 2.5 million slum dwellers in about 200 settlements, representing 60 percent of the Nairobi population. Statistics tell similar stories for Cape Town, Mexico City, Mumbai, and Karachi. The SDG Working Group has adopted an indicator from the MDG in proposing the **proportion of the urban population living in slums or informal settlements**.

In terms of access to affordable built environment and urban services, a proposed indicator is the **percentage of the urban population using basic drinking water** or **using basic sanitation**. And finally, the measurement of **mean urban air pollution of particulate matter** addresses a serious outgrowth of unmanaged and underserved urban life. The **percentage of wastewater flows treated by national standards** has been proposed as a way of capturing the lack of treatment that often characterizes urban slums.

Insofar as air and water quality are concerned, the target focuses on the ecological and land-use planning aspects of sustainable cities. Additional issues include land-use planning, urban biodiversity, actions taken to reduce climate change, and disaster relief (SDSN 2014: 117). Measures proposed include **mean urban air pollution of particulate matter, percentage of wastewater flows treated to national standards**, and **urban green space per capita**.

Conclusion

With statistics showing rapid progress over the past decade in reducing the number of people who can still be classified as being in extreme poverty, it is still the case that over 1 billion people live in such a state today, with the greatest concentration on the African continent. This chapter has set the stage for a discussion of key goals for development by discussing first some of the theoretical foundations of approaches to development, followed by a discussion of the historical evolution of trends in development. This evolution can be seen most clearly in the transition from the 2000 enumeration of MDGs to the planned 2015 adoption of SDGs for 2030. These latter goals, as their title implies, were intended for action at local, national, regional, and global levels, while stressing support for long-term approaches toward sustainable development.

In the measurement and indicator portion of the chapter, we focused first on the earliest of the indices to deal with these complex phenomena, the HDI and its later inequality-adjusted version. These measures helped the international community transition from an approach that looked at development from the point of view of nations in general to one that focused on the well-being and security of the individual. Following that, we examined in detail several of the proposed SDGs under consideration by the United Nations General Assembly for implementation as a plan for 2030. These addressed the areas of poverty, health, education, equality, agriculture, and urbanization. Collective action on these varied but clearly interrelated fronts should occupy the international community over the coming decades. Combined with other priorities that I address in other chapters, including climate change, democratization and regime consistency, and coping with ethnic diversity, there is a clear and urgent agenda for the international community.

Notes

1 One of the areas with the greatest misperception of US contributions lies in foreign aid. The most recent OECD estimate for US overseas development assistance as percentage of national income for 2006 is projected to be at 0.17 percent, the lowest of all countries. In 2005 it was at 0.22 percent GNI, above only Portugal and Greece, and at 0.17 percent GNI in 2004, above only Italy (for more information see www.oecd.org/dataoecd/14/5/38354517.pdf and www.oecd.org/dataoecd/0/41/35842562.pdf). However, Americans have historically overestimated foreign aid as a portion of the US budget by nearly 100 times the actual amount. As recently as June 2005, Gallup International asked Americans "what share of national incomes the United States actually gives in foreign aid to help development/poverty alleviation in other countries," with only 9 percent correctly estimating the amount at "higher than .1–.2 of a percentage point." Eighteen percent believed it to range from 5 to more than 25 percent, while another 11 percent thought it to range between 1 and 2 percent. Ironically, when asked to say what percentage of gross national income the US should give in foreign aid, a plurality (44 percent) preferred to give at least 1 percent and in general significantly more (www.americans-world.org/digest/overview/us_role/concerns.cfm).

2 The term "Dutch Disease" was first used by *The Economist* in 1977 to describe the decline of the manufacturing sector in the Netherlands after the discovery of a large natural gas field in 1959.

3 As of the time of writing, the list of goals, targets, and indicators is still under review prior to their formal submission to the United Nations General

Assembly. The publication from which this chapter draws is: http://unsdsn.org/wp-content/uploads/2014/05/140522-comparison-Feb14-to-May22-version_tracked-changes.pdf. All page numbers cited refer to this document only.

4 As of this writing, the list of SDGs for 2030 is still under discussion by the various groups contributing to the report to the United Nations General Assembly. This list of 10 goals is taken from http://unsdsn.org/wp-content/uploads/2014/05/140522-comparison-Feb14-to-May22-version_tracked-changes.pdf.

Chapter 5

Climate Change

The Myth and Reality of Climate Change: Setting the Scene

Many environmental problems are by their nature transboundary in scope. This makes them classic public goods or collective action issues, as members of the international community share concern over their common fate and must also share the burden of finding collective solutions. Pollution and overexploitation of resources are two main collective problems that have been magnified by intense population growth, urbanization, and industrialization (Starkey et al. 2015).

No environmental issue has engendered as much controversy as what was popularly known initially as global warming and is now commonly referred to as climate change. And just as a gradual global consensus on the need to take action has emerged over the past several decades, so too a frustrating gridlock over how to proceed has taken hold.

> Can a fragmented and often highly conflictual political system made up of over 170 sovereign states and numerous other actors achieve the high [and historically unprecedented] levels of cooperation and policy coordination needed to manage environmental problems on a global scale?
>
> (Hurrell and Kingsbury 1992: 1)

Despite a large amount of evidence that points to humanity's effect on global environmental crises, three decades of attempts to solve such crises have resulted in infrequent progress, contentious discussions, and in some cases attempts by self-interested players to undermine the efforts (Roberts et al. 2004).

> So the question is not whether we need to act. The overwhelming judgment of science—of chemistry and physics and millions of measurements—has put all that to rest. Ninety-seven percent of scientists, including...some who originally disputed the data, have

now put that to rest. They've acknowledged the planet is warming and human activity is contributing to it. So the question now is whether we will have the courage to act before it's too late. And how we answer will have a profound impact on the world that we leave behind.

(Obama 2013)

As former US Vice President Al Gore wrote, "an inconvenient truth" (Gore 2006).

Although scientists had long hypothesized that emissions of **greenhouse gases** such as carbon dioxide, methane, nitrous oxide, and chlorofluorocarbons significantly affect the environment by creating a "thick blanket" that traps heat in the atmosphere, it was not until 1990 that an official international report actually endorsed the theory. Established by the UN Environment Programme and the World Meteorological Association, the **Intergovernmental Panel on Climate Change (IPCC)** released a report that year indicating that at least one group of influential scientists and technical experts had reached a consensus on the existence of a problem. The report asserted that emissions of greenhouse gases from such modern conveniences as automobiles, refrigerators, and air conditioners would cause rapid and harmful climate change if left unabated. They projected that by 2100 the global temperature would rise between 1 and 3.5°C, with potentially profound effects on sea levels, food availability, and species survival (Houghton et al. 1990). By the time the IPCC Working Group I issued its 2013 report on the Physical Science Basis of Climate Change, it was in a position to summarize the findings of its scientists as follows:

> Human influence has been detected in warming of the atmosphere and the ocean, in changes in the global water cycle, in reductions in snow and ice, in global mean sea level rise, and in changes in some climate extremes. This evidence for human influence has grown since AR4 [4th Assessment Report, 2007]. It is *extremely likely* that human influence has been the dominant cause of the observed warming since the mid-20th century.
> (IPCC 2013a: 17: WGI AR5, Summary for Policymakers)

It is *extremely likely* that human influence has been the dominant cause of the observed warming since the mid-20th century.

To put this in perspective, recent reports have provided stark evidence of the impact of climate change on virtually every aspect of the human experience.

Humans have profoundly decreased the abundance of both large (e.g., whales) and small (e.g., anchovies) marine fauna. Such declines can generate waves of ecological change that travel both up and down marine food webs and can alter ocean ecosystem functioning.... Climate change threatens to accelerate marine defaunation over the next century. The high mobility of many marine animals offers some increased, though limited, capacity for marine species to respond to climate stress, but it also exposes many species to increased risk from other stressors. Because humans are intensely reliant on ocean ecosystems for food and other ecosystem services, we are deeply affected by all of these forecasted changes.

(McCauley et al. 2015)

During 2014, the average temperature across global land and ocean surfaces was 1.24°F (0.69°C) above the 20th century average. This was the highest among all 135 years in the 1880–2014 record, surpassing the previous records of 2005 and 2010 by 0.07°F (0.04°C). Record warmth was spread around the world, including Far East Russia into western Alaska, the western US, parts of interior South America, most of Europe stretching into northern Africa, parts of eastern and western coastal Australia, much of the northeastern Pacific around the Gulf of Alaska, the central to western equatorial Pacific, large swaths of northwestern and southeastern Atlantic, most of the Norwegian Sea, and parts of the central to southern Indian Ocean.

(State of the Climate, National Climate Data Center, National Oceanic and Atmospheric Administration (2014))

A new study by researchers at NASA and the University of California, Irvine, finds a rapidly melting section of the West Antarctic Ice Sheet appears to be in an irreversible state of decline, with nothing to stop the glaciers in this area from melting into the sea. The study presents multiple lines of evidence, incorporating 40 years of observations that indicate the glaciers in the Amundsen Sea sector of West Antarctica "have passed the point of no return," according to glaciologist and lead author Eric Rignot, of UC Irvine and NASA's Jet Propulsion Laboratory in Pasadena, California. The new study has been accepted for publication in the journal *Geophysical Research Letters*. These glaciers already contribute significantly to sea level rise, releasing almost as much ice into the ocean annually as the entire Greenland Ice Sheet. They contain enough ice to raise global sea level by 4 feet (1.2 meters) and are melting faster than most scientists had expected.

Rignot said these findings will require an upward revision to current predictions of sea-level rise.

(NASA 2014)

While the spectacular 22nd Olympic Winter Games in Sochi in February 2014 are still fresh in our minds, it might be interesting to explore the risk that these temperature rises will pose for future games. Based on extensive examination of the impact of indicators of climate change, Scott et al. conclude the following:

The negative impact of projected climate change on the climatic ability of former Olympic Winter Games locations to once again host the games was very evident by mid-century. Although all of the 19 former Olympic Winter Games hosts were classified as climatically reliable in the 1981–2010 period, by the middle of the 21st century this number had decreased to 11 . . . . In the late 21st century . . . internationally renowned Olympic sites, such as Squaw Valley [USA], Garmisch-Partenkirchen [Germany], as well as recent host cities of Vancouver [Canada] and Sochi [Russia], simply would not be cold enough to reliably host the Games.

(2014: 5)

No part of the environmental debate evokes as much unease as does the notion that after millennia of human activity, that activity is finally having a demonstrable negative effect on the planet. There is of course considerable debate as to whether this is in fact the case, or rather whether we are in the midst of a long-term, cyclical pattern attributable to natural causes, and that the ecosystem will right itself in due course. But there is a well-respected and large portion of the scientific community (some argue 97 percent), backed up by seemingly irrefutable evidence, which argues that we are approaching, or perhaps have already reached the point at which the damage that human activity is causing is irreversible.[1] Throughout the globe, there is greater commitment to "bioregionalism, the realization that ecological management must be defined by natural delineations such as watersheds and biomes rather than by national or other borders" (Khagram and Ali 2006: 403). Somewhere in the middle we presume there is a path to a solution, and hence the environmental myth:

Myth 5 While little doubt remains that human behavior has contributed to environmental degradation, a short-term technological fix is likely before this degradation becomes irreversible.

The Tragedy of the Commons

But there is a catch. Insertion of the word "global" into the accepted phraseology summarizes the dilemma: the problems which peoples and nations face arising from environmental degradation are not easily addressed by either individual or national actions and policies—they are global in scale. Sea levels will continue to rise, glaciers will continue to recede, air quality will continue to deteriorate, freshwater resources will continue to decline, and these will affect all of us. This is a classic collective action problem, perhaps best summarized by Garrett Hardin in his well-known analogy to "the tragedy of the commons":

> The tragedy of the commons develops in this way. Picture a pasture open to all. It is to be expected that each herdsman will try to keep as many cattle as possible on the commons. Such an arrangement may work reasonably satisfactorily for centuries because tribal wars, poaching, and disease keep the numbers of both man and beast well below the carrying capacity of the land. Finally, however, comes the day of reckoning, that is, the day when the long-desired goal of social stability becomes a reality. At this point, the inherent logic of the commons remorselessly generates tragedy.
>
> As a rational being, each herdsman seeks to maximize his gain. Explicitly or implicitly, more or less consciously, he asks, "What is the utility to me of adding one more animal to my herd?" This utility has one negative and one positive component.
>
> (1)   The positive component is a function of the increment of one animal. Since the herdsman receives all the proceeds from the sale of the additional animal, the positive utility is nearly +1.
>
> (2)   The negative component is a function of the additional overgrazing created by one more animal. Since, however, the effects of overgrazing are shared by all the herdsmen, the negative utility for any particular decision-making herdsman is only a fraction of −1.
>
> Adding together the component partial utilities, the rational herdsman concludes that the only sensible course for him to pursue is to add another animal to his herd. And another; and another.... But this is the conclusion reached by each and every rational herdsman sharing a commons. Therein is the tragedy. Each man is locked into a system that compels him to increase his herd without limit—in a world that is limited. Ruin is the destination toward which all men rush, each pursuing his own best interest in a society that believes in the freedom of the commons. Freedom in a commons brings ruin to all.
>
> (Hardin 1968: 1244)

Figure 5.1 A unified climate change stance.

Source: Michael de Adder artizans.com.

Reality The international community is incapable of coming together with sufficient urgency to undertake the collective action necessary to address human-induced climate change (see Figure 5.1).

Environmental Impact on Human Security

Let us consider first the circumstances that have led to the current environmental condition, and some of the consequences. There is an array of interrelated factors that fall under the rubric of environmental conditions that impact, either directly or indirectly, human security. One critical trail of intricately interconnected factors runs through energy consumption and land consumption as causes of climate change, which in turn affects variations in precipitation. A second trail focuses on resource scarcity, which is a function of land and water degradation, as well as population growth. Finally, climate change has an impact on several additional factors that threaten human security: food (in)security, natural disasters, infectious disease, and conflict. Let us briefly review the factors along these various trails.

The Trail from Climate Change to Variations in Precipitation

A recent review of global population trends and the environment (Sherbinin et al. 2007; see also IPCC 2013b, WGIII AR5, Summary for Policymakers) has identified human activity in the form of energy consumption and land consumption as the key contributor to climate change. In **energy consumption**, the extreme dependence on fossil fuels, most notably in the developed world—the US, with 4.5 percent of the world's population, accounts for 19 percent of the world total primary energy consumption—is responsible for the release of greenhouse gases. Carbon dioxide (CO_2) emissions have grown at a rate of 2.5 percent each year since 1900, a rate that most atmospheric scientists believe is dangerously unsustainable because of the resultant destabilizing effects on climate and society.

The US, with 4.5 percent of the world's population, is responsible for 19 percent of the world total primary energy consumption.

Land consumption, in the form of land change, is the most pervasive human impact on the environment. The largest contributing land-consumption factor to climate change is deforestation. Deforestation causes sizable increases in CO_2, caused by decreases in the number of trees that would transform CO_2 into oxygen. Land consumption is mostly for purposes of agricultural production and resource extraction, with timber and fuelwood consumption and urbanization also contributing factors. The **ecological footprint**—a measure of human demand on the world's ecosystem—has tripled between 1961 and 2003 (Sherbinin et al. 2007), and now constitutes about 1.5 times the **biocapacity**[2] of the planet (Global Footprint Network 2010). Figure 5.2 gives us a sense of how the ecological footprint is distributed across countries and regions. Those countries with dark shading are "biocapacity debtors"—their ecological footprint is greater than their biocapacity. Countries with light shading are "biocapacity creditors"—their biocapacity is greater than their footprint.

Human consumption patterns have a direct impact on **variations in precipitation** through their alteration of global atmospheric conditions. Evidence suggests that the climate is getting warmer and dryer (Sherbinin et al. 2007), although there is considerable regional variation. Most regions in Africa are dry and are projected to become drier due to the increase in CO_2, which would be extremely harmful because of the degree to which Africa relies on rain-fed agriculture. A small number of regions in Africa—mainly eastern and central—are wet and projected to get wetter due to increases in CO_2 levels (Collier et al. 2008a).

The Trail from Climate Change to Resource Scarcity

Renewable resource scarcity constitutes a second trail along which we can investigate the impact of environmental factors on human security (Homer-Dixon 1994). Resource decline is a function of human

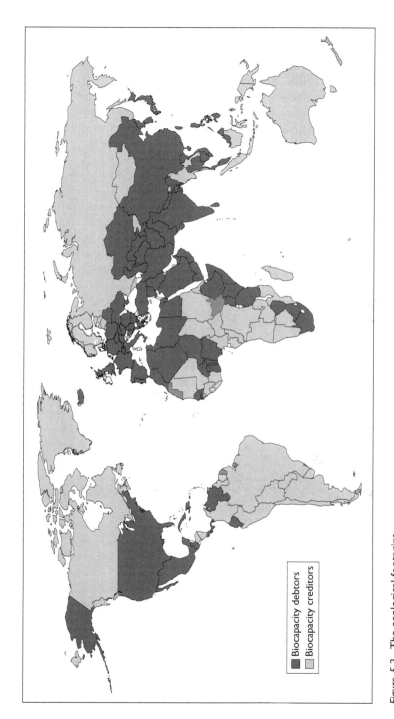

Figure 5.2 The ecological footprint.

Source: Adapted from http://issuu.com/globalfootprintnetwork/docs/ecological_wealth_of_nations/1.

consumption and settlement patterns. Contributing factors include **land degradation**, particularly in the form of deforestation, loss of arable land, and lower crop yield. For example, impoverished groups, because they lack access to good land, resources, and economic opportunity or better technology to farm current land, move to marginal lands or remote areas, such as forests, steep upland slopes, or arid or poor-growth land. Lack of technological innovation in the area of agricultural production is a particularly acute problem in Africa, as that region still relies on a narrow range of primary commodity exports.

Water degradation is also a factor, in the form of freshwater depletion, coastal erosion, loss of coral reefs, rise in sea levels, pollution, and increased nutrient loading of water. Among the causes of this degradation are the increased need for freshwater for agricultural production and livestock, economic development and urbanization in coastal areas, migration to coastal areas to extract resources, and untreated sewage (Sherbinin et al. 2007). Africa currently experiences the most acute forms of water degradation, with Northern and Southern Africa suffering absolute water scarcity (Falkenmark and Widstrand 1992). But forecasting models predict that, by 2050, Latin America and Eastern Europe/Western Asia will be most affected by this issue (De Stefano et al. 2012). Groundwater usage is one of the main concerns for both developed and middle-level economies, because it is nonrenewable and can cause land to become unsuitable or poor for growth—particularly acute in Arab countries, India, China, and the US. Movement toward large farms makes matters even worse. Coastal degradation is also a serious concern. Not only does it negatively affect ecosystems in coastal regions, but it also "reduces natural protection from storms and hurricanes" (Sherbinin et al. 2007: 359).

Population growth rounds out this dismal picture—available resources are reduced as they are divided among more people. The UN World Population Prospects (United Nations Department of Economic and Social Affairs, Population Division 2007) projection for 2050 is daunting: medium growth, all occurring in the developing world, where resource scarcity is much more of a concern, and no net growth in the developed world.

Climate change has a direct impact on three additional components of human security: food security, natural disasters, and infectious diseases. There is evidence that climate change has a significant negative effect on **food security** (McCarthy et al. 2001). While changes in precipitation and temperature have a significant effect on food security, the Intergovernmental Panel on Climate Change (2007) concludes that in the future the environmental factor that will have the greatest negative impact on food security will be an increase in **natural disasters** brought on at least in part by climate change. The most affected region is likely to be Africa (Intergovernmental Panel on Climate Change 2007).

The academic and policy communities predict that climate change will increase the frequency and intensity of natural disasters in the future, causing more destruction and serving as a greater threat to humanity (Intergovernmental Panel on Climate Change 2007). Among the recent events noted are the 2003 European heat wave, strong recent Atlantic hurricane seasons, flooding in Europe and Africa, droughts in Central and Eastern Africa (especially Kenya), and El Niño. There is evidence of a link between natural disasters and economic security through economic shock effects and decreased economic growth (Bergholt and Lujala 2012). Climatic shocks typically reduce GDP by 0.4 percent in the year of the shock (Collier et al. 2008a).

Finally, climate change has an effect on the incidence and spread of **infectious disease**, with Africa once again expected to feel the brunt of the impact. For example, there is evidence that malaria-carrying insects have begun moving to higher elevations and infecting people there (Collier et al. 2008a). Severe malaria reduces income by two-thirds, while a 10 percent reduction in malaria corresponds to 0.3 percent higher economic growth (Gallup and Sachs 2001).

The Trail from Climate Change to Conflict

To this mix we must add the complex relationship between environmental degradation and/or climate change and **conflict**. Here the theories and models are particularly complex, and are by no means unified in their findings and recommendations. The predominant view has been that scarcity of resources creates war and conflict (Adano et al. 2012). The UN Development Programme's *Human Development Report 2007/2008* emphasized the consequences of climate change for human security, with Africa termed a continent with climate-dependent economic sectors at risk of violent ethnic conflict (United Nations Development Programme 2007). Scarce water resources and associated falling agricultural yields raise the risk of violent conflict, most prominently in the Horn of Africa. Renewable-resource scarcity often affects conflict in an indirect fashion, in many cases working through its direct effect on migration. Migration can trigger conflict by altering the ethnic and sociopolitical–economic balance in the receiving region—an example is Bangladeshi and Pakistani migrants to northeast India. Typically, this takes the form of conflict between migrating farmers and local pastoralists. But this link is indirect. Conflict typically only results if scarcity and migration weaken the state sufficiently, or lead to a more unequal distribution of resources (Homer-Dixon 1994).

At the other extreme, the "resource curse," or the "paradox of plenty," have been used to explain the prevalence of violence. Resource-rich developing countries whose economies rely heavily on export of primary commodities have been found to be particularly conflict prone.

> When governments are unable to ensure fair distribution of returns from resources and provide basic public goods such as security, education and health financed through resource revenue, resource abundance stimulates violence, grievances, theft and looting caused by rebel groups, and even civil war.
>
> (Adano et al. 2012: 67)

The paradox of plenty even manifests itself in democratic countries where "state revenues from natural resources have paralyzing effects on manufacturing and economic productivity" (ibid.), often resulting in extreme inequalities in income (see Chapter 4).

So whether we are talking about extremely poor countries with limited access to resources or countries whose GDP largely consists of revenues from primary commodity exports, the impact of changing and deteriorating environmental conditions such as variation in precipitation is likely to be strongly associated with a heightened probability of conflict and violence. For example, strong deviations in precipitation levels from the norm in either direction increase the likelihood of conflict (Hendrix and Salehyan 2012), though the predominant finding is that heavy rainfall has a greater impact than abnormally dry conditions (Adano et al. 2012; Hendrix and Salehyan 2012). Others find that *type of violence* differs by precipitation deviation, with drier conditions increasing the probability of civil war, and wet conditions increasing the probability of nonstate, intercommunal violence (Raleigh and Kniveton 2012), most commonly by making conditions more favorable for cattle raiding (Adano et al. 2012). Overall, there is strong agreement that the link between environmental change and conflict is nowhere more pronounced than in sub-Saharan Africa, mainly due to the degree to which the economies rely on agriculture, particularly rain-fed agriculture (Collier et al. 2008a; see also Gleditsch 2012).

The impact of changing and deteriorating environmental conditions such as variation in precipitation is likely to be strongly associated with a heightened probability of conflict and violence.

The Ozone Layer

It is clear from the preceding discussion of the factors associated with global patterns of environmental degradation that the global community faces crisis. In particular, it has highlighted the role that climate change is playing in exacerbating the impact that these factors have had on human security writ large. Whether that crisis is already upon us as many scientists argue, or whether we are in a precrisis period of indeterminate length, collective action is now critical. We have seen that, beginning in 1985, when the annual hole in the ozone layer over Antarctica was first discovered, collective action, predominately on the part of developed states to restrict the use of chlorofluorocarbons, has stabilized the size of the hole, with some recent evidence that it is actually shrinking. So why are we stuck insofar as other greenhouse gases, predominantly CO_2, are concerned?

The Threat

When we think about environmental issues as collective goods problems, we need to focus on two types—Tragedy of the Commons problems, and **upstream–downstream problems** (usually referred to as asymmetric problems) (Mitchell 2010). These are generally distinguished by the extent to which those most concerned about environmental problems are also involved in the cause of the problem. As Mitchell notes, at one end are Tragedies of the Commons in which all relevant parties are both actors and victims. Because the perpetrators are also the victims, they would prefer that the environmental problem be resolved even while they would prefer not to contribute to its resolution. Ozone depletion is an example of this type of problem. In upstream–downstream problems, at the other end of the spectrum, none of the victims concerned about the problem have caused it, and none of those perpetrating it consider their interests harmed by it—it is only the victims who see its resolution as critical (Mitchell 2010). River pollution can be an example of this latter problem.

Additionally, both Tragedy of the Commons and upstream–downstream problems are the subject of selective attention. While some of the problems have widespread effects, these effects may be largely limited to the developing world—freshwater and environment-related illness. In contrast, issues that pose potential harm for the developed world are addressed more quickly and fully, even if their impacts are narrower or more distant in the future—ozone depletion and acid rain (Mitchell 2013).

Substantial scientific evidence has indicated for some time that an increase in the global average temperature of more than 2°C above preindustrial levels (i.e., 1860) poses severe risks to natural systems and human health and well-being. Sustained warming of this magnitude could, for example, result in the extinction of many species and extensive melting of the Greenland and West Antarctic ice sheets—causing global sea level to rise between 12 and 40 feet (Union of Concerned Scientists 2013). With more severe warming, the resultant sea level rise will inundate several island nations completely; while flooding will result in massive dislocation in coastal areas in countries like Bangladesh, the Philippines, India, and Vietnam, among others. The hardest hit will be less developed countries with less capacity for adaptation. What is needed to avoid the potentially dangerous consequences of temperatures rising more than 2°C?

Substantial scientific evidence has indicated for some time that an increase in the global average temperature of more than 2°C above preindustrial levels (i.e., 1860) poses severe risks to natural systems and human health and well-being.

Climate Change and Collective Action: Traditional Instruments

During the past 25 years, the international community has attempted to address the issues surrounding climate change through several key institutions and approaches. These include the Framework Convention on Climate Change, the Kyoto Accord, and the Intergovernmental Committee on Climate Change. Two issues have come to dominate the contentious debate surrounding the Framework Convention on Climate Change of 1992, signed in Rio de Janeiro, through the yearly Conference of the Parties, most recently in Warsaw in November 2013. These two issues clearly illustrate the difficulty in reaching agreement on action on climate change moving forward.

Differential Treatment—Developed Versus Developing World

The first issue, as alluded to above, pits the developed and developing worlds against each other as they struggle to agree upon differential treatment. Since the 1970s, there has been a major growth in the application of international law to environmental issues. However, its application has been highly contested, and there has been movement from a greater toward a smaller scope of its application, particularly in the form of a change from more to less differential treatment of developed versus developing states (Rajamani 2012).

The early period, through 1992, had developing states concerned with development, and developed states concerned with the ethics of environmental stewardship and developing an international management system for the environment. But little to no differential treatment occurred during this period, only agreement that development and environmental protection are not incompatible. From Rio 1992 to the World Summit on Sustainable Development/Earth Summit 2 in Johannesburg in 2002 (with the high point being Kyoto 1997), there was an emerging consensus around the idea of sustainable development, and multilateral environmental agreements that provided differential treatment in favor of developing countries, particularly regarding climate change. From Johannesburg 2002 to Rio+20 in 2012, climate change become the preeminent international environmental concern, with the rapid economic growth in some developing countries (e.g., India, China, Brazil, South Africa) eroding the old lines between the developed and developing worlds, and related questioning of differential treatment that favors developing countries. In line with the concerns of developed states, subsequent climate change agreements have differentiated more *among* developing countries on the basis of economics and pollution contributions, and have provided more flexibility for all countries via self-selected obligations, which implicitly erodes both the so-called Common But Differential Responsibility (CBDR) principle and mitigation requirements of developed states. There was a movement away from legal differentiation and toward symmetry (Rajamani 2012).

Rajamani argues that in the absence of new political incentives for mitigation (which seem few at this point), the changes that marked the third period may weaken the normative core (i.e., equity rather than equality of treatment) and legitimacy of the climate regime in the future, and subsequently its effectiveness at mitigating the climate change problem. A new climate agreement to replace Kyoto, particularly if the US is to be involved, will most likely involve market-friendly aspects of Kyoto, more sovereign power in the form of greater flexibility due to domestic circumstances and constraints, and "a more circumscribed role for international law" (Rajamani 2012: 621). Some contend that such an approach may in fact be more pragmatic, because it recognizes the political limits to international law. Rajamani (2012) argues that a loss of some differentiation—particularly on the issue of obligations—is both inevitable and acceptable, but too much movement toward symmetry and away from differentiation—especially if it begins to encompass issues of implementation and assistance—will decrease developing states' participation in the environmental regime due to both capacity and fairness concerns (Rajamani 2012).

Targets for Emissions Reductions

The second issue has to do with targeting goals for emissions reductions. Again we refer to the issue of preventing a 2°C rise in temperature by the end of the century. If we assume the world's developing nations pursue the most aggressive reductions that can reasonably be expected of them (see Union of Concerned Scientists 2013), the world's industrialized nations will have to reduce their emissions an average of 70–80 percent below 2000 levels by 2050. This 70–80 percent range for reductions by 2050 assumes that industrialized nations' emissions will have peaked in 2010 before starting to decline, and that those from developing nations will peak between 2020 and 2025. A delay in the peak of either group would require increasingly steep and unrealistic global reduction rates in order to stay within the cumulative emissions target for 2000–2050.

Limiting temperature to a 2°C rise by the end of the century will require the world's industrialized nations to reduce their CO_2 emissions an average of 70–80 percent below 2000 levels by 2050.

An example might be helpful here. To meet the goal outlined above, the Union of Concerned Scientists (UCS) advocated that the US reduce its CO_2 emissions by an average of 4 percent each year starting in 2010 and ending in 2050. The UCS argued that if US emissions continue to grow until 2020 according to a low projection rate and without any reductions, it will then have to reduce its emissions by an average of 8 percent each year from 2020 until 2050 in order to meet this target. The UCS derived its 80 percent target figure on the basis of: (1) the US share of all industrialized countries' CO_2 emissions; (2) assumptions about how much other industrialized nations will reduce their CO_2 emissions during this period; and (3) scientific studies that argue that global emissions must be low enough to keep atmospheric CO_2 concentrations on the order of 450 parts per million (ppm) CO_2 by 2050 in order to have a 50 percent chance of preventing the global temperature from rising more than 2°C above preindustrial levels (Union of Concerned Scientists 2013; see also discussion below of **(WRE) Carbon Emissions Trajectory**).

Adding to the complexity of setting and ratifying targeting goals is the two-level game being played out in many developed countries. This is seen most notably in the US, where it has communicated its intention not to sign the protocol, and Canada, which has actually withdrawn completely from the **Kyoto Protocol** on emission targets. The **two-level game** refers to the double set of negotiations that must be carried out both at the domestic and at the international level. This two-level game continues to be vexing to the protreaty side, as President Obama has even faced skepticism from members of Congress about the veracity of scientific claims about global warming (*New York Times* September 22, 2009).

While we have presented a rather bleak picture of the prospects for significant collective action on a global scale to address the factors contributing to climate change, there are some hopeful signs of more local and regional progress. In the area of population, actions such as access to contraception, urbanization, and education and work opportunities for women are contributing to a significant slowdown in population growth in many parts of the world (Sherbinin et al. 2007). Government policies in some states are addressing unequal resource distribution through programs such as land redistribution. Resource scarcity is being addressed through marketplace substitution and industrialization, introduction of new technologies such as fertilizers and genetically modified crops, and more efficient and effective methods like crop substitution, multi-cropping, irrigation systems, and higher labor-to-land ratios (Bremner et al. 2010; Boserup 1990; Collier et al. 2008a). The development of information bases about environmental threats, soil quality, and land vulnerability through mapping technology and remote sensing can facilitate both greater conservation and productivity (Sherbinin et al. 2007; Satterthwaite 2011). Even migration can be a positive if it facilitates urbanization and movement to coastal areas, particularly in Africa (Homer-Dixon 1994; Collier et al. 2008a).

And there are more international agreements and/or regimes which can build trust, reciprocity, and cooperation through repeated interactions (Conca and Dabelko 2002). Perhaps the most striking examples of such agreements concern regional environmental action plans in the Nile Basin and the Red Sea; and transboundary protected areas, that is, "peace parks" such as La Amistad Biosphere Reserve established by Costa Rica and Panama in 1983 to help preserve the unique biosphere that lies in the mountain region between the two countries (Khagram and Ali 2006). Water agreements in particular have been successful at the regional level, as violent conflict over freshwater has seen a significant decline due to the prevalence of such agreements (Scheffran et al. 2012; De Stefano et al. 2012). Finally, international action in the form of development and humanitarian aid and support of governments has helped to increase the adaptive capacity of affected regions—although such aid has been on the decline since the 2008 financial crisis (Scheffran et al. 2012; Collier et al. 2008a). Adaptive capacity is also necessary to increase resilience in response to recurrent crisis events such as droughts and floods (USAID 2012). Additional steps can include trade and investment in nonagricultural exports, particularly in Africa, reducing regulations that impede adaptation and diversification (genetically modified crops), and interregional integration as a way of addressing regional variation in experience with climate change (Collier et al. 2008a).

Yet the picture is still bleak when we consider the prospects for collective action to address the most pressing global climate change issues in anything more than a symbolic and haphazard fashion. Complicating matters is the fact that the developing world—particularly Africa—is most at risk of the negative effects of environmental degradation, at least in the present and for the near future; yet it contributes least to CO_2 emissions. The developed world is not expected to see significant negative effects until further into the future, yet it contributes most to CO_2 emissions (Sagar and VanDeveer 2005; Collier et al. 2008a). Generally, the extent to which the members of the international system are dedicated to curbing environmental degradation and climate change is impacted by the fact that environmental issues tend to be seen as "low politics" rather than "high politics" like military security and economic issues (Mitchell 2013). The discussion of environmental problems has been sidelined by the war on terrorism and economic recession, and, most recently, the Arab Spring and its ongoing aftermath. There is also a significant disjuncture between the way the US and the UK view climate change and the way these issues are seen by China and Russia (Scheffran et al. 2012). And finally, public opinion in the developing world shows more concern with development than with climate change, the reverse of findings for the developed world (Kvaløy et al. 2012; Gleditsch 2012).

Collective Action Plan: Climate Change

In November 2014 the presidents of the US and China announced that they had achieved a historic agreement on carbon emissions. The agreement by the world's leading carbon-emission countries calls for the US to reduce its emissions by 26 percent to 28 percent from 2005 levels by 2025. China has agreed to peak its carbon dioxide emissions by 2030 or earlier if possible, as well as to increase the proportion of renewables in its energy production mix to about 20 percent by 2030. This announcement follows the October 2014 announcement by the European Union of a commitment of a domestic 2030 greenhouse gas reduction target of at least 40 percent compared with 1990. These steps, if implemented, constitute a significant collective action plan to address climate change in the lead-up to the United Nations Climate Change Conference that will be held in Paris in late 2015.

Before beginning our discussion of policy options in the area of climate change, we need to note a critical distinction that the scientific and policy communities make between mitigation and adaptation. According to the IPCC,

> **Climate mitigation** is any action taken to permanently eliminate or reduce the long-term risk and hazards of climate change to human life and property. The International Panel on Climate Change defines mitigation as: "An anthropogenic intervention to reduce the sources or enhance the sinks of greenhouse gases." **Climate adaptation** refers to the ability of a system to adjust to climate change (including climate variability and extremes) to moderate potential damage, to take advantage of opportunities, or to cope with the consequences.
>
> (Global Greenhouse Warming 2014)

Climate mitigation is action taken to permanently eliminate or reduce the long-term risk and hazards of climate change to human life and property. *Climate adaptation* is the ability of a system to adjust to climate change.

Adaptation can be technological like sea defenses, behavioral like altered food and recreational choices, managerial like altered farming practises, and policy like planning regulation (Global Greenhouse Warming 2014). While we mentioned several adaptation measures earlier, we will focus only on climate mitigation approaches for the remainder of the chapter.

Where environmental issues are concerned, measures of short-term progress on a global or even national scale are hard to come by. Both progress and degradation involve very small incremental changes, and such changes are often subject to naturally occurring cyclical patterns in addition to the impact of human activity, and so they are difficult to untangle in the short run. Nevertheless, there are several policy initiatives that have been based on the developing science of climate change and have captured wide attention. As they begin to make a difference, enhancing their reach by taking bold political action on a global collective scale will likely result in ultimately reducing environmental degradation and enhancing sustainability.

In this section, we discuss programs that are designed to address various aspects of climate change. Each requires some degree of collective action and some level of sacrifice. The action of any individual state alone will only have a marginal effect on the overall problem. There are both political and economic costs to pay in their implementation, and the payoffs are likely to be more long term than in some of the other spheres discussed in this book. And along with a general collective action requirement, there are differentials between the way the developed and the developing world will need to approach these issues. Nevertheless, these programs are based on firm scientific approaches, and in that respect are more likely to be accepted as good for the global commons.

Wigley, Richels, and Edmonds' Carbon Emissions Trajectory

In 1996, climate scientists Tom Wigley, Richard Richels, and Jan Edmonds (WRE) published an influential paper in *Nature* entitled "Economic and Environmental Choices in the Stabilization of Atmospheric CO_2 Concentrations." Updated in 2007, the trajectory that they identified is probably the most commonly utilized **carbon mitigation** proposal. Its purpose is to try to meet two mitigation goals of the UN Framework Convention on Climate Change of 1994 (UNFCCC 1994). The first goal is achieving a stabilization of greenhouse gas concentrations at a level that would prevent dangerous interference with the climate system resulting from human activity. This translates into a level that would prevent global temperature from rising more than 2°C relative to preindustrial times. The second goal is to be cost-effective, which translates into "a realistic transition away from the current heavy dependence on fossil fuels" (Wigley et al. 1996: 240).

The goals of carbon emission reduction are stabilization of greenhouse gas concentrations at levels that would prevent damage to the climate system, and to be cost-effective as the system transitions away from heavy dependence on fossil fuels.

Examining both economic costs and environmental benefits of different trajectories, WRE arrive at a series of recommended trajectories for stabilizing CO_2 concentrations at different target volume levels: 350, 450, 550, 650, and 750 ppm. They also compare these to what are commonly known as "business as usual" or baseline trajectories, projected trajectories in the absence of action to curb emissions.[3] According to their recommended trajectories, the lower the concentration target, the sooner that more substantial emissions reductions need to occur. But countries only need to depart from business as usual immediately in order to achieve the lowest concentration target (350 ppm). For all other targets, emissions are allowed to increase in the early years of the trajectories before declining (Wigley et al. 1996).

In 2007, WRE updated their trajectories to account for an increasingly popular topic of discussion: What will happen if pathways are taken in which CO_2 concentrations initially overshoot the target before declining to it?[4] Their results show that maximum emissions reduction rates are the same in overshoot pathways, but much larger concentrations of CO_2 result and maximum emissions reduction occurs about 50 years later than under the original projections (Wigley et al. 2007).

Most of the focus has been on 450- or 550-ppm targets, which are seen as balancing environmental impact and the political and economic costs involved with reducing emissions. It is not known whether a 450- or 550-ppm target will prevent the earth's temperature from rising more than 2°C higher than it was in preindustrial times, and some vocal opponents argue that preventing a greater than 2°C increase may require a lower target than 450 or 550 ppm (Aldy et al. 2010; *New York Times*, October 2, 2009). Some would argue that we should not allow a higher concentration than we have right now, which for the US is about 400 ppm and rising. This position was adopted most notably by the IPCC Working Group I, which developed the first carbon emissions trajectories. But that solution would involve a sharp and immediate break with business as usual, which many others see as unrealistic given the economic and political costs, and the current expense of alternative technologies. WRE argue for a more gradual break with business as usual, in order to blunt the economic costs of doing so, to allow alternative technologies more time to gain traction and become cheaper, and also simply because history has shown that humans continue to use resources more efficiently over time (i.e., we will get better at this as the trajectory progresses) (Wigley et al., 2007).[5] See Figure 5.3 for overshoot trajectories.

For the 550-ppm target, the CO_2 concentration stabilization point is reached in 2150, in both the WRE and the IPCC trajectories (Wigley et al. 1996). There is wide variation in the presumed environmental impact of these targets, and there is a recent vocal movement arguing that a 350-ppm target is required to achieve the goal of limiting temperature rise to 2°C. That is, the earth is warming faster than previously expected (*New York Times*, October 2, 2009), and CO_2 concentrations are growing faster than expected. When the targets were first formulated in the 1990s, the US was around 350 ppm, whereas now the US is approaching 400 ppm.

Even if countries follow a path with greater allowable near-term CO_2 emissions, WRE recommend some immediate steps to help curb future emissions: 1.) invest in less carbon-intensive capital stock of energy production and usage, since it will be necessary in the future in all trajectories; 2.) commit to research and development of new, low-carbon technologies, since supply of new technologies typically takes years to enter the market; and 3.) adopt no-cost (i.e., "no regrets") emissions mitigation measures (Wigley et al. 1996). An example of such a measure according to UNFCCC is combined-cycle gas turbines.[6]

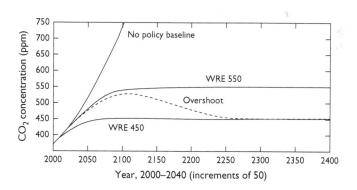

Figure 5.3   Overshoot pathways to CO_2 stabilization.

Source: Wigley et al. 2007.

Contraction and Convergence

An interesting alternative to the WRE approach is the Contraction and Convergence (C&C) approach proposed by the Global Commons Institute (GCI) in the 1990s. This approach involves a two-stage process: 1.) developing and developed states' emissions increase and decrease, respectively, until they converge at an agreed-upon point (level and date); and 2.) after convergence, all states decrease emissions at an agreed-upon contraction rate. GCI recommends a convergence date of around 2020–2050. C&C has been backed by the Royal Commission on Environmental Pollution (RCEP), GLOBE International, the German government's Advisory Council on Global Change, and the African bloc within the UN.

C&C is rooted in the idea of global inequality in terms of the ratios of population to three different factors: wealth contribution to CO_2, emissions, and environmental damages. Developed states have the smaller share of the world's population, but are the wealthiest and contribute the most to emissions and environmental degradation. Since CO_2 emissions and development are historically linked, developing states should be allowed to emit more during convergence so that they can "meet up" with developed states and more equitable economic performance can be achieved. The risks of further environmental damage caused by developing states' increased emissions would be offset by developed states' decreased emissions. The UK Department of Energy adopted RCEP's (RCEP 2000) C&C-based recommendation of a 550-ppm target and 60 percent reduction in CO_2 by 2050 relative to 1990 in order to achieve that target. In 2003, the UNFCCC Secretariat said that meeting its objective "inevitably requires Contraction and Convergence" (Meyer 2004: 189). However, costs of C&C for developed countries are high, and there has also been pushback against differential treatment since 2002 (Rajamani 2012). Thus, many see C&C as too idealistic.[7] To get developed states to agree to C&C, RCEP (2000) suggests offering them more flexibility via trading emissions (see discussion of Clean Development Mechanisms, CDM, in the next section).

Clean Development Mechanisms

While developed countries for the most part use advanced and reasonably efficient technologies for electricity generation and industrial production, many developing countries continue to use obsolete processes that waste fuel and contribute inordinately to the buildup of greenhouse gases. For example, coal-fired plants in many developing countries operate well below the efficiency level typical of those located in industrialized countries. It remains much more costly to reduce the greenhouse gas emissions of coal-burning plants based on already advanced technology in industrialized countries than it is to reduce the emissions through the replacement of obsolete plants in developing countries (for further discussion, see UNFCCC 2014a, 2014b).

The CDM is a **market-based carbon mitigation mechanism** through which developed countries are permitted to exceed their Kyoto emissions quotas by supporting emissions reduction projects in developing countries. It is an emissions trading scheme first proposed by the US and Brazil at the Kyoto negotiations of 1997, although its operational guidelines were only finalized in November 2001. It combines the goals of helping developed countries meet their emissions reduction commitments, while at the same time serving as a means by which developing countries can engage in sustainable development. In fact, CDM has become the main vehicle by which developing countries have become involved in sustainable development and therefore involved in the Kyoto process (Lecocq and Ambrosi 2007; Lederer 2013). CDM helps move the system toward a sustainable paradigm by sensitizing manufacturers in developed countries to the added costs of production that result from high-CO_2-emissions manufacturing result in, while at the same time encouraging developing countries to build from scratch industrial complexes that produce less greenhouse gases.

The Clean Development Mechanism (CDM) is a market-based carbon mitigation mechanism through which developed countries are permitted to exceed their Kyoto emissions quotas by supporting emissions reduction projects in developing countries.

CDM works as follows: The project proponent (for example, the host country) submits a proposal (called the Project Design Document or PDD) that includes a summary of methods for determining the baseline from which emissions are to be measured, additionality of emissions reduction, and monitoring. The baseline is the hypothetical level of emissions that would occur if the project were not implemented; while additionality is the requirement that emissions from the project would fall below the baseline (Clean Development Mechanism 2014). Various levels of review then take place for both the carbon buyer and seller. After the project is operational, an additional review certifies the project's emissions reductions in the form of a carbon credit unit known as Certified Emissions Reductions (CER). CERs are then placed in the project participants' account, where they become tradable. CER payments are typically only provided upon project completion, meaning that CDM is generally a performance-based mechanism (Lecocq and Ambrosi 2007).

CDM is the largest project-based carbon market. As of 2012, 3,742 projects were registered and 7,500+ were waiting to be approved or registered (Lederer 2013). From the mid-2000s until early 2012, the number of projects submitted for validation and approved, as well as the number of CERs issued, grew exponentially. Over that same time, capitalization of carbon funds from CDM grew from millions to over $100 billion. $2–3 billion in carbon finance is transferred to the developing world annually under CDM. Trade of CERs on the secondary market has become especially popular; banks and speculators play a key role. The largest percentage of CER buyers is from Europe, especially the UK. Developing countries have set up mechanisms to attract investment by promoting project opportunities (Lecocq and Ambrosi 2007). CDM has thus become a key financial market; in some ways, "the business of climate has now become more important than politics of climate" (Lederer 2013: 95; see also Bernstein et al. 2010).

CDM has some clear benefits: 1.) Performance-based incentives are viewed by many as more effective than official development assistance (ODA), which has been declining in recent years; 2.) it has gotten developing states much more heavily involved in Kyoto than initially expected (Lecocq and Ambrosi 2007) by changing perceptions, increasing climate change knowledge, and financing climate change adaptation and cost-efficient carbon mitigation (e.g., renewable industrial gas projects) (Lederer 2013). CDM has also resulted in a moderate degree of technology transfer to the developing world (United Nations Framework Convention on Climate Change 2010); 3.) despite primarily being an emissions-offset mechanism, CDM can lead to emissions reductions by "strategically important large emitters" (Lecocq and Ambrosi 2007: 148) from the developing world;[8] 4.) its centralized regulation system improves the quality and quantity of information (Michaelowa 2012).

On the supply side, CDM has provided Japan and EU states flexibility to meet their emissions commitments with limited economic and political costs. The Netherlands and the World Bank have been key players since the beginning. The World Bank views CDM as an innovative way to channel private resources to developing states as ODA has declined. Its most notable role is manager of the Prototype Carbon Fund (PCF), a closed $180 million mutual fund to purchase carbon credits. The Netherlands views CDM as the central part of its strategy to meet its Kyoto target. It is involved in PCF and developed the first carbon tenders for CDM. As of 2005, the World Bank and the Netherlands combined were involved in about one-third of all CDM-based transactions. On the demand side, the Plantar project in Brazil is a notable success story. Financed by Dutch Rabobank, a pig-iron producer substitutes sustainable charcoal for coal, and PCF purchases resulting CERs. China has used tax revenues generated by CDM projects to fund sustainable development (Lecocq and Ambrosi 2007), and CDM has helped the growth of the Chinese renewable energy sector (Lewis 2010).

Nevertheless, CDM is in trouble. The biggest problem is the extremely low price of CERs, which fell below 1 Euro for the first time in late 2012. This price drop has caused a number of companies to leave the market (Michaelowa 2012). Also, the number of submitted projects reached a seven-year low by the end of 2012, part of a growing decline from the beginning of that year. This trend continued, and 2014 saw a further decline in the number of projects submitted (United Nations Framework Convention on Climate Change June 30, 2014b). An additional blow is that starting in 2013, the EU Emissions Trading System (EU ETS)—the world's largest emissions trading market—began only accepting credits from other markets generated in least developed countries and will curb credits from CDM (especially from the industrial gas sector), due to oversupply of credits and concerns that CDM credits are not additional, not contributing sufficiently to sustainable development in host countries, and contributing too heavily to carbon leakage (Michaelowa 2012; Lederer 2013).[9] In addition, while proponents of CDM contend that by providing cheap emissions credits, CDM frees up developed states to develop more strict and ambitious commitments and reduce noncredited emissions, the evidence by and large does not support this contention (Michaelowa 2012). There is some fear of a coming "subprime carbon" or "carbon bubble" similar to what happened in the financial market. Some predict CDM's demise and others say it can be revived.

One of the ways that CDM can be improved is to increase its contribution to emissions reduction, rather than being primarily an emissions-offset mechanism. Such a move would have the benefit of demonstrating a positive contribution to a goal on which there is near universal public consensus—a decline in CO_2 levels. One way to achieve this is to set baselines below business-as-usual emissions levels in order to automatically ensure emissions reduction. The second is to mandate CER usage. This can be done supply-side by making it mandatory that host countries reinvest a portion of CDM revenues in emissions-reduction projects (e.g., China's taxation of CER revenues). A third option is to discount CERs. This can include supply-side options that are more friendly to the least developed states and aimed at increasing the contribution of emerging/middle economies, such as progressively linking discounting to either the host country's level of development or to an index that accounts for both level of development and contribution to emissions. Discounting can also be done demand-side by making CERs less valuable than carbon allowances when Kyoto Annex B (i.e., developed) countries seek to use them for compliance (e.g., the Waxman-Markey bill proposed (but defeated in 2009) in the US Congress that would have required 5 CERs to offset 4 US allowances) (Michaelowa 2012).

Emissions Trading Schemes

Emissions trading schemes (ETSs) have been implemented at the regional, national, and subnational levels, primarily in the developed world. These include programs in the EU, Canada, Japan, Switzerland, Australia, New Zealand, and the US. The EU ETS—a **cap-and-trade system**—was the first ETS in the world, with a share in roughly 97 percent of all carbon trading in 2010. EU ETS has had mixed results: a healthy market and emissions increase for sectors under the cap is smaller than those outside, but emissions are still increasing in most European countries, and the market has suffered problems of instability, transparency, cyber-theft, and low pricing of carbon credits in the wake of the 2007–2008 financial crisis (Lederer 2013). Regional ETSs also lag behind CDM in terms of generating investment in sustainable development. Most regional and national ETSs have much lower transaction costs and less regulation than CDM, though EU ETS has moved toward more central regulation (Michaelowa 2012).

In the US, ETSs have emerged on a regional basis. The Regional Greenhouse Gas Initiative (RGGI) is the first market-based regulatory program in the US to reduce greenhouse gas emissions. RGGI is a cooperative effort among the states of Connecticut, Delaware, Maine, Maryland, Massachusetts, New Hampshire, New York, Rhode Island, and Vermont to cap and reduce CO_2 emissions from the power sector. Other US programs include the California Cap-and-Trade Program and the Midwestern Greenhouse Gas Accord.

Forest Carbon Partnership Facility and UN Collaborative Programme on Reducing Emissions from Deforestation and Forest Degradation

The global impact of ongoing **deforestation** is one of the most easily grasped indicators of the impact of human activity on climate change—we can actually observe from the air and from satellite imagery the shrinkage of the forests in Brazil and Indonesia. This explains an increased push to include forestry-related conservation programs and carbon credits in new, post-Kyoto, comprehensive climate agreements. There is an understanding that deforestation must be addressed in order to make real progress on climate change, since it contributes twice as much to carbon emissions as transportation, for example (Lecocq and Ambrosi 2007), and accounts for nearly 20 percent of total global greenhouse emissions. Protecting existing forests helps to reduce emissions, while reforestation helps to achieve carbon sequestration, since forests are natural mechanisms by which carbon is captured and stored long term (ECOS December 2007/January 2008).

Deforestation must be addressed in order to make real progress on climate change, since it contributes twice as much to carbon emissions as transportation, for example, and accounts for nearly 20 percent of total global greenhouse emissions.

Reducing Emissions from Deforestation and Forest Degradation (REDD) is a proposed market mechanism to help developing countries mitigate carbon emissions and reduce their contribution to climate change. REDD+ is an enhanced version that also includes "sustainable management of forests and the conservation and enhancement of forest carbon stocks" (Burgess et al. 2010: 339–40).[10] The REDD+ idea and the forestry sector writ large have played a large role in the voluntary emissions reduction market (Lederer 2013) and discussions of Nationally Appropriate Mitigation Actions (NAMAs) for developing states (different countries may take different nationally appropriate action on the basis of equity and in accordance with common but differentiated responsibilities and respective capabilities), but a collective approach to REDD+ is also gaining more steam.[11] UNFCCC negotiations on a global REDD+ mechanism remain deadlocked due to financing issues and slow progress on a new climate agreement (Haug and Gupta 2013).

The Forest Carbon Partnership Facility (FCPF) is a fund for developing countries created by the World Bank in 2007 to help them prepare for and implement REDD+, and is viewed as a credible standard setter in that regard.[12] A secondary goal for the FCPF was to serve as an educational experience about forest-related emissions, due to slow progress on REDD+. Tertiary goals include helping to provide development resources and conserve natural resources used by indigenous and local populations (ECOS December 2007/January 2008; Davis et al. 2009; Haug and Gupta 2013).

Under the FCPF, once a country's readiness plan has been approved and initial activities are completed, countries will enter an interim stage when they will engage in policy reform and investment activities "to build institutional capacity, improve forest governance and information, scale up conservation and sustainable management of forests, and relieve pressure on forests through, for example, relocation of agribusiness activities away from forests and onto degraded lands, or improvements in agricultural productivity" (Forest Carbon Partnership Facility 2009: 9).[13] Resource requirements for the interim stage are significant and come from UN-REDD, the Global Environment Facility, traditional ODA, the countries themselves, and two new World Bank programs (REDD bonds and the Forest Investment Program).

A related program is the Carbon Finance Mechanism, a pilot program of performance-based incentives for REDD+. Countries selected into this program will sign Emission Reductions Payment Agreements (ERPAs) under which they will be financially rewarded for reducing their emissions relative to the reference scenario—"an incentive per ton of carbon dioxide of emissions reduced" (Forest Carbon Partnership Facility 2009: 6)—subject to independent verification. At present, FCPF participants are voluntarily submitting Emission Reductions Program Idea Notes (ERPINs). The World Bank estimates that about five countries will act as pilot test cases for implementation of the Carbon Fund (Forest Carbon Partnership Facility 2009).

FCPF and UN-REDD have taken on distinct yet integrated roles in REDD+ preparation activities. FCPF has focused on developing economic incentives for REDD+, while UN-REDD has focused on local capacity building and developing "effective monitoring, reporting, and verification strategies" (Thompson et al. 2011: 101; see also Haug and Gupta 2013). Some of the benefits of the FCPF and UN-REDD mechanisms are:

(1) They can help to provide other environmental goods such as biodiversity protection, water conservation, flood prevention, surface run-off reduction, erosion prevention, and river siltation reduction.

(2) They can help to provide economic goods such as fishery or hydropower facility protection.

(3) They can help "indigenous and other forest-dependent communities" (Forest Carbon Partnership Facility and UN Collaborative Programme on Reducing Emissions from Deforestation and Forest Degradation 2012: 1) share in revenues from emissions reduction or provide them with improved or alternative livelihoods (Forest Carbon Partnership Facility 2009; Larson et al. 2010).

(4) There is consistent evidence that reduction of forest-related emissions is more cost-effective than other carbon mitigation options, especially biofuel-related emissions.

(5) Since forest-related activities contribute so heavily to carbon emissions, focusing on them now can help make immediate and significant progress while buying time until a new climate agreement is signed.

(6) The FCPF's focus on performance-based economic incentives is distinct from most previous forest-related programs and viewed by many as potentially more effective.

(Kanowski et al. 2010)

The set of programs covered by the FCPF and UN-REDD mechanisms have not yet been fully implemented, and therefore our discussion has been in the realm of what may be possible if sufficient collective action on a global scale is undertaken. A reason for emphasizing these particular programs is that progress toward the joint goals of reducing deforestation and promoting reforestation as a way to reduce carbon emissions is potentially straightforward to measure, and can demonstrate progress in the relative short term. Thus, unlike the policies growing out of the WRE carbon emissions trajectory and the CDM, full implementation of the FCPF and UN-REDD, and particularly REDD+, can have immediate demonstrative impact. Thus, it is all the more disappointing that the appropriate world bodies have not yet been able to take the collective action necessary for their implementation.

Why is collective action so difficult here? One constraint surely is cost—REDD+ is expensive. The cost of reducing forest-related emissions by half by 2030 has been estimated at $17–33 billion per year. So perhaps the most significant question is whether FCPF and UN-REDD can attract consistent, long-term, and sufficient funding. Another impediment is the involvement of the World Bank, and therefore the possibility of delaying funds, too heavy involvement in the market as a buyer, poor past performance, too little transparency and accountability, and conflicts of interests due to its multiple roles. Further, REDD+ can require substantial political and economic reforms on the part of its participants. This latter may be coupled with the fact that many developing states have poor governance, and have economic development imperatives that preference resource usage over conservation (Haug and Gupta 2013). And finally, implementation of these mechanisms can pose a threat to human and land rights, culture, and traditional livelihoods of indigenous and other forest-dependent communities. These communities contend that they are underrepresented and marginalized in the top-down approaches of FCPF and UN-REDD (Larson et al. 2010; Thompson et al. 2011).

Conclusion

There is little remaining doubt that the earth is hurtling toward an environmental crisis of epic proportions. The increasing rate of global rise in temperature, with associated changing and destructive weather patterns, including both flooding and drought, the rise in sea level and the gradual melting of both the glaciers and the polar ice caps combine to provide a warning that action is urgently needed. Yet despite the heroic work over the past two-plus decades of the UN Framework Convention on Climate Change and the various Conferences of the Parties, as well as the work of hundreds of climate scientists contributing to the UN's Intergovernmental Panel on Climate Change, progress has been limited. What we have then is a classic collective action problem, with all the constraints that such problems come with.

We have proposed several policy initiatives and related measures that can begin to address climate change in a collective action framework. Long-term measures, implemented and assessed over extended periods of time include the WRE carbon emission trajectory, which requires collective action to restrict the emission of greenhouse gases to a level consistent with a sustainable increase in temperature rise by the end of this century. This approach combines reasonable trajectories with strong measurement methodologies to provide a path toward sustainability. Among medium-term policies, the CDM is a market-based carbon mitigation mechanism that couples a pathway for developed countries to meet their emission reduction commitments with economic incentives for developing economies to engage in more sustainable industrialization. Regarding shorter-term policy options, the programs clustered around the FCPF, UN-REDD and REDD+ provide an instance in which the impact of policy options taken today can be seen in the relative near-future as the size of the forest coverage can be gauged using various earth-tracking techniques now generally available.

Notes

1 According to the Emissions Gap Report of UNEP (Executive Summary), "after 2020, the world will have to rely on more difficult, costlier and riskier means of meeting the target [of limiting temperature increase to 1.5°C at the end of the century]—the further from the least-cost level in 2020, the higher these costs and the greater the risks will be. If the gap is not closed or significantly narrowed by 2020, the door to many options...will be closed, further increasing the need to rely on accelerated energy-efficiency increases and biomass with carbon capture and storage for reaching the target" (2013: 1).

2 The biological capacity of an ecosystem like our planet is calculated from the production of useful biological materials and the amount of absorption of wastes like carbon dioxide emissions. It is estimated that we are currently using about 1.5 earths to cover the growing needs of the Earth's population.

3 In deriving their trajectories, they operate under four critical assumptions: 1.) States will slowly depart from their "business as usual" emissions, given costs of departure and entrenchment of behavior; 2.) The higher the concentration targets, the longer states will stick to business-as-usual emissions, in order to lower costs of mitigation; 3.) "In the absence of policy intervention, CO_2 emissions will continue to grow" (Wigley et al. 1996: 241); and 4.) Current supply of "economically competitive low-carbon alternatives" is "insufficient...to arrest future growth in carbon emissions" (ibid.: 242).

4 The most common causes of overshoot are setting too-high an initial target and having to readjust downward later, or economic, political, or technological factors. Their updated analysis also accounts for non-CO_2 emissions and climate feedbacks on the carbon cycle.

5 On the other hand, the IPCC Working Group III has determined that "most aspects of climate change will persist for many centuries even if emissions of CO_2 are stopped." Thus, immediate departure from business as usual would be required to meet any of the above targets (IPCC 2013b).

6 "In electric power generation a **combined cycle** is an assembly of heat engines that work in tandem from the same source of heat, converting it into mechanical energy, which in turn usually drives electrical generators" (Wikipedia, http://en.wikipedia.org/wiki/Combined_cycle). The principle is that the exhaust of one heat engine is used as the heat source for another, thus extracting more useful energy from the heat, increasing the system's overall efficiency (ibid.).

7 C&C was discussed at the 1997 Kyoto negotiations, but despite some strong support was not adopted in practise.

8 A common criticism of CDM is that, because it is an emissions offset rather than emissions reduction mechanism, it does not help to achieve the global 2°C goal. But it is unfair to judge CDM on those terms, because emissions reduction is not its intent. Also, many critics ignore possible positive indirect effects (Michaelowa 2012).

9 Carbon leakage occurs when emissions reduction in one area leads to emissions increase in another area, a process driven by market forces (Murray et al. 2004).

10 Enhancement of forest stock component of REDD+ includes "forest regeneration and rehabilitation, negative degradation, negative emissions, carbon uptake...or removals" (Angelsen 2009: 2) of CO_2 from the atmosphere.

11 Recent trends also show moves toward more "nested" (i.e., decentralized within states) and context-specific approaches to REDD+, given the diversity of state experiences with deforestation and land degradation as well as the concerns and contributions of local populations (United Nations Collaborative Programme on Reducing Emissions from Deforestation and Forest Degradation in Developing Countries 2008; Kanowski et al. 2010).

12 The World Bank is also involved in forest-related carbon mitigation through its BioCarbon Fund. This fund finances CDM projects related to afforestation, reforestation, and forest protection (Forest Carbon Partnership Facility 2009).

13 Forest governance is a large concern for REDD+ practitioners and analysts. Some key causes of deforestation and forest degradation are symptoms of poor forest governance: "illegal logging, unplanned forest conversion, and conflicts over access to land and resources" (Williams and Davis 2012: 2). Good governance is also necessary for successful implementation of REDD+ activities such as "monitoring, information sharing, and revenue management" (ibid.).

Conclusion

Global Challenges to Human Security in the 21st Century

Recent generations have experienced dramatic improvements in the quality of human life across the globe. Wars between states are fought less frequently and are less lethal. Food is more plentiful and more easily accessed. In most parts of the world, birthrates are down and life expectancy up. Significantly less people live in extreme poverty relative to the overall population. Statistics would argue that the human race has never flourished as it does in this moment.

And yet even with the aforementioned progress, we face a number of seemingly intractable challenges to the welfare of both states and individuals, including:

- *Persistent and recurring intrastate conflict* due to ineffective conflict management strategies.
- *Internecine conflict in multiethnic societies*, manifested by exclusion, discrimination, and, ultimately, violence; the inevitable consequence of an insufficient focus on managing the inherent tensions in diverse societies.
- *Governmental instability* undermining the lives of citizens both within and beyond their borders.
- *Marginally successful development efforts* and *growing income inequality*, both within and between nations, a result of uncoordinated and ineffective global development strategies.
- *Global climate change* with the possibility of catastrophic long-term consequences, following an inability to effectively come to terms with and respond to the impact of human activity on our environment.

This book began with a challenge to global leaders. Many of the most severe threats to human security cannot be adequately addressed through the actions of single countries. Climate change, conflict, regime instability, and the consequences of ethnic diversity and underdevelopment are global phenomena, and thus the solutions must be global in nature. They require collective action that is timely and coordinated, action that can be systematically measured to assess impact and then adjusted to achieve optimal outcomes. Solutions will require a level of boldness and collaboration on the part of leaders and nations that they have only rarely exhibited in the past.

Many of the most severe threats to human security cannot be adequately addressed through the actions of single countries. They require collective action that is timely and coordinated.

This concluding chapter begins by reviewing key challenges to human security. It summarizes the measures and indicators that have been proposed to assess progress toward addressing these challenges and creating the conditions for improvements to human security. We close with a discussion of policies and measures that can inform an action agenda for leadership in the 21st century.

Challenges to Human Security

Conflict Resolution

Conflict has evolved over the past several decades from predominantly interstate or between nations, to one typified by intrastate or subnational conflict, often based on local religious, ethnic, cultural, and linguistic differences. While this shift has been accompanied by a significant decrease in the number of fatalities associated with conflict, this positive outgrowth is more than offset by an increase in the destruction wreaked on the productive capacities of states. Yet the mechanisms that have been available to the international community to address these localized conflicts are largely left over from collective responses to interstate conflict. Their inadequacy is reflected in the persistence of intractable conflicts, and the dramatic increase in conflict recurrence. Our discussion therefore touched upon the complex sources of conflict today, and obstacles to the types of negotiated settlements that might move us from conflict management to conflict resolution. In short, we face this dilemma:

Subnational conflict has now replaced interstate conflict as the dominant threat to human security today. But we have not adapted conflict resolution mechanisms and institutions to deal with this threat, and the consequence has been a surge in the recurrence of conflicts that have been managed but not resolved.

Ethnic Diversity

While applauding the creativity and innovation that ethnic diversity brings to nations and the world, we also recognize a darker side. One in seven citizens of the globe are members of a persecuted ethnic minority. At the extreme, this discrimination and unequal treatment has spawned conflict and in some cases terrorism, spilling over borders. We argue that successful collective protection of group rights is best achieved through negotiation and mutual accommodation. This accommodation is facilitated by an evolving global doctrine for managing ethnic conflict (Gurr 2002) that includes recognition and protection of racial, ethnic, and religious minorities, promotion of democratic institutions for guaranteeing group rights, arrangements for regional autonomy within existing states, enhancing the responsibilities and capabilities of regional and global organizations, and intervention with military sanctions and peace enforcement when all else fails. In sum:

While collectively celebrating the creativity, imagination, and invention that ethnic diversity has fostered globally and nationally, we have not come to grips with the flip-side of this phenomenon that can carry with it political, economic, social, and cultural discrimination.

Stability and Democracy

A complex relationship exists between stability and democracy. While we am unapologetic in our support for democratic regimes, we acknowledge that the process of transitioning from autocracy to a democratic form of government is likely to bring on a sustained period of instability. In this transition state, referred to as anocracy, underdeveloped national institutions and rising aspirations for participation, often in the form of early elections, can combine to produce a level of instability and even violence that is far worse than can be anticipated even under extreme authoritarian rule. In this environment, we argue that we need to be extremely mindful of the warning signs of deteriorating regimes, and possible points of intervention through collective action by the international community. Several indicators can assist in pinpointing the vulnerability of societies to regime inconsistency—regime durability, magnitude of regime change, direction of regime change, and leadership change. Policy recommendations designed to address the vulnerability experienced by states in the midst of democratic transitions should include the development of institutions that blunt or discourage factionalism when opening up political participation (Goldstone et al. 2010), strengthening political parties, approaching elections gradually, exploring caretaker governments as a transition phase, and the preservation of local democratic practices whenever possible.

Important gains have been made in the spread of democracy through the international system and the decline in the number of autocratic regimes. And yet we still face the daunting challenge of helping societies transition from autocracy to democracy while passing through a dangerously unstable period during which the societal institutions are not yet up to the task of simultaneously delivering democracy *and* stability.

Development and Inequality

Tremendous inequalities of wealth and opportunity exist among nations. Development aid began flowing first as a means of addressing the destruction of the Second World War, and then turned by the 1960s to addressing the development issues facing other regions, in particular Africa and Asia. But in a world in which nation-states themselves have not managed to deal with problems of severe inequality internally, the prospect for collective action on a global scale would seem quite remote. The consequences of ignoring or inadequately dealing with these development issues include, at the extreme, state instability, fragility, and failure, with consequences for the nations in which they occur, their immediate neighbors, and the system as a whole. Policy options that are being captured by the Sustainable Development Goals for 2030, presented to the United Nations General Assembly in 2014, address in particular the areas of health, education, equality, poverty, agriculture, and urbanization. In sum:

There are many success stories that chronicle the transition of societies out of extreme poverty during the past few decades. And yet the impact of development aid is still outpaced by the regional and global economic costs resulting from instability, fragility, and state failure. And within many states, aid is still not being distributed in ways that will effectively address tremendous local disparities in wealth and the attendant instability that results.

Climate Change

Climate change is the poster child for the opportunities and difficulties facing the international community as it seeks a collective action approach. In the face of overwhelming scientific evidence that human activity is the primary contributing factor to adverse climate change, we have seen the enormous difficulty in developing agreed measures of the impact of various types of activity on climate, and on the proper way to divide responsibility for addressing these problems going forward. One critical divide is between the developed and the developing worlds, when competing visions of development and sustainability have erupted into arguments that have halted progress in achieving conventions that will address these issues for the remainder of the century. It is the Tragedy of the Commons played out on a global stage, with easily identifiable negative consequences, but seemingly no easy way to reach agreement on sets of policies that will constitute a so-called off-ramp. We suggest several goals and attendant strategies for achieving them, but all require some sacrifice, and in the current political climate, reaching such agreements is exceedingly difficult. In sum:

In climate change, Al Gore's "inconvenient truth" remains as real today as it was years ago. While little doubt remains that human behavior is a key contributor to the deterioration of our environment, the international community remains incapable of coming together in collective action programs designed to address this universal threat.

Components of a Collective Action Plan to Address Global Challenges

This book has attempted to address these seemingly insolvable challenges through a call for a collective action approach. Elements of such an approach are the development of universally accepted measures for assessing problems and progress, the monitoring of these indicators so that we can set up better early warning systems for addressing emerging problems, the provision of targeted assistance, and, in the extreme, intervention with force to address problems that are not being addressed, or cannot be addressed locally. Here are some examples, drawn from the chapters of this book.

In the area of conflict, we have called for the use of tools like the *Peace and Conflict Instability Ledger* as a measurement and monitoring mechanism. The *Instability Ledger* provides an assessment of the risk of future conflict and instability covering the majority of countries in the world. Drawing on indicators from the political, economic, security, and social domains, a ratio is produced on which the countries are ranked in terms of their risk of instability. As a supplement, we have also examined the applicability of crowd sourcing as a means of monitoring conflict and crisis in real time. With the deployment of such indicators and tools, the international community is better equipped to anticipate potential trouble spots, and to act collectively on conflict through mechanisms like mediation, peacekeeping, and enforcement missions.

Our approach to the challenges of ethnic diversity is guided by the principle that disputes between communal groups and states are best settled by negotiation and mutual accommodation. This requires the active engagement of major powers, the UN, and regional organizations applying a mix of diplomacy, mediation, inducements, and pressure to encourage negotiated settlements of ethnic conflicts (Gurr 2000). Measures of discrimination are derived from *Minorities at Risk* (MAR) political and economic discrimination indicators, to provide a basis for assessing the degree to which various minorities around the world are in need of support by the international community. This then can take the form of providing assistance in the areas of democracy promotion and power sharing, regional autonomy, stability promotion programs, the promotion of membership in international and regional organizations with minority rights agendas, and at the extreme, international prevention of ethnic violence in low-intensity conflicts.

In the realm of regime consistency and democracy, we have highlighted the challenge of achieving stability through consistency, while promoting democracy. We have taken the strong position that the road to stability must pass through a transition to democracy. We have noted the inherent instability of the transition process from autocracy to democracy. Hence, it is the responsibility of the international community to provide technical and financial resources for state institution building and consolidation, strengthening judicial institutions and the political party structure, and supporting pro-democracy civil society organizations. The *Polity Score* serves as a static indicator of regime type, an important starting point in a collective action approach to the promotion of stability and democracy. A number of other Polity-based indicators help us create measures of regime durability, the magnitude and direction of regime change, and an assessment of how leadership change can come about in positive circumstances.

Underdevelopment and the inequalities both within and between societies constitute areas where measurement has been substantial, but severe problems remain. Here we have recommended the use of both the original *Human Development Index* (HDI) and the *Inequality-adjusted Development Index* (IHDI) as a frame of reference for both social and economic development. With these measures in hand, we go on to explore a number of the *Sustainable Development Goals* which the United Nations General Assembly is considering for adoption for 2030, as well as a number of proposed indicators for measuring progress toward achieving those goals. Among the goals discussed are ending extreme poverty, ensuring effective learning, achieving gender equality, achieving health and well-being, improving agricultural systems, and empowering inclusive, productive, and resilient cities.

Of all the issues addressed in this book, climate change may turn out to be the most extreme manifestation of failed collective action in the face of looming threat. There are a very large number of indicators of the deterioration of conditions on this planet resulting from the impact of human behavior on climate. A key measure identified here is a relatively straightforward indicator that measures concentrations of greenhouse gases in terms of parts per million of CO_2 concentrations. With this measure in hand, we proposed the WRE *Carbon Emissions Trajectory* as a way to focus on the policy options and likely outcomes from the application of these policies at various concentrations. Based on a sense of the desired level of CO_2 emissions by the end of the century, several options were explored: *CDM*, a market-based carbon mitigation mechanism; emission trading schemes; and the *Forest Carbon Partnerships Facility* to reduce emissions from deforestation and forest degradation.

Conclusion

The challenges and opportunities facing the international system today are easily recognized. They differ from those identified by previous generations only to the extent that their impact is on a grander scale—organizations with conflicting agendas and interests become societies and nations with the use of violence and war at their disposal; local pollution becomes a contributor to global warming and climate change; and poverty and income disparities become a flood of illegal immigration in Southern Europe and the southwestern United States. And our leaders, caught in the midst of difficult political situations and coalitions that do not allow for flexibility and long-term planning, are forced to deal piecemeal with complex long-term issues.

Garrett Hardin wrote many decades ago: "Ruin is the destination toward which all men rush, each pursuing his own best interest in a society that believes in the freedom of the common. Freedom in a commons brings ruin to all" (Hardin 1968: 1248). Our challenge is to rise above the collective tendency to regress toward undesired outcomes, to convince our leaders that we will tolerate sacrifice in pursuit of the common good, and that the human spirit, which has been capable of such great imagination and creativity in the past, can act collectively to address the immense global challenges we face today.

Our challenge is to convince our leaders that we will tolerate sacrifice in pursuit of the common good, that the human spirit can act collectively to address the immense global challenges we face today.

References

Adano, Wario R., Ton Dietz, Karen Witsenburg, and Fred Zaal. 2012. "Climate Change, Violent Conflict and Local Institutions in Kenya's Drylands." *Journal of Peace Research*, 49(1): 65–80.

Aggestam, Karin. 2002. "Mediating Asymmetrical Conflict." *Mediterranean Politics*, 7(1): 69–91.

Aldy, Joseph E., Alan J. Krupnick, Richard G. Newell, Ian W. H. Parry, and William A. Pizer. 2010. "Designing Climate Mitigation Policy." *Journal of Economic Literature*, 48(4): 903–34.

Angelsen, Arild. 2009. "Introduction." In *Realising REDD+: National Strategy and Policy Options*, edited by Arild Angelsen. Bogor, Indonesia: Center for International Forestry Research (CIFOR), pp. 1–9.

Asal, Victor, and R. Karl Rethemeyer. 2008. "The Nature of the Beast: Organizational Structures and the Lethality of Terrorist Attacks." *The Journal of Politics*, 70(2): 437–49.

Asal, Victor, and Jonathan Wilkenfeld. 2013. "Ethnic Conflict: An Organizational Perspective." *Penn State Journal of Law & International Affairs*, 2(1): 91–102.

Asal, Victor, Carter Johnson, and Jonathan Wilkenfeld. 2008. "Ethnopolitical Violence and Terrorism in the Middle East." In *Peace and Conflict 2008*, edited by J. Joseph Hewitt, Jonathan Wilkenfeld, and Ted Robert Gurr. Boulder, CO: Paradigm Publishers, pp. 55–66.

Backer, David, and Paul Huth. 2014a. "The Peace and Conflict Instability Ledger: Ranking States on Future Risks." In *Peace and Conflict 2014*, edited by David Backer, Jonathan Wilkenfeld, and Paul Huth. Boulder, CO: Paradigm Publishers, pp. 4–17.

——2014b. "Global Trends in Armed Conflict, 1946–2012." In *Peace and Conflict 2014*, edited by David Backer, Jonathan Wilkenfeld, and Paul Huth. Boulder, CO: Paradigm Publishers, pp. 18–22.

Ball, Nicole, with Tammy Halevy. 1996. *Making Peace Work: The Role of the International Development Community*. Washington, DC: Overseas Development Council.

Barrett, R.E., and M.K. Whyte. 1982. "Dependency Theory and Taiwan: Analysis of a Deviant Case." *American Journal of Sociology*, 87(5): 1064–89.

Bates, Robert H. 2008. *When Things Fell Apart: State Failure in Late-Century Africa*. Cambridge, UK: Cambridge University Press.

Beardsley, Kyle. 2011. *The Mediation Dilemma*. Ithaca, NY: Cornell University Press.

Beardsley, Kyle, and Holger Schmidt. 2012. "Following the Flag or Following the Charter? Examining the Determinants of UN Involvement in International Crises, 1945–2002." *International Studies Quarterly*, 56(1): 33–49.

Beardsley, Kyle, David Quinn, Bidisha Biswas, and Jonathan Wilkenfeld. 2006. "Mediation Style and Crisis Outcomes." *Journal of Conflict Resolution*, 50(1): 58–86.

Bercovitch, Jacob. 1992. "The Structure and Diversity of Mediation in International Relations." In *Mediation in International Relations: Multiple Approaches to Conflict Management*, edited by Jacob Bercovitch and Jeffrey Z. Rubin. New York: St. Martin's Press, pp. 1–29.

——1997. "Mediation in International Conflict: An Overview of Theory, a Review of Practice." In *Peacemaking in International Conflict*, edited by I. William Zartman and J. Lewis Rasmussen. Washington, DC: U.S. Institute of Peace Press, pp. 125–53.

Bercovitch, Jacob, and Allison Houston. 1996. "The Study of International Mediation: Theoretical Issues and Empirical Evidence." In *Resolving International Conflicts*, edited by Jacob Bercovitch. Boulder, CO: Lynne Reinner, pp. 11–35.

Bercovitch, Jacob, J. Theodore Anagnoson, and Donnette L. Wille. 1991. "Some Conceptual Issues and Empirical Trends in the Study of Successful Mediation in International Relations." *Journal of Peace Research*, 28(1): 7–17.

Bergholt, Drago, and Päivi Lujala. 2012. "Climate-related Natural Disasters, Economic Growth, and Armed Civil Conflict." *Journal of Peace Research*, 49(1): 147–62.

Berlinski, S., S. Galiani, and P. Gertler. 2009. "The Effect of Pre-Primary Education on Primary School Performance." *Journal of Public Economics*, 93(1–2): 219–34.

Bernstein, Steven, Michele Betsill, Matthew Hoffmann, and Matthew Paterson. 2010. "A Tale of Two Copenhagens: Carbon Markets and Climate Governance." *Millennium: Journal of International Studies*, 39(1): 161–73.

Birdsall, Nancy. 2007. "Do No Harm: Aid, Weak Institutions, and the Missing Middle in Africa." Washington DC: Center for Global Development, Working paper number 113, March.

Bloom, Mia M. 2005. *Dying to Kill*. New York: Columbia University Press.

Boserup, Esther. 1990. *Economic and Demographic Relationships in Development*. Baltimore, MD: Johns Hopkins University Press.

Brancati, Dawn, and Jack L. Snyder. 2011. "Rushing to the Polls: The Causes of Premature Postconflict Elections." *Journal of Conflict Resolution*, 55(3): 469–92.

——2013. "Time to Kill: The Impact of Election Timing on Postconflict Stability." *Journal of Conflict Resolution*, 57(5): 822–53.

Brass, J.N. 2008. "Djibouti's Unusual Resource Curse." *Journal of Modern African Studies*, 46(4): 523–45.

Bremner, Jason, David López-Carr, Laurel Suter, and Jason Davis. 2010. "Population, Poverty, Environment, and Climate Dynamics in the Developing World." *Interdisciplinary Environmental Review*, 11(2/3): 112–26.

Browne, Stephen. 1990. *Foreign Aid in Practice*. Washington Square, NY: New York University Press.

Bueno De Mesquita, Bruce, George W. Downs, Alastair Smith, and Feryal Marie Cherif. 2005. "Thinking Inside the Box: A Closer Look at Democracy and Human Rights." *International Studies Quarterly*, 49(3): 439–57.

Buhaug, Halvard. 2006. "Relative Capability and Rebel Objective in Civil War." *Journal of Peace Research*, 43(6): 691–708.

Buhaug, Halvard, Scott Gates, and Päivi Lujala. 2009. "Geography, Rebel Capability, and the Duration of Civil Conflict." *Journal of Conflict Resolution*, 53(4): 544–69.

Burgess, Neil D., Bruno Bahane, Tim Clairs, Finn Danielsen, Søren Dalsgaard, Mikkel Funder, Niklas Hagelberg, Paul Harrison, Christognus Haule, Kekilia Kabalimu, Felician Kilahama, Edward Kilawe, Simon L. Lewis, Jon C. Lovett, Gertrude Lyatuu, Andrew R. Marshall, Charles Meshack, Lera Miles, Simon A.H. Milledge, Pantaleo K.T. Munishi, Evarist Nashanda, Deo Shirima, Ruth D. Swetnam, Simon Willcock, Andrew Williams, and Eliakim Zahabu. 2010. "Getting Ready for REDD+ in Tanzania: A Case Study of Progress and Challenges." *Oryx*, 44(3): 339–51.

Burton, John W. 1990. *Conflict: Resolution and Prevention*. New York: St. Martin's Press.

Caprioli, Mary, Rebecca Nielsen, and Valerie M. Hudson. 2010. "Women and Post-Conflict Settings." In *Peace and Conflict 2010*, edited by J. Joseph Hewitt, Jonathan Wilkenfeld, and Ted Robert Gurr. Boulder, CO: Paradigm Publishers, pp. 91–102.

Carnevale, Peter J. D. 1986. "Strategic Choice in Mediation." *Negotiation Journal*, 2(1): 41–56.

Casper, Gretchen, and Michelle M. Taylor. 1996. *Negotiating Democracy: Transitions from Authoritarian Rule*. Pittsburgh, PA: University of Pittsburgh Press.

Cederman, Lars-Erik, Simon Hug, and Lutz F. Krebs. 2010a. "Democratization and Civil War: Empirical Evidence." *Journal of Peace Research*, 47(4): 377–94.

Cederman, Lars-Erik, Andreas Wimmer, and Brian Min. 2010b. "Why Do Ethnic Groups Rebel? New Data and Analysis." *World Politics*, 62(1): 87–119.

Center for Global Development. n.d. "Education and the Developing World: Why Is Education Essential for Development?" www.cgdev.org/files/2844_file_EDUCATON1.pdf (accessed May 12, 2015).

Chapman, S. 2004. *Sociology*. London: Letts Educational.

Clean Development Mechanism (CDM). 2014. *CDM Rulebook: Clean Development Mechanism Rules, Practices and Procedures*. www.cdmrulebook.org/ (accessed July 23, 2014).

Cleary, Matthew R. 2000. "Democracy and Indigenous Rebellion in Latin America." *Comparative Political Studies*, 33(9): 1123–53.

Clinton, Hillary Rodham. 2010. "Leading Through Civilian Power: Redefining American Diplomacy and Development." *Foreign Affairs*, 89(6): 13–24.

Collier, Paul. 2009. *Wars, Guns, and Votes: Democracy in Dangerous Places*. New York: HarperCollins.

Collier, Paul, and Anke Hoeffler. 2004. "Greed and Grievance in Civil War." *Oxford Economic Papers*, 56(4): 563–95.

Collier, Paul, Lani Elliott, Håvard Hegre, Anke Hoeffler, Marta Reynal-Querol, and Nicholas Sambanis. 2003. *Breaking the Conflict Trap: Civil War and*

Development Policy. Washington, DC: The International Bank for Reconstruction and Development/The World Bank.

Collier, Paul, Gordon Conway, and Tony Venables. 2008a. "Climate Change and Africa." *Oxford Review of Economic Policy*, 24(2): 337–53.

Collier, Paul, Anke Hoeffler, and Måns Söderbom. 2008b. "Post-Conflict Risks." *Journal of Peace Research*, 45(4): 461–78.

Conca, Ken, and Geoffrey D. Dabelko. 2002. "The Problems and Possibilities of Environmental Peacemaking." In *Environmental Peacemaking*, edited by Ken Conca and Geoffrey D. Dabelko. Washington, DC: Woodrow Wilson Center Press, pp. 220–33.

Crenshaw, Martha. 1988. "Theories of Terrorism: Instrumental and Organizational Approaches." In *Inside Terrorist Organizations*, edited by David C. Rapoport. New York, NY: Columbia University Press, pp. 13–31.

Crocker, Chester A., Fen Osler Hampson, and Pamela Aall. 2001. "Introduction." In *Turbulent Peace: The Challenges of Managing International Conflict*, edited by Chester A. Crocker, Fen Osler Hampson, and Pamela Aall. Washington, DC: United States Institute of Peace Press, pp. xv–xxix.

——(eds.). 2005. *Grasping the Nettle: Analyzing Cases of Intractable Conflict.* Washington, DC: United States Institute of Peace Press.

——2011. "Regional Security through Collective Conflict Management." In *Rewiring Regional Security in a Fragmented World*, edited by Chester A. Crocker, Fen Osler Hampson, and Pamela Aall. Washington, DC: United States Institute of Peace Press, pp. 529–56.

Cunningham, David E. 2006. "Veto Players and Civil War Duration." *American Journal of Political Science*, 50(4): 875–92.

Davenport, Christian. 1995. "Multi-Dimensional Threat Perception and State Repression: An Inquiry into Why States Apply Negative Sanctions." *American Journal of Political Science*, 39(3): 683–713.

——1996. "'Constitutional Promises' and Repressive Reality: A Cross-National Time-Series Investigation of Why Political and Civil Liberties are Suppressed." *The Journal of Politics*, 58(3): 627–54.

——2007. "State Repression and Political Order." *Annual Review of Political Science*, 10: 1–23.

Davenport, Christian, and David A. Armstrong, II. 2004. "Democracy and the Violation of Human Rights: A Statistical Analysis from 1976 to 1996." *American Journal of Political Science*, 48(3): 538–54.

Davies, James C. 1962. "Toward a Theory of Revolution." *American Sociological Review*, 27(1): 5–19.

Davis, Crystal, Florence Daviet, Smita Nakhooda, and Alice Thuault. 2009. "A Review of 25 Readiness Plan Idea Notes from the World Bank Forest Carbon Partnership Facility." World Resources Institute (WRI) Working Paper, February 2009. Washington, DC: World Resources Institute.

DeRouen, Jr., Karl. 2003. "The Role of the UN in International Crisis Termination, 1945–1994." *Defence and Peace Economics*, 14(4): 251–60.

DeRouen, Jr., Karl, Jenna Lea, and Peter Wallensteen. 2009. "The Duration of Civil War Peace Agreements." *Conflict Management and Peace Science*, 26(4): 367–87.

De Stefano, Lucia, James Duncan, Shlomi Dinar, Kerstin Stahl, Kenneth M. Strzepek, and Aaron T. Wolf. 2012. "Climate Change and the Institutional Resilience of International River Basins." *Journal of Peace Research*, 49(1): 193–209.

Doyle, Michael W., and Nicholas Sambanis. 2000. "International Peacebuilding: A Theoretical and Quantitative Analysis." *The American Political Science Review*, 94(4): 779–801.

——2006. *Making War and Building Peace: United Nations Peace Operations*. Princeton, NJ: Princeton University Press.

Dudley, Ryan, and Ross A. Miller. 1998. "Group Rebellion in the 1980s." *Journal of Conflict Resolution*, 42(1): 77–96.

Easterly, W. 2006. *The White Man's Burden: Why the West's Efforts to Aid the Rest Have Done so Much Ill and so Little Good*. Penguin Group USA.

ECOS. December 2007/January 2008. "In Brief: Fund to Save Forests for Carbon Sequestration." *ECOS Magazine*, 140: 5.

ElBaradei, Mohamed. 2010. "Sadat Lecture 2006." In *The Sadat Lectures: Words and Images on Peace, 1997–2008*, edited by Shibley Telhami. Washington DC: United States Institute of Peace, pp. 86–94.

Epstein, David L., Robert Bates, Jack Goldstone, Ida Kristensen, and Sharyn O'Halloran. 2006. "Democratic Transitions." *American Journal of Political Science*, 50(3): 551–69.

Esty, Daniel C., Jack A. Goldstone, Ted Robert Gurr, Barbara Harff, Marc Levy, Geoffrey D. Dabelko, Pamela T. Surko, and Alan N. Unger. 1999. *State Failure Task Force Report: Phase II Findings*. McLean, VA: Science Applications International Corporation (SAIC).

Falkenmark, Malin, and Carl Widstrand. 1992. "Population and Water Resources: A Delicate Balance." *Population Bulletin*, 47(3): 2–35.

Fearon, James D. 1995. "Rationalist Explanations for War." *International Organization*, 49(3): 379–414.

——2003. "Ethnic and Cultural Diversity by Country." *Journal of Economic Growth*, 8(2): 195–222.

——2004. "Why Do Some Civil Wars Last So Much Longer than Others?" *Journal of Peace Research*, 41(3): 275–301.

Fearon, James D., and David D. Laitin. 1999. "Weak States, Rough Terrain, and Large-Scale Ethnic Violence since 1945." Paper presented at the Annual Conference of the American Political Science Association, Atlanta, GA, September 2–5.

——2000. "Violence and the Social Construction of Ethnic Identity." *International Organization*, 54(4): 845–77.

——2003. "Ethnicity, Insurgency, and Civil War." *The American Political Science Review*, 97(1): 75–90.

Findley, Michael G., and Joseph K. Young. 2011. "Terrorism, Democracy, and Credible Commitments." *International Studies Quarterly*, 55(2): 357–78.

Fish, M. Steven. 2001. "The Dynamics of Democratic Erosion." In *Postcommunism and the Theory of Democracy*, edited by Richard D. Anderson, Jr., M. Steven Fish, Stephen E. Hanson, and Philip G. Roeder. Princeton, NJ: Princeton University Press, pp. 54–95.

———2006. "Stronger Legislatures, Stronger Democracies." *Journal of Democracy*, 17(1): 5–20.

Fisher, R.J. 1972. "Third Party Consultation: A Method for the Study and Resolution of Conflict." *Journal of Conflict Resolution*. 16: 67–94.

Fjelde, Hanne. 2010. "Generals, Dictators, and Kings: Authoritarian Regimes and Civil Conflict, 1973–2004." *Conflict Management and Peace Science*, 27(3): 195–218.

Flores, Thomas Edward, and Irfan Nooruddin. 2009. "Democracy under the Gun: Understanding Postconflict Economic Recovery." *Journal of Conflict Resolution*, 53(1): 3–29.

Food Research and Action Center. 2010. "Why Low-Income and Food Insecure People are Vulnerable to Overweight and Obesity." http://frac.org/initiatives/hunger-and-obesity/why-are-low-income-and-food-insecure-people-vulnerable-to-obesity/ (accessed May 12, 2015).

Forest Carbon Partnership Facility (FCPF). 2009. Forest Carbon Partnership Facility Brochure: Demonstrating Activities that Reduce Emissions from Deforestation and Forest Degradation. Washington, DC: Forest Carbon Partnership Facility.

Forest Carbon Partnership Facility (FCPF) and United Nations Collaborative Programme on Reducing Emissions from Deforestation and Forest Degradation in Developing Countries (UN-REDD). 2012. "Guidelines on Stakeholder Engagement in REDD+ Readiness With a Focus on the Participation of Indigenous Peoples and Other Forest-Dependent Communities." Working draft, April 20, 2012 version. Washington, DC and Geneva.

Fortna, Virginia Page. 2003. "Scraps of Paper? Agreements and the Durability of Peace." *International Organization*, 57(2): 337–72.

———2004. "Does Peacekeeping Keep Peace? International Intervention and the Duration of Peace After Civil War." *International Studies Quarterly*, 48(2): 269–92.

Francisco, Ronald A. 1996. "Coercion and Protest: An Empirical Test in Two Democratic States." *American Journal of Political Science*, 40(4): 1179–1204.

Frank, A.G. 1966. *The Development of Underdevelopment*. Boston: New England Free Press.

Frantz, Erica. 2014. "Global Trends in Democratization: Leadership Transitions and Systemic Change." In *Peace and Conflict 2014*, edited by David Backer, Jonathan Wilkenfeld, and Paul Huth. Boulder, CO: Paradigm Publishers, pp. 23–8.

Freedom House. 2011. *Freedom in the World 2011: The Authoritarian Challenge to Democracy*. https://freedomhouse.org/report/freedom-world-2011/essay-authoritarian-challenge-democracy#.VT6IMEtboU4 (accessed May 12, 2015).

Freeman, Mark. 2006. *Truth Commissions and Procedural Fairness*. Cambridge, UK: Cambridge University Press.

Friedman, Thomas. 2014. Op-ed: "WikiLeaks, Drought, and Syria." *New York Times*, January 21.

Gallup, John Luke, and Jeffrey D. Sachs. 2001. "The Economic Burden of Malaria." *American Journal of Tropical Medicine and Hygiene*, 64(1, supplement): 85–96.

Gartner, Scott Sigmund. 2011. "Signs of Trouble: Regional Organization Mediation and Civil War Agreement Durability." *The Journal of Politics*, 73(2): 380–90.

Gates, B., and M. Gates. 2014. "2014 Gates Annual Letter: 3 Myths that Block Progress for the Poor." http://annualletter.gatesfoundation.org (accessed May 12, 2015).

Gates, Scott, Håvard Hegre, Mark P. Jones, and Håvard Strand. 2006. "Institutional Inconsistency and Political Instability: Polity Duration, 1800–2000." *American Journal of Political Science*, 50(4): 893–908.

Geddes, Barbara. 1999. "What Do We Know About Democratization After Twenty Years?" *Annual Review of Political Science*, 2: 115–44.

Geertz, Clifford. 1973. *The Interpretation of Cultures*. New York: Basic Books.

Gelb, Leslie H. 2013. "The Democracy-Election Trap in Egypt." *The Daily Beast*, July 22, 2013. New York: Council on Foreign Relations. www.thedaily beast.com/articles/2013/07/22/leslie-h-gelb-on-the-democracy-elections-trap-in-egypt.html (accessed May 12, 2015).

George, Alexander L. 1984. "Crisis Management: The Interaction of Political and Military Considerations." *Survival*, 26(5): 223–34.

——1991. *Avoiding War: Problems of Crisis Management*. Boulder, CO: Westview Press.

Gillies, A. 2010. "Giving Money Away? The Politics of Direct Distribution in Resource Rich States." Center for Global Development, working paper 231.

Gilligan, Michael, and Stephen John Stedman. 2003. "Where Do the Peacekeepers Go?" *International Studies Review*, 5(4): 37–54.

Glassman, A. 2014. "Spatial Relationships: Does Global Health Aid Go Where It's Needed?" www.cgdev.org/blog/spatial-relationships-does-global-health-aid-go-where-its-needed (accessed May 12, 2015).

Gleditsch, Kristian Skrede, and Michael D. Ward. 2000. "War and Peace in Space and Time: The Role of Democratization." *International Studies Quarterly*, 44(1): 1–29.

——2006. "Diffusion and the International Context of Democratization." *International Organization*, 60(4): 911–33.

Gleditsch, Nils Petter. 2012. "Whither the Weather? Climate Change and Conflict." *Journal of Peace Research*, 49(1): 3–9.

Global Footprint Network. 2010. http://issuu.com/globalfootprintnetwork/docs/ecological_wealth_of_nations/1 (accessed May 12, 2015).

Global Greenhouse Warming. 2014. "Climate Mitigation and Adaptation." www.global-greenhouse-warming.com/climate-mitigation-and-adaptation.html (accessed July 22, 2014).

Goemans, Henk E., Kristian Skrede Gleditsch, and Giacomo Chiozza. 2009. "Introducing Archigos: A Dataset of Political Leaders." *Journal of Peace Research*, 46(2): 269–83.

Goldstone, Jack A., Ted Robert Gurr, Barbara Harff, Marc A. Levy, Monty G. Marshall, Robert H. Bates, David L. Epstein, Colin H. Kahl, Pamela T. Surko, John C. Ulfelder, Jr., and Alan N. Unger. 2000. State Failure Task Force Report: Phase III Findings. McLean, VA: Science Applications International Corporation (SAIC).

Goldstone, Jack A., Robert H. Bates, David L. Epstein, Ted Robert Gurr, Michael B. Lustik, Monty G. Marshall, Jay Ulfelder, and Mark Woodward. 2010. "A Global Model for Forecasting Political Instability." *American Journal of Political Science*, 54(1): 190–208.

Gore, Al. 2006. *An Inconvenient Truth: The Planetary Emergency of Global Warming and What We Can Do about It*. New York: Rodale.

Gupta, Dipak K., Harinder Singh, and Tom Sprague. 1993. "Government Coercion of Dissidents: Deterrence or Provocation?" *Journal of Conflict Resolution*, 37(2): 301–39.

Gurr, Ted Robert. 1970. *Why Men Rebel*. Princeton, NJ: Princeton University Press.

——1974. "Persistence and Change in Political Systems, 1800–1971." *The American Political Science Review*, 68(4): 1482–1504.

——1993. *Minorities at Risk: A Global View of Ethnopolitical Conflicts*. Washington, DC: United States Institute of Peace Press.

——2000. *Peoples versus States: Minorities at Risk in the New Century*. Washington, DC: United States Institute of Peace Press.

——2002. "Attaining Peace in Divided Societies: Five Principles of Emerging Doctrine." *International Journal on World Peace*, 19(2): 27–51.

Gurr, Ted Robert, and Barabara Harff. 1994. *Ethnic Conflict in World Politics*. Boulder, CO: Westview Press.

Gurr, Ted Robert, and Will H. Moore. 1997. "Ethnopolitical Rebellion: A Cross-Sectional Analysis of the 1980s with Risk Assessments for the 1990s." *American Journal of Political Science*, 41(4): 1079–1103.

Hannum, Hurst. 1990. *Autonomy, Sovereignty, and Self-Determination: The Accommodation of Conflicting Rights*. Philadelphia: University of Pennsylvania Press.

Hardin, Garrett. 1968. "The Tragedy of the Commons." *Science*, 162(3859): 1243–48.

Harff, Barbara, and Ted Robert Gurr. 2004. *Ethnic Conflict in World Politics*, Second Edition. Boulder, CO: Westview Press.

Hartzell, Caroline, and Matthew Hoddie. 2003. "Institutionalizing Peace: Power Sharing and Post-Civil War Conflict Management." *American Journal of Political Science*, 47(2): 318–32.

——2007. *Crafting Peace: Power-Sharing Institutions and the Negotiated Settlement of Civil Wars*. University Park, PA: The Pennsylvania State University Press.

Hartzell, Caroline, Matthew Hoddie, and Donald Rothchild. 2001. "Stabilizing the Peace after Civil War: An Investigation of Some Key Variables." *International Organization*, 55(1): 183–208.

Haug, Constanze, and Joyeeta Gupta. 2013. "The Emergence of REDD on the Global Policy Agenda." In *Climate Change, Forests, and REDD*, edited by Joyeeta Gupta, Nicolien van der Grijp, and Onno Kuik. London: Routledge, pp. 77–98.

Hechter, Michael. 2004. "Containing Ethnonationalist Violence." In *Facing Ethnic Conflicts: Toward a New Realism*, edited by Andreas Wimmer, Richard J. Goldstone, Donald L. Horowitz, Ulrike Joras, and Conrad Schetter. Lanham, MD: Rowman & Littlefield, pp. 283–300.

Hechter, Michael, and Dina Okamoto. 2001. "Political Consequences of Minority Group Formation." *Annual Review of Political Science*, 4: 189–215.

Hegre, Håvard, and Nicholas Sambanis. 2006. "Sensitivity Analysis of Empirical Results on Civil War Onset." *Journal of Conflict Resolution*, 50(4): 508–35.

Hegre, Håvard, and Hanne Fjelde. 2010. "Democratization and Post-Conflict Transitions." In *Peace and Conflict 2010*, edited by J. Joseph Hewitt, Jonathan Wilkenfeld, and Ted Robert Gurr. Boulder, CO: Paradigm Publishers, pp. 79–90.

Hegre, Håvard, Tanja Ellingsen, Scott Gates, and Nils Petter Gleditsch. 2001. "Toward a Democratic Civil Peace? Democracy, Political Change, and Civil War, 1816–1992." *The American Political Science Review*, 95(1): 33–48.

Hegre, Håvard, Ranveig Gissinger, and Nils Petter Gleditsch. 2003. "Globalization and Internal Conflict." In *Globalization and Armed Conflict*, edited by Gerald Schneider, Katherine Barbieri, and Nils Petter Gleditsch. Lanham, MD: Rowman & Littlefield, pp. 251–76.

Hendrix, Cullen S., and Idean Salehyan. 2012. "Climate Change, Rainfall, and Social Conflict in Africa." *Journal of Peace Research*, 49(1): 35–50.

Hewitt, J. Joseph. 2008. "The Peace and Conflict Instability Ledger: Ranking States on Future Risks." In *Peace and Conflict 2008*, edited by J. Joseph Hewitt, Jonathan Wilkenfeld, and Ted Robert Gurr. Boulder, CO: Paradigm Publishers, pp. 5–20.

———2010. "The Peace and Conflict Instability Ledger: Ranking States on Future Risks." In *Peace and Conflict 2010*, edited by J. Joseph Hewitt, Jonathan Wilkenfeld, and Ted Robert Gurr. Boulder, CO: Paradigm Publishers, pp. 5–18.

———2012a. "The Peace and Conflict Instability Ledger: Ranking States on Future Risks." In *Peace and Conflict 2012*, edited by J. Joseph Hewitt, Jonathan Wilkenfeld, and Ted Robert Gurr. Boulder, CO: Paradigm Publishers, pp. 4–17.

———2012b. "Trends in Global Conflict, 1946–2009." In *Peace and Conflict 2012*, edited by J. Joseph Hewitt, Jonathan Wilkenfeld, and Ted Robert Gurr. Boulder, CO: Paradigm Publishers, pp. 25–30.

Hjertholm, Peter, and Howard White. 2000. *Survey of Foreign Aid: History, Trends and Allocation*, www.econ.ku.dk/wpa/pink/2000/0004.pdf, p. 10 (accessed May 12, 2015).

Hobsbawm, Eric. 1990. *Nations and Nationalism since 1780: Programme, Myth, Reality*. Cambridge, UK: Cambridge University Press.

Hoddie, Matthew, and Caroline Hartzell. 2005. "Power Sharing in Peace Settlements: Initiating the Transition from Civil War." In *Sustainable Peace: Power and Democracy After Civil Wars*, edited by Philip G. Roeder and Donald Rothchild. Ithaca, NY: Cornell University Press, pp. 83–106.

Hoeffler, Anke. 2010. "State Failure and Conflict Recurrence." In *Peace and Conflict 2010*, edited by J. Joseph Hewitt, Jonathan Wilkenfeld, and Ted Robert Gurr. Boulder, CO: Paradigm Publishers, pp. 65–78.

Hoffman, Bruce. 1999. "Terrorism Trends and Prospects." In *Countering the New Terrorism*, edited by Ian O. Lesser, Bruce Hoffman, John Arquilla, David Ronfeldt, and Michele Zanini. Santa Monica, CA: Rand, pp. 7–38.

Homer-Dixon, Thomas F. 1994. "Environmental Scarcities and Violent Conflict: Evidence from Cases." *International Security*, 19(1): 5–40.

Hopmann, P. Terrance. 1996. *The Negotiation Process and the Resolution of International Conflicts.* Columbia, SC: University of South Carolina Press.

Horowitz, Donald L. 1985. *Ethnic Groups in Conflict.* Berkeley: University of California Press.

Houghton, J.T., G.J. Jenkins, and J.J. Ephraums (eds.). 1990. *1990 Intergovernment Panel on Climate Change.* Cambridge, UK: Cambridge University Press.

Humphreys, Macartan. 2005. "Natural Resources, Conflict, and Conflict Resolution: Uncovering the Mechanisms." *Journal of Conflict Resolution,* 49(4): 508–37.

Humphreys, Macartan, and Jeremy M. Weinstein. 2008. "Who Fights? The Determinants of Participation in Civil War." *American Journal of Political Science,* 52(2): 436–55.

Huntington, Samuel P. 1991. *The Third Wave: Democratization in the Late Twentieth Century.* Norman, OK: Oklahoma University Press.

———1996. *The Clash of Civilizations and the Remaking of World Order.* New York, NY: Simon & Schuster.

Hurrell, Andrew, and Benedict Kingsbury (eds.). 1992. *The International Politics of the Environment.* Oxford: Oxford University Press.

Intergovernmental Panel on Climate Change (IPCC). 2007. *Climate Change 2007: Synthesis Report.* Contribution of Working Groups I, II and III to the Fourth Assessment Report of the Intergovernmental Panel on Climate Change, edited by The Core Writing Team, Rajendra K. Pachauri, and Andy Reisinge. Geneva, Switzerland: Intergovernmental Panel on Climate Change.

———2013a. "Summary for Policymakers." In *Climate Change 2013: The Physical Science Basis.* Contribution of Working Group I to the Fifth Assessment Report of the Intergovernmental Panel on Climate Change, edited by Thomas F. Stocker, Dahe Qin, Gian-Kasper Plattner, Melinda M.B. Tignor, Simon K. Allen, Judith Boschung, Alexander Nauels, Yu Xia, Vincent Bex, and Pauline M. Midgley. Cambridge, UK: Cambridge University Press, pp. 1–29.

———2013b. *Climate Change 2014: Mitigation of Climate Change.* Contribution of Working Group III to the Fifth Assessment Report of the Intergovernmental Panel on Climate Change, edited by Ottmar Edenhofer, Ramón Pichs-Madruga, Youba Sokona, Ellie Farahani, Susanne Kadner, Kristin Seyboth, Anna Adler, Ina Baum, Steffen Brunner, Patrick Eickemeier, Benjamin Kriemann, Jussi Savolainen, Steffen Schlömer, Christoph von Stechow, Timm Zwickel, and Jan C. Minx. Cambridge, UK: Cambridge University Press.

International Institute for Democracy and Electoral Assistance (International IDEA). 2003. *Reconciliation After Violent Conflict: A Handbook.* Stockholm: International Institute for Democracy and Electoral Assistance.

———2006. *Democracy, Conflict and Human Security: Pursuing Peace in the 21st Century,* Volume 1. Stockholm: International Institute for Democracy and Electoral Assistance.

Jenne, Erin K. 2004. "A Bargaining Theory of Minority Demands: Explaining the Dog that Did not Bite in 1990s Yugoslavia." *International Studies Quarterly,* 48(4): 729–54.

———2007. *Ethnic Bargaining: The Paradox of Minority Empowerment.* Ithaca, NY: Cornell University Press.

Jentleson, Bruce W. 2000. *Coercive Prevention: Normative, Political, and Policy Dilemmas*, Peaceworks No. 35. Washington, DC: United States Institute of Peace Press.

Juergensmeyer, Mark. 2003. *Terror in the Mind of God: The Global Rise of Religious Violence*, 3rd edition. Berkeley: University of California Press.

Justino, Patricia, Tilman Bruck and Phillip Verwimp (eds.). 2013. *A Micro-level Perspective on the Dynamics of Conflict, Violence, and Development*. Oxford: Oxford University Press: pp. 12–13.

Kanowski, Peter J., Constance L. McDermott, Benjamin W. Cashore. 2010. "Implementing REDD+: Lessons from Analysis of Forest Governance." *Environmental Science and Policy*, 14(2): 111–17.

Kapstein, Ethan B., and Nathan Converse. 2008. *The Fate of Young Democracies*. Cambridge, UK: Cambridge University Press.

Kaufmann, Chaim. 1996. "Possible and Impossible Solutions to Ethnic Civil Wars." *International Security*, 20(4): 136–75.

Kedourie, Elie. 1960. *Nationalism*. London: Hutchinson & Co.

Khagram, Sanjeev, and Saleem Ali. 2006. "Environment and Security." *Annual Review of Environment and Resources*, 31: 395–411.

Kishi, R. 2014. "Does Foreign Aid Lead to Armed Civil Conflict? Examining Horizontal Inequalities and Ethnic Exclusion." Unpublished doctoral dissertation. University of Maryland, College Park.

Kleiboer, Marieke. 1998. *The Multiple Realities of International Mediation*. Boulder, CO: Lynne Rienner.

Knack, S. 2001. "Aid Dependence and the Quality of Governance: Cross-Country Empirical Tests." *Southern Economic Journal*, 68(2): 310–29.

Kolb, Deborah M., and Eileen Babbitt. 1995. "Mediation Practice on the Home Front: Implications for Global Conflict Resolution." In *Beyond Confrontation: Learning Conflict Resolution in the Post-Cold War Era*, edited by John A. Vasquez, James Turner Johnson, Sanford Jaffee, and Linda Stamato. Ann Arbor, MI: University of Michigan Press, pp. 63–85.

Korchumova, S. 2007. "Development Projects that Work: Multidisciplinarity in Action." Globalhood Research Paper. www.globalhood.org/articles/briefingnotes/Development_Projects_that_work.pdf (accessed May 12, 2015).

Kvaløy, Berit, Henning Finseraas, and Ola Listhaug. 2012. "The Public's Concern for Global Warming: A Cross-national Sudy of 47 Countries." *Journal of Peace Research*, 49(1): 11–22.

Kymlicka, Will. 1998. "Is Federalism a Viable Alternative to Secession?" In *Theories of Secession*, edited by Percy B. Lehning. London: Routledge, pp. 111–50.

Laqueur, Walter. 1999. *The New Terrorism: Fanaticism and the Arms of Mass Destruction*. New York: Oxford University Press.

Larson, Anne M., Esteve Corbera, Peter Cronkleton, Chris van Dam, David Bray, Manuel Estrada, Peter May, Gabriel Medina, Guillermo Navarro, and Pablo Pacheco. 2010. "Rights to Forests and Carbon under REDD+ Initiatives in Latin America." CIFOR Infobrief, No. 33, November 2010. Bogor, Indonesia: Center for International Forestry Research (CIFOR).

Lecocq, Franck, and Philippe Ambrosi. 2007. "The Clean Development Mechanism: History, Status, and Prospects." *Review of Environmental Economics and Policy*, 1(1): 134–51.

Lederer, Markus. 2013. "The Future of Carbon Markets: Carbon Trading, the Clean Development Mechanism and Beyond." In *Low Carbon Development: Key Issues*, edited by Frauke Urban and Johan Nordensvärd. New York: Routledge, pp. 94–106.

Lee, Chris, Sandra Maline, and Will H. Moore. 2000. "Coercion and Protest: An Empirical Test Revisited." In *Paths to State Repression: Human Rights Violations and Contentious Politics*, edited by Christian Davenport. Lanham, MD: Rowman & Littlefield, pp. 127–147.

Lenhardt, A. 2013. "Measuring Poverty Below the Averages." www.developmentprogress.org/blog/2013/05/23/measuring-poverty-below-averages (accessed May 12, 2015).

Lewis, Joanna I. 2010. "The Evolving Role of Carbon Finance in Promoting Renewable Energy Development in China." *Energy Policy*, 38(6): 2875–86.

Lichbach, Mark. 1987. "Deterrence or Escalation?: The Puzzle of Aggregate Studies of Repression and Dissent." *Journal of Conflict Resolution*, 31(2): 266–97.

——1995. *The Rebel's Dilemma*. Ann Arbor: the University of Michigan Press.

Lichbach, Mark, and Ted Robert Gurr. 1981. "The Conflict Process: A Self-Generative Model." *Journal of Conflict Resolution*, 25(1): 3–29.

Lijphart, Arend J. 1977. *Democracy in Plural Societies: A Comparative Exploration*. New Haven: Yale University Press.

Lobell, D.B., K.G. Cassman, and C.B. Field. 2009. "Crop Yield Gaps: Their Importance, Magnitudes, and Causes." *Annual Review of Environment and Resources*, 34(1): 1–26.

Londregan, John B., and Keith T. Poole. 1996. "Does High Income Promote Democracy?" *World Politics*, 49(1): 1–30.

Lund, Michael S. 1996. *Preventing Violent Conflicts: A Strategy for Preventive Diplomacy*. Washington, DC: United States Institute of Peace Press.

McAdam, Doug. 1996. "Conceptual Origins, Current Problems, Future Directions." In *Comparative Perspectives on Social Movements: Political Opportunities, Mobilizing Structures, and Cultural Framings*, edited by Doug McAdam, John D. McCarthy, and Mayer N. Zald. Cambridge, UK: Cambridge University Press, pp. 23–40.

McCarthy, John D. 1996. "Constraints and Opportunities in Adopting, Adapting, and Inventing." In *Comparative Perspectives on Social Movements: Political Opportunities, Mobilizing Structures, and Cultural Framings*, edited by Doug McAdam, John D. McCarthy, and Mayer N. Zald. Cambridge, UK: Cambridge University Press, pp. 141–51.

McCarthy, John D., and Mayer N. Zald. 1977. "Resource Mobilization and Social Movements: A Partial Theory." *American Journal of Sociology* 82(6): 1212–41.

McCarthy, James J., Osvaldo F. Canziani, Neil A. Leary, David J. Dokken, and Kasey S. White (eds.). 2001. *Climate Change 2001: Impacts, Adaptation, and Vulnerability*. Cambridge, UK: Cambridge University Press.

McCauley, Douglas J., Malin L. Pinsky, Stephen R. Palumbi, James A. Estes, Francis H. Joyce, and Roert R. Warner. 2015. Abstract. ScienceMag.org. 347(6219): 247. www.sciencemag.org/content/347/6219/1255641 (accessed January 16, 2015).

Machado, Fabiana, Carlos Scartascini, and Mariano Tommasi. 2011. "Political Institutions and Street Protests in Latin America." *Journal of Conflict Resolution*, 55(3): 340–65.

McQuade, M. 2011. "The Importance of Broadband to Economic Development," website. *Selection Magazine*, September. http://bit.ly/NdLnnB (accessed May 12, 2015).

Managing Intrastate Low-level Conflict. 2007. *Codebook for the Dataset Managing Intrastate Low-level Conflict (MILC)*, Version 1.0. Uppsala Conflict Data Program (UCDP), Department of Peace and Conflict Research, Uppsala University.

Mansfield, Edward D., and Jack Snyder. 2007. "The Sequencing 'Fallacy'." *Journal of Democracy*, 18(3): 5–10.

Maoz, Zeev. 2004. "Conflict Management and Conflict Resolution: A Conceptual and Methodological Introduction." In *Multiple Paths to Knowledge in International Relations: Methodology in the Study of Conflict Management and Conflict Resolution*, edited by Zeev Maoz, Alex Mintz, T. Clifton Morgan, Glenn Palmer, and Richard J. Stoll. New York: Lexington Books, pp. 1–32.

Marshall, Monty G., Ted Robert Gurr, and Keith Jaggers. 2013. *Polity IV Project: Political Regime Characteristics and Transitions, 1800–2012*, Dataset Users' Manual. Vienna, VA: Center for Systemic Peace.

Meernik, James, Rosa Aloisi, Angela D. Nichols, and Marsha Sowell. 2010. "The Impact of Tribunals and Truth Commissions on Post-Conflict Peace Building." In *Peace and Conflict 2010*, edited by J. Joseph Hewitt, Jonathan Wilkenfeld, and Ted Robert Gurr. Boulder, CO: Paradigm Publishers, pp. 103–16.

Meier, Patrick. 2014. "Crowdsourcing to Map Conflict, Crises, and Humanitarian Responses." In *Peace and Conflict 2014*, edited by David Backer, Jonathan Wilkenfeld, and Paul Huth. Boulder, CO: Paradigm Publishers, pp. 122–41.

Melander, Erik, Frida Möller, and Magnus Öberg. 2009. "Managing Intrastate Low-Intensity Armed Conflict 1993–2004: A New Dataset." *International Interactions*, 35(1): 58–85.

Meyer, Aubrey. 2004. "Briefing: Contraction and Convergence." Proceedings of the ICE: *Engineering Sustainability*, 157(4): 189–92.

Michaelowa, Axel. 2012. "Strengths and Weaknesses of the CDM in Comparison with New and Emerging Market Mechanisms." Paper No. 2 for the CDM Policy Dialogue panel, June 2012.

Minorities at Risk. 2009. *Minorities at Risk (MAR) Codebook*, Version 2/2009. College Park, MD: Center for International Development and Conflict Management, University of Maryland.

Minority Rights Group International. 2012. *State of the World's Minorities and Indigenous Peoples 2012: Events of 2011*, edited by Beth Walker. London: Minority Rights Group International.

Mitchell, Christopher. 1981. *Peacemaking and the Consultant's Role*. New York: Nichols.

Mitchell, Ronald B. 2010. *International Politics and the Environment*. Los Angeles: SAGE.

——2013. "International Environmental Politics." In *Handbook of International Relations*, 2nd edition, edited by Walter Carlsnaes, Thomas Risse, and Beth A. Simmons. Los Angeles: SAGE, pp. 801–26.

Moore, Will H. 1998. "Repression and Dissent: Substitution, Context, and Timing." *American Journal of Political Science*, 42(3): 851–73.

Morgan, T. Clifton. 1994. *Untying the Knot of War: A Bargaining Theory of International Crises*. Ann Arbor: University of Michigan Press.

Muller, Edward, and Mitchell Seligson. 1987. "Inequality and Insurgency." *The American Political Science Review*, 81(2): 425–52.

Murray, Brian C., Bruce A. McCarl, and Heng-Chi Lee. 2004. "Estimating Leakage from Forest Carbon Sequestration Programs." *Land Economics*, 80(1): 109–24.

National Aeronautics and Space Administration. 2014. "West Antarctic Glacier Loss Appears Unstoppable." www.jpl.nasa.gov/news/news.php?release=2014-148 (accessed May 12, 2014).

New York Times. September 22, 2009. "Obama's Speech on Climate Change." www.nytimes.com/2009/09/23/us/politics/23obama.text.html?pagewanted=all &_r=0 (accessed July 29, 2014).

——October 2, 2009. "The Economics of Climate Stabilization," by John Lorinc. *New York Times*, Green: Energy, the Environment, and the Bottom Line blog, 8:30AM. http://green.blogs.nytimes.com/2009/10/02/the-economics-of-climate-stabilization/ (accessed July 23, 2014).

Noble, K.B. 1992. "U.S. Reaping Zairians' Anger Toward Mobutu." *The New York Times*, March 30, 1992 issue.

Obama, Barack. 2013. Remarks by the President on Climate Change. Georgetown University.

Oberschall, Anthony. 1973. *Social Conflict and Social Movements*. Englewood Cliffs, NJ: Prentice-Hall.

O'Brien, Sean P. 2010. "Crisis Early Warning and Decision Support: Contemporary Approaches and Thoughts on Future Research." *International Studies Review*, 12(1): 87–104.

Olinto, P., and H. Uematsu. 2013. "The State of the Poor: Where Are the Poor and Where Are They Poorest?" www.worldbank.org/content/dam/Worldbank/document/State_of_the_poor_paper_April17.pdf (accessed May 12, 2015).

Olzak, Susan. 2006. *The Global Dynamics of Racial and Ethnic Mobilization*. Stanford, CA: Stanford University Press.

Pape, Robert A. 2003. "The Strategic Logic of Suicide Terrorism." *The American Political Science Review*, 97(3): 343–61.

Paris, Roland. 2004. *At War's End: Building Peace After Civil Conflict*. Cambridge, UK: Cambridge University Press.

Pedahzur, Ami, Arie Perliger, and Leonard Weinberg. 2003. "Altruism and Fatalism: The Characteristics of Palestinian Suicide Terrorists." *Deviant Behavior*, 24(4): 405–23.

Petersen, D. Roger. 2002. *Understanding Ethnic Violence: Fear, Hatred, and Resentment in Twentieth-Century Eastern Europe*. Cambridge, UK: Cambridge University Press.

Pevehouse, Jon C. 2002. "With a Little Help from My Friends? Regional Organizations and the Consolidation of Democracy." *American Journal of Political
Science*, 46(3): 611–26.

Polity IV Database. 2014. Center for Systemic Peace, www.systemicpeace.org/
polity/polity4.htm (accessed May 12, 2015).

Posen, Barry R. 1993. "Security Dilemma and Ethnic Conflict." *Survival*, 35(1):
27–47.

Powell, Robert. 1999. *In the Shadow of Power*. Princeton, NJ: Princeton
University Press.

——2004. "The Inefficient Use of Power: Costly Conflict with Complete Information." *The American Political Science Review*, 98(2): 231–41.

——2006. "War as a Commitment Problem." *International Organization*, 60(1):
169–203.

Przeworski, Adam, and Fernando Limongi. 1997. "Modernization: Theories and
Facts." *World Politics*, 49(2): 155–83.

Przeworski, Adam, Michael E. Alvarez, José Antonio Cheibub, and Fernando
Limongi. 2000. *Democracy and Development: Political Institutions and Well-
Being in the World, 1950–1990*. Cambridge, UK: Cambridge University Press.

Quinn, David. 2008. "Self-Determination Movements and Their Outcomes." In
Peace and Conflict 2008, edited by J. Joseph Hewitt, Jonathan Wilkenfeld, and
Ted Robert Gurr. Boulder, CO: Paradigm Publishers, pp. 33–8.

Quinn, David, Jonathan Wilkenfeld, Kathleen Smarick, and Victor Asal. 2006.
"Power Play: Mediation in Symmetric and Asymmetric International Crises."
International Interactions, 32(4): 441–70.

Quinn, David, Jonathan Wilkenfeld, Pelin Eralp, Victor Asal, and Theodore
McLauchlin. 2013a. "Crisis Managers but not Conflict Resolvers: Mediating
Ethnic Intrastate Conflict in Africa." *Conflict Management and Peace Science*,
30(4): 387–406.

Quinn, David, Roudabeh Kishi, Jonathan Wilkenfeld, Michele Gelfand, Pelin
Eralp, Elizabeth Salmon, and Daniel Owens. 2013b. "Adapting Mediation
to the Intrastate Crisis Context." Paper presented at the Annual Conference of the American Political Science Association, Chicago, August
28–31.

Rajamani, Lavanya. 2012. "The Changing Fortunes of Differential Treatment
in the Evolution of International Environmental Law." *International Affairs*,
88(3): 605–23.

Raleigh, Clionadh, and Dominic Kniveton. 2012. "Come Rain or Shine: An
Analysis of Conflict and Climate Variability in East Africa." *Journal of Peace
Research*, 49(1): 51–64.

Rauchhaus, Robert W. 2006. "Asymmetric Information, Mediation, and Conflict
Management." *World Politics*, 58(2): 207–41.

Regan, Patrick M., and Errol A. Henderson. 2002. "Democracy, Threats and
Political Repression in Developing Countries: Are Democracies Internally Less
Violent?" *Third World Quarterly*, 23(1): 119–36.

Regan, Patrick M., and Sam R. Bell. 2010. "Changing Lanes or Stuck in the
Middle: Why Are Anocracies More Prone to Civil Wars?" *Political Research
Quarterly*, 63(4): 747–59.

Reidpath, D.D., and P. Allotey. 2003. "Infant Mortality Rate as an Indicator of Population Health." *Journal of Epidemiology & Community Health*, 57: 344–6.

Richmond, Oliver. 1998. "Devious Objectives and the Disputants' View of International Mediation: A Theoretical Framework." *Journal of Peace Research*, 35(6): 707–22.

Roberts, J. Timmons, Bradley C. Parks, and Alexis A. Vásquez. 2004. "Who Ratifies Environmental Treaties and Why? Institutionalism, Structuralism and Participation by 192 Nations in 22 Treaties." *Global Environmental Politics*, 4(3): 22–64.

Rostow, W.W. 1960. *The Stages of Economic Growth: A Non-Communist Manifesto*. Cambridge, UK: Cambridge University Press.

Rothchild, Donald. 1997. *Managing Ethnic Conflict in Africa: Pressures and Incentives for Cooperation*. Washington, DC: Brookings Institution Press.

Rothchild, Donald, and Caroline Hartzell. 2000. "Security in Deeply Divided Societies: The Role of Territorial Autonomy." In *Identity and Territorial Autonomy in Plural Societies*, edited by William Safran and Ramon Maiz. London: Frank Cass, pp. 254–71.

Royal Commission on Environmental Pollution (RCEP). 2000. "Energy: The Changing Climate," 22nd report, Norwich, UK: Crown.

Rubin, Jeffrey Z. 1980. "Experimental Research on Third-Party Intervention in Conflict: Toward some Generalizations." *Psychological Bulletin*, 87(2): 379–91.

Ruel, M.T. 2003. "Is Dietary Diversity an Indicator of Food Security or Dietary Quality? A Review of Measurement Issues and Research Needs." *Food and Nutrition Bulletin*, 24(2): 143–242.

Sachs, J.D. 2005. *The End of Poverty: Economic Possibilities for Our Time*, 1st edn. London, UK: Penguin Press.

Sagar, Ambuj D., and Stacy D. Van Deveer. 2005. "Capacity Development for the Environment: Broadening the Scope." *Global Environmental Politics*, 5(3): 14–22.

Salehyan, Idean. 2009. *Rebels without Borders: Transnational Insurgencies in World Politics*. Ithaca, NY: Cornell University Press.

Sambanis, Nicholas. 2001. "Do Ethnic and Nonethnic Civil Wars Have the Same Causes? A Theoretical and Empirical Inquiry (Part 1)." *Journal of Conflict Resolution*, 45(3): 259–82.

Satterthwaite, David. 2011. "Climate Change and Urbanization: Effects and Implications for Urban Governance." In *Population Distribution, Urbanization, Internal Migration, and Development: An International Perspective*, edited by United Nations Department of Economic and Social Affairs (UN DESA), Population Division. New York: United Nations Department of Economic and Social Affairs, Population Division, pp. 340–63.

Savun, Burcu, and Daniel C. Tirone. 2011. "Foreign Aid, Democratization, and Civil Conflict: How Does Democracy Aid Affect Civil Conflict?" *American Journal of Political Science*, 55(2): 233–46.

Scheffran, Jürgen, Michael Brzoska, Jasmin Kominek, P. Michael Link, and Janpeter Schilling. 2012. "Disentangling the Climate-Conflict Nexus: Empirical and Theoretical Assessment of Vulnerabilities and Pathways." *Review of European Studies*, 4(5): 1–13.

Schelling, Thomas C. 1960. *The Strategy of Conflict*. Cambridge, MA: President and Fellows of Harvard College.

Schrodt, Philip A., and Deborah J. Gerner. 2004. "An Event Analysis of Third-party Mediation in the Middle East and Balkans." *Journal of Conflict Resolution*, 48(3): 310–30.

Scott, Daniel, Robert Steiger, Michelle Rutty, and Peter Johnson. 2014. *The Future of the Winter Olympics in a Warmer World*. Waterloo, CA: Interdisciplinary Centre on Climate Change.

Sherbinin, Alex de, David Carr, Susan Cassels, and Leiwen Jiang. 2007. "Population and Environment." *Annual Review of Environment and Resources*, 32: 345–73.

Simon, Steven, and Daniel Benjamin. 2001. "The Terror." *Survival*, 43(4): 5–18.

Smith, Alastair, and Allan C. Stam. 2003. "Mediation and Peacekeeping in a Random Walk Model of Civil and Interstate War." *International Studies Review*, 5(4): 115–35.

Snyder, Jack. 2000. *From Voting to Violence: Democratization and Nationalist Conflict*. New York: W.W. Norton and Company.

——2010. "Elections as Milestones and Stumbling Blocks for Peaceful Democratic Consolidation." In *Friedrich-Ebert-Stiftung (FES) International Policy Analysis Series*, September 2010. Berlin: Friedrich-Ebert-Stiftung. http://library.fes.de/pdf-files/iez/07438.pdf (accessed May 12, 2015).

Snyder, Richard, and James Mahoney. 1999. "The Missing Variable: Institutions and the Study of Regime Change." *Comparative Politics*, 32(1): 103–22.

Starkey, Brigid, Mark A. Boyer, and Jonathan Wilkenfeld. 2015. *International Negotiation in a Complex World*, 4th edition. Lanham, MD: Rowman & Littlefield.

State of the Climate, National Climate Data Center, National Oceanic and Atmospheric Administration. 2014. www.ncdc.noaa.gov/sotc/summary-info (accessed May 12, 2015).

Stedman, Stephen J. 1997. "Spoiler Problems in Peace Processes." *International Security*, 22(2): 5–53.

Susskind, Lawrence, and Eileen Babbitt. 1992. "Overcoming the Obstacles to Effective Mediation of International Disputes." In *Mediation in International Relations: Multiple Approaches to Conflict Management*, edited by Jacob Bercovitch and Jeffrey Z. Rubin. New York: St. Martin's Press, pp. 30–51.

Sustainable Development Solutions Network. 2014. "Indicators for Sustainable Development Goals." http://unsdsn.org/wp-content/uploads/2014/02/140214-SDSN-indicator-report-DRAFT-for-consultation.pdf (accessed May 12, 2015).

Tambiah, Stanley Jeyaraja. 1996. *Leveling Crowds: Ethnonationalist Conflicts and Collective Violence in South Asia*. Berkeley, CA: University of California Press.

The Economist. 1977. "The Dutch Disease." *The Economist*, November 26, 1977 issue, pp. 82–3.

——2013. "Making Up." *The Economist*, November 23, 2013 issue.

——2014. "China's Cities: The Great Transition." *The Economist*, March 22, 2014 issue.

The Economist Intelligence Unit. 2014. Democracy Index 2013: Democracy in Limbo. London: The Economist Intelligence Unit.

Therkildsen, O. 2002. "Keeping the State Accountable: Is Aid No Better than Oil?" *IDS Bulletin*, 33(3): 41–9.

Thompson, Mary C., Manali Baruah, and Edward R. Carr. 2011. "Seeing REDD+ as a Project of Environmental Governance." *Environmental Science & Policy*, 14(2): 100–10.

Tilly, Charles. 1973. "Does Modernization Breed Revolution?" *Comparative Politics*, 5(3): 425–47.

——1978. *From Mobilization to Revolution*. Reading, MA: Addison-Wesley.

——2003. *The Politics of Collective Violence*. Cambridge, UK: Cambridge University Press.

Toft, Monica D. 2003. *The Geography of Ethnic Violence: Identity, Interests, and the Indivisibility of Territory*. Princeton: Princeton University Press.

Touval, Saadia. 1994. "Why the UN Fails." *Foreign Affairs* 73(5): 44–57.

Touval, Saadia, and I. William Zartman. 1985. "Introduction: Mediation in Theory." In *International Mediation in Theory and Practice*, edited by Saadia Touval and I. William Zartman. Boulder, CO: Westview Press, pp. 7–17.

UK Parliament. 2012. "Chapter 2: The Global Aid Context: Who Gives What?" www.publications.parliament.uk/pa/ld201012/ldselect/ldeconaf/278/27805.htm (accessed May 12, 2015).

Ulfelder, Jay, and Michael Lustik. 2007. "Modelling Transitions To and From Democracy." *Democratization*, 14(3): 351–87.

Union of Concerned Scientists (UCS). 2013. *Causes of Sea Level Rise. Rapidly Rising Seas: What the Science Tells Us*. Cambridge, MA: Union of Concerned Scientists. www.ucsusa.org/assets/documents/global_warming/Causes-of-Sea-Level-Rise.pdf (accessed July 29, 2014).

United Nations. 2012. "United Nations Peacekeeping Operations: Partnerships." www.un.org/en/peacekeeping/operations/partnerships.shtml (accessed May 12, 2015).

——2013. "MONUSCO (United Nations Organization Stabilization Mission in the Democratic Republic of the Congo): Protecting civilians and consolidating peace in the Democratic Republic of the Congo." www.un.org/en/peacekeeping/missions/monusco/ (accessed May 12, 2015).

——2014. "We Can End Poverty: Millennium Development Goals and Beyond 2015." www.un.org/millenniumgoals/bkgd.shtml (accessed May 12, 2015).

United Nations Agenda for Peace. 1992. United Nations.

United Nations Collaborative Programme on Reducing Emissions from Deforestation and Forest Degradation in Developing Countries (UN-REDD). 2008. FAO, UNDP, UNEP Framework Document. Geneva: United Nations Collaborative Programme on Reducing Emissions from Deforestation and Forest Degradation in Developing Countries. June 20, 2008.

United Nations Department of Economic and Social Affairs, Population Division. 2007. "World Population Prospects: The 2006 Revision, Highlights." Working Paper No. ESA/P/WP.202. New York: United Nations.

United Nations Development Programme (UNDP). 2004. *Human Development Report 2004: Cultural Liberty in Today's Diverse World*. New York: United Nations Development Programme.

———2007. Human Development Report 2007/2008. *Fighting Climate Change: Human Solidarity in a Divided World*. New York: United Nations Development Programme.

———2013a. "Human Development Reports: About Human Development." http://hdr.undp.org/en/humandev (accessed May 12, 2015).

———2013b. "Human Development Reports: Human Development Index (HDI)." http://hdr.undp.org/en/statistics/hdi (accessed May 12, 2015).

———2014. "Empowered Lives. Resilient Nations." www.undp.org/content/undp/en/home.html (accessed May 12, 2015).

United Nations Environment Programme (UNEP). 2013. *Emissions Gap Report: Executive Summary*. Nairobi: United Nations Environment Programme.

United Nations Framework Convention on Climate Change (UNFCCC). 1994. http://unfccc.int/essential_background/convention/items/2627.php (accessed June 18, 2015).

———2010. *The Contribution of the Clean Development Mechanism under the Kyoto Protocol to Technology Transfer*. Bonn: United Nations Framework Convention on Climate Change.

———2014a. "Clean Development Mechanism." http://unfccc.int/kyoto_protocol/mechanisms/clean_development_mechanism/items/2718.php (accessed July 29, 2014).

———2014b. "Projects Entering Validation." CDM Project Activities, Clean Development Mechanism (CDM). http://cdm.unfccc.int/Statistics/Public/files/201406/valnum.pdf (accessed July 24, 2014).

United Nations Security Council Resolution 2085 (2012). *Security Council Authorizes Deployment of African-led International Support Mission in Mali for Initial Year-Long Period*, S/RES/2085 (December 20, 2012), available from undocs.org/S/RES/2085(2012).

Uppsala Conflict Data Program (2008). Department of Peace and Conflict Research, Uppsala University.

U.S. Agency for International Development (USAID). 2005. *Fragile States Strategy*. Washington, DC: U.S. Agency for International Development.

———2012. "Building Resilience in Recurring Crisis: USAID Policy and Program Guidance." Washington, DC: U.S. Agency for International Development. www.usaid.gov/sites/default/files/documents/1870/USAIDResiliencePolicyGuidanceDocument.pdf (accessed July 29, 2014).

———2013. "Violent Conflict and Instability Affect at Least 50 Countries and 1.5 Billion People Worldwide." Washington, DC: U.S. Agency for International Development. www.usaid.gov/what-we-do/working-crises-and-conflict/conflict-mitigation-and-prevention (accessed July 18, 2014).

Van der Berg, S. et al. 2011. "Low Quality Education as a Poverty Trap." Research paper by the Social Policy Research Group. www.andover.edu/GPGConference/Documents/Low-Quality-Education-Poverty-Trap.pdf (accessed May 12, 2015).

Vanhanen, Tatu. 1999. "Domestic Ethnic Conflict and Ethnic Nepotism: A Comparative Analysis." *Journal of Peace Research*, 36(1): 55–73.

Vinck, Patrick, and Phuong Pham. 2014. "Localizing Peace, Reconstruction, and the Effects of Mass Violence." In *Peace and Conflict 2014*, edited by David Backer, Jonathan Wilkenfeld, and Paul Huth. Boulder, CO: Paradigm Publishers, pp. 105–21.

Walter, Barbara F. 2002. *Committing to Peace: The Successful Settlement of Civil Wars*. Princeton, NJ: Princeton University Press.

——2004. "Does Conflict Beget Conflict? Explaining Recurring Civil War." *Journal of Peace Research*, 41(3): 371–88.

——2013. "Civil Wars, Conflict Resolution, and Bargaining Theory." In *Handbook of International Relations*, edited by Walter Carlsnaes, Thomas Risse, and Beth A. Simmons. Los Angeles: SAGE, pp. 656–72.

Weidmann, Nils B. 2009. "Geography as Motivation and Opportunity: Group Concentration and Ethnic Conflict." *Journal of Conflict Resolution*, 53(4): 526–43.

Weinstein, Jeremy M. 2005. "Resources and the Information Problem in Rebel Recruitment." *Journal of Conflict Resolution*, 49(4): 598–624.

Werner, Suzanne. 1999. "The Precarious Nature of Peace: Resolving the Issues, Enforcing the Settlement, and Renegotiating the Terms." *American Journal of Political Science*, 43(3): 912–34.

Wigley, T.M.L., R. Richels, and J.A. Edmonds. 1996. "Economic and Environmental Choices in the Stabilization of Atmospheric CO_2 Concentrations." *Nature*, 379: 240–43.

——2007. "Overshoot Pathways to CO_2 Stabilization in a Multi-Gas Context." In *Human-Induced Climate Change: An Interdisciplinary Assessment*, edited by Michael E. Schlesinger, Haroon Kheshgi, Joel B. Smith, Francisco C. de la Chesnaye, John M. Reilly, Tom Wilson, and Charles Kolstad. Cambridge, UK: Cambridge University Press, pp. 84–92.

Wikipedia. "Combined cycle." http://en.wikipedia.org/wiki/Combined_cycle (accessed July 23, 2014).

Wilkenfeld, Jonathan. 2011. "Structural Challenges for American Foreign Policy in the Obama Administration." In *Obama in Office*, edited by James Thurber. Boulder, CO: Paradigm Publishers, pp. 227–42.

——2014. "Profiles of Active Armed Conflict." In *Peace and Conflict 2014*, edited by David Backer, Jonathan Wilkenfeld, and Paul Huth. Boulder, CO: Paradigm Publishers, pp. 142–68.

Wilkenfeld, Jonathan, Kathleen Young, Victor Asal, and David Quinn. 2003. "Mediating International Crises: Cross-National and Experimental Perspectives." *Journal of Conflict Resolution*, 47(3): 279–301.

Wilkenfeld, Jonathan, Kathleen Young, David Quinn, and Victor Asal. 2005. *Mediating International Crises*. London: Routledge.

Wilkenfeld, Jonathan, Amy Pate, and Victor Asal. 2009. "Mosaic of Minority Violence: Ethno-Political Mobilization in the Middle East." In *START 2009 Research Review*, edited by Gary A. Ackerman and Matthew Rhodes. College Park, MD: National Consortium for the Study of Terrorism and Responses to Terrorism (START), University of Maryland, pp. 8–9.

Williams, Lauren Goers, and Crystal Davis. 2012. "Getting Ready with Forest Governance: A Review of the Forest Carbon Partnership Facility Readiness Preparation Proposals and the UN-REDD National Programme Documents." World Resources Institute (WRI) Working Paper, March 2012. Washington, DC: World Resources Institute.

Wimmer, Andreas, Lars-Erik Cederman, and Brian Min. 2009a. "Ethnic Politics and Armed Conflict: A Configurational Analysis of a New Global Data Set." *American Sociological Review*, 74(2): 316–37.

——2009b. "Ethnic Politics and Armed Conflict: A Configurational Analysis of a New Global Data Set," Online Appendix. *American Sociological Review*, 74(2).

World Bank. 2011. Poverty Gap at $1.25 Per Day. Washington DC http://data.worldbank.org/indicator/SI.POV.GAPS (accessed May 12, 2015).

World Economic Forum. 2013. "The Global Gender Gap Report 2013." www3.weforum.org/docs/WEF_GenderGap_Report_2013.pdf (accessed May 12, 2015).

World Ethnic Diversity Map. 2000. www.mappery.com/map-of/world-ethnic-diversity-map (accessed May 12, 2015).

Zakaria, Fareed. 1997. "The Rise of Illiberal Democracy." *Foreign Affairs*, 76(6): 22–43.

——2014. "The Rise of Putinism." *Washington Post*. August 3, 2014.

Zanger, Sabine Z. 2000. "A Global Analysis of the Effect of Political Regime Changes on Life Integrity Violations, 1977–93." *Journal of Peace Research*, 37(2): 213–33.

Zartman, I. William. 1989. *Ripe for Resolution: Conflict and Intervention in Africa*. New York: Oxford University Press.

——1997. "Introduction: Toward the Resolution of International Conflicts." In *Peacemaking in International Conflict: Methods and Techniques*, edited by I. William Zartman and J. Lewis Rasmussen. Washington, DC: United States Institute of Peace Press, pp. 3–19.

Index

Diagrams, drawings and graphs are given in *italics*